OF TIDE & THYME

THE JUNIOR LEAGUE OF ANNAPOLIS, INC.

Contemporary & Classic Recipes

Celebrating Annapolis, Maryland

THE JUNIOR LEAGUE
OF ANNAPOLIS

is an organization of women committed to promoting
voluntarism and to improving the community through
the effective action and leadership of trained volunteers.
Its purpose is exclusively educational and charitable.

Additional copies of OF TIDE & THYME may be ob-
tained by sending $18.95 plus $3.00 per book for postage and handling to:

Junior League of Annapolis, Inc.
19 Loretta Avenue
Annapolis, Maryland 21401

First Printing, April, 1995
Second Printing, May, 1995

Printed in the USA by

WIMMER
The Wimmer Companies, Inc.
Memphis • Dallas

WELCOME TO ANNAPOLIS

Founded in 1649, Annapolis is one of the United States' earliest colonial settlements. Unlike other early colonial cities, she did not become a busy metropolis. After the American Revolution, industry and commerce moved to Baltimore or inland, and this charming place on the cusp of the Severn River became a colonial Brigadoon — rousing annually to assume her role as Maryland's state capital and entertain the visiting legislators, gracefully hosting summer visitors from Baltimore and Washington, D.C., and providing a home to the U.S. Naval Academy.

Too poor to raze and rebuild in more modern fashions, Annapolis maintained the early residences, inns and places of commerce. The beautiful old buildings and baroque street plan remain intact today, not as pristine museums or carefully restored paths for the tourist, but as vibrant homes and businesses and enchanting walkways. A stroll through the historic district can find a homeowner tending her roses or a glimpse of sailboats moored in the harbor at the end of a street lined with colonial homes. Under the Liberty Tree on the grounds of St. John's College, students debate where the Sons of Liberty once argued for revolution. At city dock midshipmen from the United States Naval Academy mingle with boaters on the porch of a historic tavern, and near the old market young mothers give their toddlers bread to feed the ducks waiting hopefully in the water. Annapolis reminds both residents and visitors of a grand old lady, proud of her heritage and still relishing life. She wears her age gracefully.

Life here has a casual charm and vigor as well. For more than three hundred years the great natural beauty of the Chesapeake Bay has attracted people to Anne Arundel County. This marvelous broad expanse of water provides bountiful land, wonderful food, and scenic vistas that enrich the soul. Annapolitans celebrate their lifestyle with a vivacity that only hints at their deep contentment.

So, in compiling a cookbook that would reflect the spirit of this appealing town, what comes to mind is the timeless beauty and constant abundance which surrounds Annapolis. We cherish the bounty of the land and the Bay that fed the native Americans and early colonists and still provides nourishment, an almost four hundred year old reputation for lively entertainment and warm hospitality, and the times we celebrate as families or as a community.

Of Tide & Thyme is a product of Annapolis's casual lifestyle. We have learned to provide quick, elegant meals using the fresh vegetables and seafood available locally and to season our dishes with lively herbs and spices. This cookbook is a compilation of our favorite dishes. Some are traditional Maryland fare, others are family secrets, still others favorites we'd like to share with you. We welcome you to our town, and we invite you to enjoy our recipes, our cooking secrets and our memories.

TABLE OF CONTENTS

THE COVER

Annapolis's harbor forms the backdrop for a classic Maryland crabfeast. Local Chesapeake sailboats, powerboats and working vessels travel the water, while colonial buildings reflect the late morning sun. An arrangement of Maryland's state flower, the Black-eyed Susan, overflows an antique Chesapeake Bay oyster can.

COVER ARTIST

Annapolis artist Jennifer Heyd Wharton is widely known for her richly textured watercolors. Her work has won many awards in juried shows throughout the Mid-Atlantic area and can be found in several private collections. She trained at the Moore College of Art in Philadelphia, Pennsylvania and is a member of the Baltimore Watercolor Society, the Annapolis Watercolor Club, the Maryland Federation of Art, and the Academy of the Arts. Mrs. Wharton is a sustaining member and former vice president of the Junior League of Annapolis.

GRAPHIC ARTIST ILLUSTRATOR

Marti Betz is a graphic designer, illustrator, portrait artist and owner/creative director of Marti Betz Design/Illustration. The business founded in 1982 provides design services to organizations and businesses in the Baltimore/Washington/Annapolis area. As a multi-talented designer/illustrator, she has proven ability in all phases of print graphics. Quality and creative design are her trademarks. She trained at Wittenbery University and the University of Maryland and has won several honors for her poster designs. Marti has been involved in the following professional organizations: Graphic Artists' Guild, AIGA Baltimore, Art Directors Club of Washington, Maryland Society of Portrait Painters and Women In Communication, Inc.

The Big Moments

ENTERTAINMENT
HINTS & MENUS

The United States Naval Academy

Founded in 1845 on the site of an old Army fort, the United States Naval Academy commands the point at the mouth of the Severn River and Annapolis Harbor. The Academy grounds cover more than 1300 acres and constitute one of the finest collections of Beaux Arts buildings in the country. Bancroft Hall, the huge complex which contains the living quarters for the Brigade, has constant reminders of the career to which the midshipmen have committed themselves. Catwalks crossing the roof recall the decks of naval vessels. In Memorial Hall, somber roll calls and battle mementoes bring to mind the ultimate sacrifice that some graduates have made for their country.

The midshipmen of the Academy are an important element of the economic, social, and even romantic life of Annapolis. These diligent future officers spend four years in rigorous study and training in "The Yard," and they come to have great affection for the town in which they became adults. Families all over the county sponsor midshipmen and provide them with a local home. Many Academy graduates return to live or retire here.

More than one million visitors tour the grounds annually and get a glimpse of a midshipman's life. From the parade grounds at Worden Fields and the Olympic size swimming pool in Lejeune Hall to the Tiffany stained glass windows and John Paul Jones' crypt in the Chapel, the Academy's splendor and traditions are rich and inviting year-round.

In the fall Annapolis becomes awash in blue and gold during Navy football games. Navy fans gather in the Memorial stadium parking lot for festive tailgate parties and cheer the Brigade of Midshipmen as they march into the stadium to support their team.

During Commissioning Week, held in late May, proud families stream into town to celebrate the transformation from midshipmen to an ensign in the U.S. Navy or a second lieutenant in the U.S. Marine Corps. This may also be a time to welcome a new spouse to the family. The Naval Academy Chapel holds weddings every hour immediately after graduation. Newly-married couples radiate happiness as they exit the chapel under the crossed swords of the honor guard, and the new spouse is always "Welcomed to the Navy" with a polite sword swat on the behind, courtesy of the final guard. Sentimental Annapolitans can never resist standing outside the Chapel and applauding the bride and groom.

PARADE OF LIGHTS WARM-UP BUFFET

SHERRY WASSAIL (79)

CHAFING DISH CRAB DIP (20)

PATE WITH PINE NUTS AND PROSCIUTTO (50)

STEAK PESTO ROUNDS (25)

GRUYERE AND MIXED GREENS SALAD (145)

SWEDISH SALMON WITH MUSTARD SAUCE (27)

SLICED PROVIDENCETOWN HOLIDAY TURKEY WITH
CRANBERRY CHUTNEY (209, 33)

OR

TARRAGON CHICKEN IN PHYLLO (202)

COTTAGE DILL ROLLS (95)

HONEY WHEAT ROLLS (96)

GINGER-ORANGE GLAZED CARROTS (173)

SPINACH MUSHROOM GAME RICE (184)

MOCHA RASPBERRY TRIFLE (345)

GRAND MARNIER POUND CAKE (355)

A magical part of Annapolis's holiday season is the Eastport Yacht Club's annual Boat Parade of Lights. Sailboats and motoryachts adorned in elaborate light designs move in a glimmering procession through the harbor. Thousands of people, heavily bundled against the chilly night wind, line the shore to watch. Invite friends back to your house afterwards to get warm with this plentiful buffet.

The Big Moments

MAY DAY BREAKFAST

SCARLETT O'HARAS (72)

OR

CARIBBEAN FRUIT PUNCH (64)

COLD STRAWBERRY SOUP (137)

VEGETABLE FRITTATA (112)

SOUR CREAM ALMOND COFFEE CAKE (100)

FRESHLY BREWED COFFEE

A engaging spring rite in Annapolis is the annual Historic District May basket display. On May 1, businesses, historic sites, and private homes hang baskets of fresh flowers on their doors. The cheery displays range from a simple bouquet to elaborate arrangements festooned with ribbons. Celebrate the arrival of spring with an impromptu May Day breakfast. Invite your neighbors by placing a small basket of flowers and the invitation on their doorstep! Make a centerpiece brimming with lilacs and tulips from your garden.

SUNDAY BRUNCH

FRESH SQUEEZED ORANGE JUICE

BAKED CINNAMON PANCAKE WITH FRUIT
BUTTER (104)

EXTRAORDINARY CRAB QUICHE (106)

HERBED SAUSAGE PUFFS (110)

GRANNY APPLE MUFFINS (90)

Greet a clear summer morning with a leisurely breakfast on the deck. Place a basket of garden roses on the table and put classic jazz on the stereo. Complete your contentment with a quick trip to the newsstand. Buy an assortment of Sunday newspapers and magazines for the family to absorb in companiable quiet.

Entertainment Hints & Menus

BLUE AND GOLD TAILGATE

FALL APPLE PUNCH (63)

SESAME CHICKEN WINGS (47)

PASTA SHISH KEBABS (34)

SWEET AND TANGY GRILLED SHRIMP SALAD (158)

ITALIAN TORTA (111)

GREEN BEANS VINAIGRETTE (172)

BLUEBERRY STREUSEL MUFFINS (92)

CARAMEL PECAN BARS (379)

Fans of U.S. Naval Academy football games feast on lavish brunches before the games. Serve this brunch on a blue tablecloth trimmed with Navy pennants and decorated with a vase overflowing with gold mums or Black-Eyed Susans, the Maryland state flower.

A TWILIGHT CRUISE

MARINA CAY SALMON SPREAD (24)

BROCCOLI CHEESE DIP (59)

CURRIED CHICKEN SALAD WITH CANTALOUPE AND CHUTNEY (155)

ROASTED VEGETABLE PASTA (318)

ENGLISH MATRIMONIALS (381)

SAILOR'S COFFEE (82)

Early evening is a magic time for a cruise. The deep violets and roses of the twilight sky throw shimmering reflections on the water, and the air itself seems quiet and serene. Escape with close friends for an intimate dinner on board. Cruise for a while, then anchor and admire the setting sun as you savor these transportable goodies.

The Big Moments

A MODERN THANKSGIVING

OYSTERS SALISBURY (26)

PUMPKIN AND APPLE BISQUE (133)

PARSLEY SALAD (147)

ROAST DUCKLING WITH GREEN PEPPERCORN SAUCE (208)

SPINACH AND MUSHROOM GAME RICE (184)

PEAR BREAD (85)

SWEET POTATO AND TANGERINE SOUFFLÉ (179)

BLACK WALNUT CAKE (353)

Try this menu for a different twist to the traditional Thanksgiving dinner. Use Birds of Paradise to create an original autumn colored floral centerpiece. Instead of placecards, write your guest's names on tiny pumpkins.

CLASSIC WINTER DINNER

FRUIT WASSAIL (74)

SAVORY HERBED BAKED BRIE (38)

CRAB BISQUE (120)

TOSSED SALAD WITH SWEET DIJON MUSTARD
DRESSING (163)

ANNAPOLIS STUFFED PORK ROAST (226)

YORKSHIRE PUDDING (98)

CHEDDAR SQUASH BAKE (181)

HONEY-GLAZED GREEN BEANS ALMANDINE (171)

CRÊPES WITH LEMON LISBON SAUCE (340)

Celebrate winter and snow! Festoon the mantel and create a centerpiece of white roses and lilies in traditional greenery. Place white ceramic angels and candlesticks with long white tapers on the table. Use a white lace tablecloth over a green undercloth. Tie white ribbons around green napkins and tuck snowy white sprays of baby's breath in the ribbon.

Entertainment Hints & Menus

SPRING LUNCHEON

CHICKEN SATAY WITH SPICY PEANUT SAUCE (48)

MEDITERRANEAN DIP (58)

HEARTS OF PALM SALAD WITH AVOCADO AND
GRAPEFRUIT (146)

HERB AND MUSTARD GLAZED RACK OF LAMB (222)

GARLIC NEW POTATOES (178)

GLAZED SNOWPEAS (167)

POPPY SEED MUFFINS (89)

CHOCOLATE MOUSSE TORTE (346)

Make your own Spring Bonnets while the lamb is cooking. Have ribbons, silk flowers and other goodies to glue on party hats. Use them as a centerpiece with bright flowers and colored grass or let your guests wear their festive attire through lunch!

INDEPENDENCE DAY PICNIC

CHILLED CRAB DIP (19)

HONEY MUSTARD GRILLED CHICKEN (193)

CHESAPEAKE GRILLED CORN (175)

DILL AND ARTICHOKE POTATO SALAD (153)

MARINATED VEGETABLE SALAD (148)

FOURTH OF JULY BLUEBERRY CREAM PIE (337)

Neighborhood parades are an Anne Arundel County tradition on the Fourth of July. Gather the neighborhood children together to decorate bikes, wagons and pets in red, white, and blue. Let them parade around the block waving flags and playing every conceivable instrument, including pots and pans. Serve your picnic to the little revolutionaries and their parents early enough so everyone can see the fireworks over the water in Annapolis harbor!

The Big Moments

THE GANG'S ALL HERE!!!

CALIFORNIA SALSA WITH TORTILLA CHIPS (42)

SPINACH AND STRAWBERRY SALAD (154)

CHALUPAS (223)

WHITE CHILI AND/OR

ESTOFADO (206/234)

FABULOUS CHOCOLATE SHEET CAKE (354)

Sixteen for the Super Bowl. "Hey Mom, everybody's home on break and they're coming over." The annual Booster Club potluck dinner. This crowd-pleasing menu can turn aggravations into ovations.

EVERYTHING NICE FIRESIDE PICNIC

TOMATO BRUSCHETTA (44)

MAHI MAHI WITH WHITE WINE AND FRESH MANGOES (266)

ANGEL HAIR FLANS (299)

BROCCOLI IN LIME BUTTER (169)

GRAND MARNIER SPICED PECANS (390)

CHOCOLATE HAZELNUT TRUFFLES (381)

Banish winter with an intimate dinner by the fire. Use a bright blanket for your tablecloth, set votive candles on the mantel, and throw dried rosemary stems on the logs for a fragrant fire. For true romance, play that most romantic opera, La Traviata!

Entertainment Hints & Menus

SUPER DAD'S DINNER

APPLE RUM PORK CHOPS (227)
ZUCCHINI IN HERBED TOMATO SAUCE (182)
CREAMY CHOCOLATE MACADAMIA COOKIES (365)

Emily has student government, Christopher has soccer, and Mom has a meeting. Today's Dad will find this meal easy to prepare before the evening carpool revs up. Our hero even made the cookies with the kids on Sunday so the cookie jar was stocked for the week. What a guy!

BANISH THE BLUES BASKET

THE BEST CHEESE CRACKERS (32)
SUNDRIED TOMATO AND BASIL SPREAD (39)
MEXICAN LASAGNA (322)
OATMEAL AND TOFFEE COOKIES (372)
TANGY TOASTED NUTS (392)

Take an under-the-weather friend to the rainbow's end with a glowing basket of goodies. Wrap your containers in iridescent paper and use rainbow colored dishes and flatware. Sprinkle with chocolate coins and wrap it all with a big gold ribbon for a true pot o' gold.

The Big Moments

THE FANCIEST FEAST

MUSHROOM BISQUE (136)

SWEET RED PEPPER SALAD WITH NICOISE SAUCE (151)

STUFFED TENDERLOIN (215)

BLUE CHEESE BISCUITS (93)

BROILED CAULIFLOWER WITH ROSEMARY (174)

GLAZED ASPARAGUS (167)

CHAMPAGNE PUNCH WITH BRANDIED
STRAWBERRIES (69)

TANGERINE MOUSSE WITH CHOCOLATE SAUCE (343)

Certain family occasions demand a lavish dinner — a child's graduation, your parents' golden anniversary, the welcoming of a new spouse to the family. Polish grandmother's candlesticks, put out your best tablecloths, and don't forget plenty of glasses to toast the best of times.

SEE "THE ART OF THE CRABFEAST" ON PAGE 252 FOR A CLASSIC MARYLAND CRABFEAST.

Brilliant Beginnings

APPETIZERS

Colonial Times

Annapolis sits on the banks of the Severn River in the heart of Maryland. Settled in 1649, colonial Annapolis was a sparkling economic and social center for the Mid-Atlantic area. Annapolitans were known for their congeniality and enthusiasm for social activities.

The early settlers had high hopes and vigorous ambitions for the colony they were establishing. Anne Arundel County boasts many stately homes whose elegance speaks eloquently of the care that went into building them and the loving tending of subsequent generations. Their names are redolent of the dreams and aspirations of their owners. Titles such as My Lord's Bounty or Obligation speak of debts owed to benefactors, while places like Whitehall or Tulip Hill resound with pride. Great townhomes built prior to the American Revolution still line the streets of Annapolis.

A certain wistfulness is apparent in the titles bestowed by the early colonists — the echo of places left behind but fondly remembered. The Severn River has her namesake in the river that divides England and Wales. Glen Burnie, in northern Anne Arundel County, recalls the many Scotsmen who emigrated here.

Annapolis's harbor bustled with trade. The brigs of colonial times unloaded goods from England and other colonies at the City Dock. Walking down to the harbor today, it is not difficult to imagine the dock teeming with activity. City Dock also contains a grim reminder of a sadder trade. A brass plaque marks the spot where Kunta Kinte arrived on a slave ship and was sold to a plantation owner.

The town of today differs very little from colonial Annapolis in its design, purpose, and baroque street plan. Tour guides in Colonial garb will cheerfully point out the many relics of that time: the Old Treasury House(1737); taverns where Revolutionary War heroes planned their separation from English rule; 300 year old masonry containing oyster shells to hold the mortar together, and a church whose roof was built by shipwrights during the winter months without the use of nails and is so well joined today that it is impossible to slip a credit card between the joists.

Annapolis's many charms lie in a rare ability to combine the past with the present in a seamless line, each era building onto the previous one and respecting each one in the process. Little has been lost in the transition from Colonial times to the present.

CHILLED CRAB DIP

Serves 10 to 12

Easy, can be made ahead

Serve this tasty dip in a glass bowl to highlight its pink color.

2 finely diced hard boiled eggs

1 pound fresh backfin crabmeat

½ cup mayonnaise

½ cup chili sauce

1 teaspoon horseradish

1 tablespoon Worcestershire sauce

¼ teaspoon salt

⅛ teaspoon hot pepper sauce

1 finely grated small onion

◢ Remove any shells from crabmeat.

◢ Put into medium bowl with all other ingredients and mix thoroughly.

◢ Serve with corn chips, potato chips or plain crackers.

◢ Keeps for up to two days in refrigerator.

To keep dips from spoiling in the summertime, serve them in small bowls nesting in larger bowls of chipped ice.

19

CHAFING DISH CRAB DIP

Serves 10 to 12 `

Easy, can be made ahead
Perfect for a party!

1 pound fresh backfin crabmeat, picked

1 (8 ounce) package softened cream cheese

2 tablespoons milk

1 medium onion, chopped

2 tablespoons horseradish

dash hot pepper sauce

salt and white pepper to taste

4 tablespoons mayonnaise

dash paprika

3 tablespoons sherry/wine

pinch seafood seasoning

toasted almonds

crackers

◢ Combine all ingredients, bake at 375° for 10 to 15 minutes.

◢ Sprinkle with toasted almonds, serve in chafing dish with crackers.

The old brick sidewalks in Annapolis's historic district are notoriously uneven. Local legend has it that the Naval Academy midshipmen gain their sea legs by negotiating the sidewalks.

20

C A V I A R   M O U S S E

Serves 10-12

Average, must be made ahead

Parsley and dill give this elegant appetizer a fresh taste.

3 grated hard boiled eggs

¾ cup sour cream

¼ cup chopped onion

3 tablespoons mayonnaise

2 teaspoons fresh lemon juice

½ teaspoon Worcestershire sauce

1½ teaspoons unflavored gelatin

2 tablespoons cold water

3 ounces black or red caviar

3 tablespoons minced fresh parsley

1 tablespoon chopped fresh dill

crackers, thinly sliced pumpernickel bread, or rye triangles

▲ Spray 2 cup pan or decorative mold with cooking spray.

▲ Mix eggs, sour cream, onion, mayonnaise, lemon juice, and Worcestershire sauce in a bowl.

▲ Mix gelatin with cold water in small bowl, set in pan of boiling water until gelatin dissolves. Stir gelatin into sour cream mixture, fold in caviar, parsley and dill.

▲ Put in pan or mold, refrigerate for at least 3 hours.

▲ To serve, set mold in warm water for a minute and unmold on serving plate.

▲ Garnish with additional caviar, parsley and/or dill, serve with toast triangles, crackers or bread.

21

Brilliant Beginnings

CLOVERHILL ROAD CLAM PUFFS

Serves 6 dozen

Average, can be made ahead and frozen

The secret of these easy puffs is the clam juice in the pastry adding immeasurably to the flavor.

3   (8 ounce) cans of minced clams

½   cup butter

1   cup flour

4   room temperature eggs

4   (3 ounce) packages chive cream cheese

4   dashes hot pepper sauce

¼   teaspoon pepper

¾   teaspoon seasoned salt

▲ Preheat oven to 400*.

▲ Drain juice from clams into measuring cup and add enough water to make 1 cup.

▲ Mix clams, cream cheese, hot pepper sauce, pepper, and seasoned salt in a bowl.

▲ Heat juice in pan over low heat, add butter and bring to a boil.

▲ Add flour all at once and stir vigorously over low heat until mixture leaves sides of pan.

▲ Add eggs one at a time beating after each.

▲ Place level tablespoon of batter on ungreased cookie sheet and bake at 400° for 10 minutes.

▲ Reduce heat to 300°, bake for an additional 20 to 25 minutes.

▲ Cool, cut in half and fill with mixture of cream cheese, clams and spices.

▲ Puffs can be frozen, defrosted & filled just prior to serving.

MARINATED SHRIMP

Serves 20 to 25

Easy, can be made ahead

This crowd pleaser is great for a cocktail party, even the onions are delicious!

5   pounds cooked and peeled medium shrimp

10 thinly sliced mild white onions

1   pint vegetable oil

1½ cups good cider vinegar

1   large bottle of capers and juice

1   teaspoon salt

2   teaspoons hot pepper sauce

2   tablespoons Worcestershire sauce

2   cups sugar

▲ Mix all together in big bowl, marinate for at least 2 days.

▲ Stir occasionally, drain and serve with toothpicks.

Add interest to your buffet by placing food at different heights. Stack sturdy and steady containers or books under the tablecloth and place cracker baskets, cheeses or desserts on top.

23

MARINA CAY SALMON SPREAD

Serves 12

Easy, can be made ahead

Tastes like a summer evening at the beach.

1 (7.5 ounce) can pink salmon

1 (8 ounce) package softened cream cheese

2½ tablespoons lime juice

½ teaspoon dried dill or 1½ tablespoons fresh dill

hot pepper sauce

▲ Remove any bones and skin from salmon.

▲ Cream salmon with cream cheese until mixed.

▲ Squeeze lime and blend into cream cheese mixture.

▲ Stir in dill and hot pepper sauce (about 6 drops for mild).

▲ Serve with a sturdy cracker.

CURRIED SHRIMP DIP

Serves 12 to 16

Easy, can be made ahead and reheated

A never fail party pleaser.

1 can shrimp soup

1 (8 ounce) package cream cheese

4 ounces drained and chopped black olives

2 tablespoons lemon juice

1 teaspoon curry

1 clove minced garlic

1 small bag frozen salad shrimp

▲ Melt soup and cheese in double boiler.

▲ Use mixer to add olives, lemon juice, curry, and garlic.

▲ Add frozen shrimp and heat until shrimp are warm.

▲ Serve warm with large dipping corn chips.

PESTO ROUNDS WITH STEAK OR SHRIMP

Serves 20-25

Average, can be made ahead, partially

This versatile appetizer is delicious as either a seafood or a meat hors d'oeuvre.

½ cup pesto sauce

2 tablespoons grated Parmesan cheese

1 French bread baguette, sliced

1 pound shrimp, cooked and peeled

1 pound flank steak, grilled and sliced thinly to fit baguettes

◢ Combine pesto and cheese.

◢ Spread on one side of each bread slice.

◢ If making the shrimp rounds, top each slice with shrimp and broil for 2 minutes until lightly toasted. Serve immediately.

◢ If making the steak rounds, broil bread and pesto mixture for 2 minutes, then top with grilled flank steak. Serve warm or at room temperature.

Brilliant Beginnings

OYSTERS SALISBURY

Serves 4 dozen

Average, can be made ahead, partially

These excellent oysters are an elegant first course.

4   dozen Maryland oysters in shell

2   tablespoons butter

2   tablespoons flour

2   cups milk

½   cup shredded Swiss cheese

¾   teaspoon Worcestershire sauce

¼   teaspoon nutmeg

⅛   teaspoon pepper

½   package (10 ounce) frozen chopped spinach

     salt to taste

     Parmesan cheese for topping

▲ Open oysters, letting oysters remain in deep half of shell (fish and seafood shops will do this for you).

▲ Melt butter in 1 quart sauce pan. Blend in flour and slowly add milk. Simmer slowly for 5 minutes (low heat) stirring occasionally.

▲ Add Swiss cheese and stir until melted. Stir in Worcestershire sauce, nutmeg, salt and pepper.

▲ Cook spinach as directed on the package and squeeze out all additional moisture.

▲ Blend spinach into cheese sauce and let mixture cool. Top each oyster with 1 tablespoon spinach mixture.

▲ Sprinkle with grated Parmesan cheese (can be covered and refrigerated to this point).

▲ Bake at 400° for 10 to 15 minutes. Serve immediately.

SWEDISH SALMON WITH MUSTARD SAUCE

Serves 20

Gourmet, must be made ahead.

Sensational for holiday buffets!

1	8 pound fresh salmon
⅔	cup salt
½	cup sugar
1	tablespoon whole black peppers, crushed
1	teaspoon allspice
6	tablespoons cognac
2	bunches dill, chopped finely

Mustard Sauce

9	tablespoons olive oil
3	tablespoons white vinegar
2½	tablespoons prepared mustard
¾	teaspoon salt
¼	teaspoon white pepper
½	cup sugar
⅛	teaspoon cardamom

Bone salmon, rinse in icy water, dry with towel.

Mix salt, sugar, and spices. Rub on all sides of fish.

Sprinkle cognac and dill around and on fish.

Place fish in deep bowl and seal with cover.

Refrigerate for 36 hours.

Serve with lemon wedges, fresh pepper, and mustard sauce.

To make mustard sauce, combine all ingredients in blender. Make 2 hours before serving.

Whisk before serving.

This traditional salmon can also be halved and served as the main course for a dinner party.

Brilliant Beginnings

REMOULADE SAUCE

Makes 2 1/2 cups

Gourmet, may be prepared ahead

This is superb as a seafood dip or sauce.

¾ cup olive oil

¼ cup lemon juice

¼ cup Creole mustard or prepared brown mustard

2 tablespoons prepared horseradish

⅔ cup finely chopped onion

⅔ cup finely chopped celery

2 tablespoons finely sliced green onions with tops

2 tablespoons finely chopped parsley

2 teaspoons paprika

1 teaspoon salt

⅛ teaspoon pepper

⅛ teaspoon cayenne

1 clove minced garlic

◤ Combine all ingredients and mix well, chill.

◤ Serve over seafood or with sliced meats.

◤ May be stored covered in the refrigerator 4 days.

My uncle, a chef, catered an unforgettable outdoor luncheon in my honor after my college graduation. We sat in the park eating shrimp and salmon and lamb under a clear May sky. It was quite a celebration!

COCKTAIL SAUCE

Makes 1 1/2 cups

Easy, can be made ahead
The essential seafood sauce.

1½ cups chili sauce

1   tablespoon tarragon
     vinegar

2   tablespoons prepared
     horseradish

1   teaspoon
     Worcestershire sauce

     dash hot pepper sauce

     ground pepper to taste

◤ Combine all ingredients, chill well
  before serving.

WYE RIVER CRAB FONDUE

Serves 4

Average, can be made ahead

Your guests will keep coming back for more!

1	pound lump backfin crabmeat
⅛	teaspoon pepper
¼	teaspoon seasoning salt
1	(8 ounce) package cream cheese
1	(6 ounce) package grated Gruyère cheese
½	cup milk
¼	teaspoon lemon-pepper seasoning
1	tablespoon chopped parsley
	salt and pepper to taste
¼	cup white wine
1	teaspoon Worcestershire sauce
	French bread cut into 1½ inch cubes

◢ Combine cheeses, milk, seasonings, and wine in a pan or fondue pot over a low flame.

◢ Stir often until blended and smooth.

◢ Add crabmeat and continue stirring and heating until hot and bubbly, about 5 minutes.

◢ Serve with bread cubes (speared) or crackers.

St. Anne's Episcopal Church, in the center of Church Circle, was founded in 1695. King William III gave the church its communion plate. Surrounding the church are elaborate colonial tombs of which William O. Stephens wryly observed: "There are no common sinners here."

CHEDDAR BEER FONDUE

Serves 8

Average, cannot be made ahead

Serve this hearty appetizer in front of a roaring fire after skiing.

1   clove garlic

1   pound well-aged sharp cheddar cheese

3   tablespoons flour

1-2 teaspoons Worcestershire sauce

½   teaspoon dry mustard

2   cups beer (good quality)

3-4 drops hot sauce, optional

2   tablespoons chopped chives

     cubes of sourdough bread

▲ Rub inside of fondue pot with garlic, discard garlic.

▲ In fondue pot, heat beer (start with 1½ cups of beer and add up to 2 cups as needed) until almost boiling.

▲ Add cheese, dredged in flour, by handfuls, making sure each addition has melted and blended before adding more.

▲ When all cheese has melted and the mixture is smooth and thick, stir in Worcestershire sauce, dry mustard, and hot sauce.

▲ Garnish with chives, serve with bread cubes for dunking.

31

THE BEST CHEESE CRACKERS

Makes 48 crackers

Easy, can be made ahead

Use different cookie cutters to create these crackers for parties with a theme, such as stars for the Fourth of July or numbers for birthdays.

½   pound grated mild cheddar cheese

1   cup overflowing with flour

1   stick softened margarine

1   teaspoon cayenne pepper

▲ Put all ingredients into a mixing bowl.

▲ Using hands, knead the mixture until the butter and cheese and flour are well mixed. Cheese will still look a bit separated, but make sure that all is well incorporated.

▲ Grease a cookie sheet, roll out dough on floured surface and cut into 2 inch round shapes. Make sure it is of uniform thickness.

▲ Bake crackers on cookie sheet at 300° until they are showing just a slight raising (about 15 to 20 minutes). After cooling can be stored in tins or frozen.

CRANBERRY CHUTNEY

Makes 2 cups

Must be made ahead

Keep on hand for a quick appetizer. Serve on top of cream cheese or use in baked brie.

1   quartered and seeded lemon

1   quartered and seeded orange

1½   cups fresh or frozen whole cranberries

2   cups dark brown sugar

1½   cups raisins

½   cup white vinegar

½   teaspoon ground cinnamon

½   teaspoon ground cloves

½   teaspoon freshly grated nutmeg

½   cinnamon stick

1   cup fresh pitted cherries or dried cherries (optional)

▲ Cut lemon and orange into pieces no bigger than ½ inch.

▲ Place them in a large saucepan with all the other ingredients.

▲ Bring the mixture to a boil over medium heat and reduce the heat.

▲ Simmer for 15 minutes.

▲ Remove the cinnamon stick, cool and refrigerate.

Use different antique china bowls or jam jars for serving dips.

33

PASTA SHISH KEBAB

Serves 24

Average, must be made ahead

A fun nibbler for a casual party.

1   (12 to 16 ounce) package frozen cheese tortellini

2   tablespoons freshly squeezed lemon juice

¼   cup olive oil

3   tablespoons fresh chopped parsley

1-2 cloves crushed garlic

1½ teaspoons oregano

⅛   teaspoon black ground pepper

1   sliced or cubed red pepper

1   sliced or cubed green pepper

1   small jar green or black pitted olives

1   (8 ounce) package cubed mozzarella cheese

▲ Cook tortellini according to package directions. Do not overcook.

▲ To make dressing, mix lemon juice, olive oil, parsley, garlic, oregano, and black pepper in small bowl.

▲ Immediately place hot pasta into dressing so flavors will be absorbed.

▲ Add peppers, olives and cheese, marinate for 24 hours.

▲ Either serve as a salad or place one of each ingredient on skewers for hors d'oeuvres.

▲ Refrigerate until ready to serve.

THYME PESTO CHEESECAKE

Serves 18

Gourmet, must be made ahead

A Showstopper! Can top with sun-dried tomato pesto or julienned roasted vegetables for variation.

1   tablespoon softened butter

¼   cup fine, dry breadcrumbs

½   cup plus 2 tablespoons grated Parmesan cheese

2   (8 ounce) packages softened cream cheese

1   cup ricotta cheese

¼   teaspoon salt

¼   teaspoon cayenne

3   large eggs

½   cup thyme pesto (see recipe in Pasta) or purchased pesto sauce

¼   cup lightly toasted pine nuts

     fresh basil sprigs

     hearty crackers

▲ Preheat oven to 325°.

▲ Rub 1 tablespoon butter over bottom and sides of 9-inch springform pan. Mix breadcrumbs with 2 tablespoons grated cheese. Coat pan with crumb mixture.

▲ Using electric mixer, beat cream cheese, ricotta, remaining ½ cup Parmesan cheese, salt and cayenne in a large bowl until fluffy. Add eggs one at a time, beating well after each addition.

▲ Transfer half of mixture to medium bowl, mix pesto into remaining half.

▲ Pour pesto mixture into prepared pan, smooth top. Carefully spoon plain mixture on top; smooth. Sprinkle with pine nuts.

▲ Bake cake until center no longer moves when shaken, about 45 minutes. Transfer to rack and cool completely. Cover tightly with plastic wrap and chill overnight.

▲ Run small sharp knife around pan sides to loosen cheesecake and remove sides. Transfer cake to a platter or raised cake plate, garnish with basil sprigs and surround with crackers to serve.

EAST INDIAN CHEESE BALL

Serves 12

Easy, must be made ahead

A tangy treat to add variety to your buffet. Wonderful on the boat!

2 (8 ounce) packages softened cream cheese

1 cup cottage cheese

1 teaspoon curry powder

1 cup finely chopped green onions, including tops

1 cup chopped dry roasted peanuts

1 cup raisins

½ cup shredded coconut

¾ cup mango chutney

▲ Beat cream cheese, cottage cheese and curry together with electric mixer until smooth.

▲ Beat remaining ingredients except chutney by hand. Refrigerate over night.

▲ Form into 2 balls and wrap in wax paper. Chill at least 6 hours.

▲ To serve, place ball on platter, spoon chutney on top and surround with toasted pita triangles or crackers.

PINEAPPLE CHEESE BALL

Serves 12

Easy, must be made ahead

For a different look shape and serve this in a hollowed out pineapple sliced sideways.

2 (8 ounce) packages softened cream cheese

1 (13½ ounce) can crushed pineapple

2 cups finely crushed pecans

¼ cup finely chopped green pepper

2 tablespoons chopped onion

1 tablespoon seasoned salt

crackers

◢ Beat cream cheese until smooth.

◢ Stir drained pineapple into cheese with one cup of nuts.

◢ Add rest of ingredients.

◢ Chill one hour, form into 2 large or 3 small balls and roll in remaining 1 cup nuts.

◢ Serve with crackers.

37

SAVORY HERBED BAKED BRIE

Serves 12-16

Average

Superb for a cocktail reception.

1   2 pound wheel brie (8 inch diameter)

1   sheet frozen puffed pastry

¼   cup chopped parsley

1   clove garlic, minced

1   teaspoon dried rosemary

1   teaspoon dried thyme

1   teaspoon dried marjoram

2   ounces hard salami, chopped

1   egg, lightly beaten

▲ Place brie in freezer for 30 minutes. Let pastry stand at room temperature for 20 minutes.

▲ Mix parsley, garlic, and herbs in a small bowl.

▲ Slice brie into two layers. Spread herb mixture on bottom layer. Sprinkle with salami. Replace top layer.

▲ Unfold pastry sheet. Roll into 12 inch by 8 inch rectangle on floured surface.

▲ Place brie on center of pastry. Cover with pastry and cut off excess. Brush edges with egg and press to seal. Brush pastry with remaining egg and cut 4 steam vents.

▲ Bake at 350° for 30 minutes until pastry is golden and puffed. Let stand 15 minutes before serving. Serve with crackers.

Appetizers

SUN-DRIED TOMATO AND BASIL SPREAD

Serves 8

Easy, can be made ahead

A delectable stuffing for mushrooms as well.

1   (8 ounce) package cream cheese

12-14 chopped sun-dried tomatoes, softened in boiling water and drained

¼   cup grated fresh Parmesan cheese

1   clove minced garlic

4-5 leaves chopped fresh basil

▲ Combine all ingredients in food processor and process until smooth.

▲ Garnish with chopped basil leaves. Serve at room temperature or slightly warmed in the microwave.

TORTILLA PINWHEELS

Makes 24

Easy, can be made ahead

Very colorful. Watch them disappear!

1   (8 ounce) package softened cream cheese

2   tablespoons sour cream

½   teaspoon garlic powder

1   tablespoon dried Italian dressing mix

4   tablespoons finely chopped scallions

1   roasted red pepper, peeled and cut into fine slices

5   large flour tortillas

▲ Mix cream cheese, sour cream and garlic powder or seasoning. Spread lightly on tortillas.

▲ Sprinkle scallions and red pepper pieces onto tortillas, leaving a half inch of spread open for sealing. Roll tightly.

▲ Refrigerate to chill, cut into ¾ inch pieces and lay on side for serving.

40

SPICY TORTILLA ROLL UPS

Serves 6

Terrific for football parties.

1   (8 ounce) package
    softened cream cheese

2   tablespoons sour
    cream

1   (4 ounce) can chopped
    green chilies

1   (4 ounce) can chopped
    black olives

1   cup grated cheddar
    cheese

5   large flour tortillas

◢ Mix all ingredients except tortillas.

◢ Spread lightly over tortillas, then roll up tightly. Cover and refrigerate to chill.

◢ Cut into 1½ inch pieces, cut off ends and discard. Serve with salsa for dipping.

41

Brilliant Beginnings

CALIFORNIA SALSA

Serves 12

Easy, must be made ahead

You'll never have leftovers with this dip!

2   cups shredded Monterey jack cheese

2   large chopped tomatoes

4   chopped scallions

1   (4 ounce) can chopped mild green chilies

4   ounces chopped black olives

1   package dried Italian dressing

   red wine vinegar

▲ Make Italian dressing according to package directions using red wine vinegar.

▲ Mix all ingredients together.

▲ Marinate overnight to blend flavors, drain the dressing and serve with sturdy tortillas chips.

FRESH SALSA

Serves 8

Easy, can be made ahead

A spicy way to use summer tomatoes.

10 fresh tomatoes chopped into large pieces

1 bunch spring onions

1 green pepper

1 tablespoon fresh cilantro

1 teaspoon apple cider vinegar

1 clove garlic or powder to taste

1 teaspoon salt to taste

½ teaspoon pepper to taste

3-4 tablespoons finely chopped jalapeño peppers to taste

◢ Place chopped tomatoes into food processor a handful at a time and use the pulse setting to dice the tomatoes. Drain excess liquid if necessary. Pour mixture into large mixing bowl.

◢ Dice the green pepper in the processor and transfer to mixing bowl.

◢ Next put the cilantro, onions, and garlic into processor and add to the mixing bowl when done.

◢ Add vinegar, salt and pepper to bowl and mix thoroughly. Add finely chopped jalapeño peppers to desired heat.

43

◢ Let sit for 1 hour to blend flavors. Lasts for 4 days in the refrigerator.

TOMATO BRUSCHETTA

Serves 18

Average, can be made ahead, partially

A satisfying first course for a pasta dinner.

1 baguette, sliced in ½ inch pieces

2 chopped tomatoes

2 tablespoons fresh chopped basil

½ teaspoon salt

½ teaspoon minced garlic

½ teaspoon coarse pepper

2 tablespoons olive oil

¼ teaspoon garlic powder

1 pound thinly sliced fresh mozzarella

▲ Combine tomatoes, basil, salt, minced garlic and pepper. Drain.

▲ Toast baguette slices under broiler until light golden brown. (Approximately 1 to 2 minutes, watch carefully).

▲ Mix olive oil and garlic powder, brush over toast.

▲ Top each slice with tomato mixture.

▲ Reduce oven heat to 350°, bake for 5 minutes just before serving.

▲ Top with sliced mozzarella and serve.

Freeze cheese for 10-15 minutes before slicing or grating to prevent crumbling.

QUESADILLAS

Serves 12

Average

These can be made hot and spicy or mild.

1 (10 ounce) package shredded Pepper Jack cheese or 5 ounces Monterey jack and 5 ounces sharp cheddar cheese

1 (6 ounce) can drained and chopped green chilies, optional

1 (2¼ ounce) can drained and sliced ripe olives

⅔ cup picante sauce

½ cup chopped toasted almonds

¼ cup loosely packed chopped cilantro

8 7 to 8 inch flour tortillas

3 tablespoons melted butter or margarine

◢ Preheat oven to 450°.

◢ For mild: use 5 ounces cheddar and 5 ounces Monterey jack cheese, omit chilies. For hot and spicy: use 10 ounces Pepper Jack cheese and chopped green chilies.

◢ Combine cheese, chilies, olives, picante sauce, almonds, and cilantro in a large bowl. Mix well.

◢ Brush one side of 4 tortillas with butter, place butter side down on baking sheet.

◢ Place 1 cup cheese mixture on each tortilla, spread to within ¾ inch of edge.

◢ Top each with remaining tortillas, pressing firmly, brush tops with butter. Bake about 10 minutes or until tops are lightly browned.

◢ Remove from oven and let stand 3 to 5 minutes. Cut each quesadilla into 8 wedges.

◢ Serve with additional picante sauce.

Cilantro or coriander is used in many ethnic dishes and blends well with pungent spices like curry and cumin. It has a fresh aromatic flavor and should be used sparingly.

SPICY CHESAPEAKE CHICKEN SPREAD

Makes 3 cups

Average, must be made ahead

Good for tea sandwiches as well.

2 (8 ounce) packages softened cream cheese

1 tablespoon bottled steak sauce

½ teaspoon curry powder

red and black pepper to taste

1½ cup minced cooked chicken

⅓ cup minced celery

¼ cup chopped parsley

¼ cup chopped toasted almonds

crackers

◢ Beat together cream cheese, steak sauce, curry powder and pepper.

◢ Blend in cooked chicken and celery and 2 tablespoons parsley. Refrigerate remaining parsley.

◢ Shape mixture into 9 inch log. Wrap in plastic and chill for 4 hours or overnight.

◢ Toss together remaining parsley and almonds and coat log with this mixture.

◢ Serve with crackers.

SESAME CHICKEN WINGS

Serves 12

Average, can be made ahead

Serve on the porch at sunset.

12 chicken wings

1 tablespoon light soy sauce

1 tablespoon Chinese rice wine or dry sherry

½ teaspoon freshly grated ginger

2 beaten egg whites

2 tablespoons ground almonds

2 tablespoons flour

2 tablespoons sesame seeds

   peanut oil for deep frying

Oriental Sauce

2 tablespoons soy sauce

2 tablespoons vinegar

½ teaspoon sesame oil

1 teaspoon freshly grated ginger

2 tablespoons sugar

◢ Cut each wing into 3 pieces, discard tip. Combine light soy sauce, wine, and ginger for a marinade.

◢ Soak the wing pieces in the marinade for 15 minutes.

◢ Blend the almonds, flour and sesame seeds for coating the wings and heat the oil. Remove wings from marinade and dip in the egg whites.

◢ Dredge the wings in coating mixture. Deep fry at 360° until each piece is golden brown, about 5 minutes.

47

◢ Serve hot with dip sauce.

◢ Combine soy sauce, vinegar, sesame oil, ginger, and sugar for dip sauce.

CHICKEN SATAY WITH SPICY PEANUT SAUCE

Makes 50 pieces

Gourmet, must be made ahead

A spectacular appetizer when you're hosting the gourmet club.

1¼ pounds boneless, skinless chicken breast

Marinade

2 tablespoons sesame oil

2 tablespoons corn oil

¼ cup dry sherry

¼ cup soy sauce

2 tablespoons lemon juice

1½ teaspoons minced garlic

1½ teaspoons minced ginger

¼ teaspoon salt

¼ teaspoon pepper

1 dash hot pepper sauce

▲ Cut the chicken into ½ inch wide by 3 inch long strips.

▲ Combine with the ingredients and leave to marinate in the refrigerator anywhere from 1 to 3 hours.

Continued on next page

Use the garden year-round to provide inexpensive color for the table. Decorate appetizer platters with fresh flowers tied with a ribbon or frost pine boughs or holly leaves by dipping them in egg whites and sugar. Scatter scarlet and gold autumn leaves across a green tablecloth.

CHICKEN SATAY WITH SPICY PEANUT SAUCE (Continued)

Satay Sauce

4	teaspoons corn oil
2	teaspoons sesame oil
½	tablespoon minced red onion
2	tablespoons minced garlic
1½	teaspoons minced ginger
1	tablespoon brown sugar
1	tablespoon red wine vinegar
⅓	cup smooth peanut butter
½	teaspoon ground coriander
3	tablespoons ketchup
3	tablespoons soy sauce
1	tablespoon lime or lemon juice
½	teaspoon pepper
1	dash hot pepper sauce
⅓-½ cup hot water	
½	teaspoon turmeric for color (optional)

To prepare Satay Sauce

▲ Heat the corn and sesame oils in a small saucepan. Add the onion, garlic and ginger. Sauté over medium heat until softened.

▲ Add vinegar and sugar, continue to cook and stir until sugar dissolves.

▲ Remove from heat and stir in remaining ingredients (or combine in a food processor for a completely smooth sauce).

▲ Preheat oven to 375°.

▲ Thread each piece of chicken onto wooden toothpick or small skewer and arrange on baking sheets.

▲ Bake for 5 to 10 minutes or until just cooked.

▲ Serve hot with bowl of room temperature sauce for dipping.

▲ Since the sauce can be made in advance, it may thicken or separate before you use it. Whisk in a little hot water until the sauce is the consistency you desire.

49

PÂTÉ WITH PINE NUTS AND PROSCIUTTO

Serves 12

Average, must be prepared ahead

Deceptively easy to make and delicious.

1 pound ground pork

½ pound ground veal

¼ pound pork fat cut in strips or 1 pound of bacon

⅓ cup chopped oil-cured olives

¼ cup lightly toasted pine nuts

¼ cup diced prosciutto ham

¼ cup soft white bread crumbs moistened in 2 tablespoons dry vermouth

1½ teaspoons dried basil

½ teaspoon dried thyme

¼ teaspoon fresh ground pepper

1 minced large clove garlic

½ teaspoon salt

1 egg lightly beaten

50

◢ Combine all the above ingredients except pork fat or bacon.

◢ Line the bottom of a 4 to 5 cup loaf pan with the thin strips of pork fat or bacon.

◢ Turn the meat mixture into the loaf pan and pat down firmly.

◢ Cover the top of the mixture with the remaining thin strips of pork fat or bacon.

◢ Bake the pâté in a preheated 350° for 1½ hours.

◢ Cover with a double layer of tin foil and weight the pâté down with a brick. Chill for 24 hours.

◢ Unmold the pâté onto a serving platter and remove the pork fat or bacon.

◢ Serve the sliced pâté at room temperature with thin toast points.

TERIYAKI MEATBALLS

Makes 150 meatballs

Gourmet, must be made ahead

These meat balls are worth the effort. Keep on hand for the holidays!

3   pounds ground pork

2   (8 ounce) cans drained, finely chopped water chestnuts

1½ cups finely chopped green onions

1   tablespoon finely chopped fresh or crystallized ginger

2   tablespoons salt

3   tablespoons soy sauce

4   lightly beaten eggs

1½ cups bread crumbs

¼   cup cornstarch

1   (8 ounce) can chopped pineapple

½   cup vegetable oil

2   cups unsweetened pineapple juice

1   cup cider vinegar

¼   cup soy sauce

⅔   cup sugar

1½ cups beef broth

2   tablespoons finely chopped fresh or crystallized ginger

⅓   cup cornstarch

⅔   cup cold water

◢ Combine pork, water chestnuts, green onions, 1 tablespoon ginger, salt, 3 tablespoons soy sauce and eggs in a large bowl. Mix well with hands.

◢ Add bread crumbs and mix until just combined, chill mixture.

◢ Shape into ¾ to 1 inch balls, roll the balls in cornstarch.

◢ Brown meat on all sides in hot oil. Remove balls and put on a roasting pan.

◢ To freeze, place meatballs in a single layer on the roasting pan and put into freezer bags when frozen. Take out as needed.

◢ Preheat oven to 350° and bake meatballs for 15 to 20 minutes until cooked through.

◢ To make sauce, combine pineapple with juice, vinegar, ¼ cup soy sauce, ⅔ cup sugar, beef broth and ginger in large saucepan, bring to boiling.

◢ Mix cornstarch with cold water, add to boiling mixture stirring constantly. Continue cooking and stirring until sauce is thick and clear.

◢ Sauce will keep in refrigerator for up to a week.

◢ To serve, place in chafing dish with enough sauce to coat balls. Serve with toothpicks.

SWEET AND SOUR SMOKED SAUSAGES

Serves 30

Easy, can be made ahead

A proven favorite.

3	pounds sliced and browned smoked sausage
1	(20 ounce) can drained chunk pineapple
2	tablespoons butter
½	chopped onion
2	cups chili sauce
¼	cup vinegar
1	teaspoon Worcestershire sauce
½	cup lemon juice
¼	cup brown sugar
½	teaspoon paprika
2	teaspoons dry mustard
1	teaspoon salt
½	teaspoon pepper

▲ Sauté onion in butter, add everything except sausage and heat.

▲ Add previously browned sausage.

▲ Serve with toothpick in a chafing dish or fondue pot.

TEXAS CAVIAR

Makes 2 cups

Easy
A colorful low-fat dip.

2 (8 ounce) cans black-eyed peas

1 (8 ounce) can hominy

2 chopped tomatoes

1 chopped green pepper

4 chopped scallions

1 teaspoon minced garlic

1 tablespoon fresh parsley

½ bottle Italian dressing

corn chips

▲ Mix all ingredients together and marinate for 2 hours.

▲ Serve with corn chips.

Ground peppers add different qualities to dishes. A handy guide is to use black for flavor, white for bite, and red for heat.

MARINATED PINEAPPLE

Serves 6

Easy, must be made ahead

Perfect for a warm weather party.

2   fresh pineapples cut into bite size chunks

1   cup sugar

½   cup water

½   cup Grand Marnier

½   cup lime juice

1   tablespoon finely grated orange rind (about 1 medium orange)

▲ Boil sugar and water for one minute.

▲ Add Grand Marnier, orange rind and lime juice.

▲ Place pineapple in serving bowl, pour sauce over pineapple.

▲ Let pineapple marinate in refrigerator for 1 to 2 hours before serving, stirring occasionally.

▲ Serve cold with toothpicks for appetizer or in bowl for dessert.

54

SWEET SPICE DIP FOR FRESH FRUIT

Makes 1 cup

Easy, must be made ahead
Serve in a hollowed out
melon surrounded by fruit.

⅛   teaspoon cinnamon

⅛   teaspoon nutmeg

dash allspice

dash salt

2   tablespoons sugar

1   cup sour cream

½   teaspoon pure vanilla extract

⅛   teaspoon rum extract

◢ Mix cinnamon, nutmeg, allspice and salt with sugar.

◢ Stir into sour cream, add extracts and mix well.

◢ Chill two hours to allow flavors to blend.

◢ Serve with fresh fruit such as strawberries, bing cherries, green grapes, apples, pineapple and bananas.

55

ANTIPASTO WEDGES

Serves 24 wedges

Easy, can be prepared ahead

Great starter to an Italian meal.

1	(8 ounce) package softened cream cheese
1	teaspoon oregano
¼	teaspoon garlic powder
¼	teaspoon dried marjoram
¼	teaspoon crushed dried basil
3	tablespoons lemon juice
3	pita shells or toasted pita chips
2	small jars marinated artichoke hearts
1	small can of pitted black olives
6	slices of Genoa salami

▲ Combine cream cheese, lemon juice, and herbs until smooth.

▲ Cut pita shells into quarters and separate each quarter.

▲ Toast the pita pieces lightly.

▲ Cut the Genoa salami and artichoke hearts into quarters. Cut olives in half.

▲ Spread the cream cheese mixture onto the pita chips and place a piece of salami onto each chip.

▲ Put a dab of the cheese spread on top of the salami and fix an artichoke piece and half of an olive there.

Appetizers

S P I C E D   G R E E N   O L I V E S

Serves 2 1/2 cups

Average, must be made ahead

An addictive nibbler to start a Spanish meal.

2   cups large green olives

10   sprigs coarsely chopped fresh rosemary

1   thinly sliced large lemon

4   peeled and minced garlic cloves

¼   teaspoon fresh ground pepper

¼   teaspoon crushed red pepper

1½   cups extra virgin olive oil

◢ Wash olives under running cold water.

◢ Crack olives gently with meat mallet, so they crack slightly and pits remain inside.

◢ Place olives in sterilized mason jars alternately with lemon slices.

◢ Combine rosemary, spices and olive oil, divide evenly among jarred olives.

◢ Seal jars and leave at room temperature for 4 days before serving.

MEDITERRANEAN DIP

2 cups

Average, can be made ahead and frozen

Low-fat but watch your guests devour it.

1	large eggplant
2	tablespoons sugar
½	cup plus 2 tablespoons olive oil
2½	cups sliced onions
1	cup diced celery
2	(8 ounce) cans tomato sauce
¼	cup red wine vinegar
2	tablespoons drained capers
12	sliced pitted large olives
	dash of salt and pepper

▲ Wash eggplant, cut into ½ inch cubes and sauté in ½ cup olive oil until tender and golden brown. Can be grilled for added flavor.

▲ Remove eggplant and set aside.

▲ Sauté onion and celery in 2 tablespoons olive oil in same skillet until tender.

▲ Return eggplant, stir in tomato sauce and bring to boil. Lower heat, cover, simmer 15 minutes.

▲ Add remaining ingredients. Simmer in covered skillet about 20 minutes, stirring occasionally.

▲ Purée in a food processor. Refrigerate overnight in a covered container. Can be frozen.

▲ Serve with crackers or pita chips.

BROCCOLI CHEESE DIP

Makes 3 cups

Easy

This pretty and unusual dip is guaranteed to draw crowds. Serve in two bowls to prevent riots.

2   bunches finely chopped fresh broccoli, excluding stems

1   (8 ounce) package grated cheddar cheese

1   pound cooked crumbled bacon

1   small finely chopped onion, optional

1   cup mayonnaise

2   tablespoons vinegar

½   cup sugar

crackers

◢ Mix broccoli, cheese, bacon and onion in serving bowl.

◢ Mix mayonnaise, vinegar and sugar in small bowl. Sauce should be sweet, adjust with more sugar if not sweet.

◢ Pour sauce over broccoli mixture and lightly toss.

◢ Serve with crackers.

59

LEMON PEPPER PARMESAN DIP

Makes one cup

Easy, can be made ahead
Serve with crisp vegetables.

½ cup sour cream

½ cup mayonnaise

¼ cup lemon juice

½ teaspoon ground black pepper

3-4 tablespoons Parmesan cheese

½ teaspoon crushed garlic

60

▲ Combine mayonnaise, sour cream and lemon juice.

▲ Add cheese and spices, refrigerate until serving.

▲ Can add more Parmesan if desired.

To brighten the color of raw broccoli and carrots, plunge them into boiling water for a minute, then drain and chill before serving with cold dips.

Early Risers

BEVERAGES, BREADS, & BRUNCHES

The Steeplechase

Annapolis in the spring is a city that bursts with the vigorous celebration of old customs to herald the new season. In an area where the maritime history dominates, other parts of the British colonial heritage remain. Come April, thousands of casual spectators and steeplechase fans gather on a placid farm in Davidsonville, the horse country south of Annapolis, to watch the steeplechase. Roedown, as these races are known locally, is the latest manifestation of the passion for horses that made colonial Annapolitans well-known both for their superb horses and for the fine racetrack just outside the city gates on West street. This track drew sporting gentlemen from all over the middle colonies and led to the establishment of a Jockey Club in the town. George Washington attended the Annapolis races on more than one occasion and enjoyed the conviviality of the Jockey Club.

The Roedown races are an opportunity both to extend modern hospitality and to enjoy the centuries-old tradition of the steeplechase, races in which the horses jump over different types of fences on a grass course. Before the races, spectators set up tailgate parties along the course fence ranging from simple picnics to elaborate buffets decorated with silver, candles and flowers. Friends wander from one group to another, reveling in the brisk spring weather. The knowledgeable horse fans view the competition at the holding paddock, noting the energetic stepping of a glossy chestnut or the beautiful economy of motion in a stately gray.

The races themselves are a poetry of movement as the horses prance toward the start and then head around the grassy course in a magnificent rush. Spectators become intent as the jockeys urge their spirited charges over heart-stopping fences then race at a full gallop toward the finish. Out in the spring air away from the grandstands and betting stalls of flat racing, Roedown remains much like the races of colonial days, a meeting of good friends, a generous array of appetizing tidbits, and a celebration of good sportsmanship.

FALL APPLE PUNCH

Serves 8

Easy, can prepare ahead
Great for a Halloween party.

1   quart plus 1 cup
     chilled ginger ale

2⅔   cups chilled apple juice
     or cider

2   lemons, thinly sliced

⅓   cup lemon juice

1   tablespoon plus 1
     teaspoon grenadine
     syrup

◢ Combine all ingredients except
lemon slices. Stir to mix and chill
well. Pour into a punch bowl and
float lemon slices on top.

All drink recipes
are based on two 6-8
ounce servings per person.

63

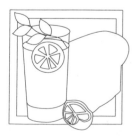

CARIBBEAN FRUIT PUNCH

Serves 25

Easy, can prepare ahead

Add a touch of the islands to your next party!

4   cups sugar

6   cups warm water

1   (46 ounce) can
     pineapple juice

2   (12 ounce) cans frozen
     orange juice
     concentrate

1   (12 ounce) can frozen
     lemonade concentrate

5   puréed bananas

6   (20 ounce) bottles
     lemon-lime carbonated
     drink

▲ Mix sugar and water. Add pine-apple juice, orange juice concentrate, lemonade concentrate and puréed bananas and mix well.

▲ Refrigerate until serving time. Add lemon-lime drink just before serving punch.

64

BUBBLY PEACH PUNCH

Serves 20

Easy

This punch made its debut at a romantic wedding in the historic district.

2   (10 ounce) cans frozen peach daiquiri mix

1   (12 ounce) can frozen orange juice concentrate

1   (12 ounce) can frozen limeade concentrate

4   cups water

2   liters ginger ale

1   bottle champagne or seltzer

    lots of ice cubes

    orange and lime slices for garnish

◢ Mix frozen fruit concentrates with water. Pour over ice. Add ginger ale and champagne or seltzer.

◢ Garnish glasses with fresh peach slices.

65

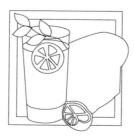

MOCHA PUNCH

Serves 12

Easy

Men will love this punch!

3   cups milk

1   cup double-strength chilled coffee

½   teaspoon almond extract or amaretto

Dash of salt

¼   cup sugar

1   quart chocolate ice cream, slightly softened

1   cup heavy cream, whipped

½   teaspoon nutmeg

1   cup dark rum (optional)

◢ Combine milk, coffee, rum (optional), almond extract, salt and sugar in a punch bowl. Spoon in half of the chocolate ice cream and stir until partially melted.

◢ Fold in whipped cream and remainder of ice cream. Sprinkle with nutmeg. Serve immediately.

PERFECT PARTY PUNCH

Serves 24

Easy

This long lasting punch holds up well to melting ice.

3   liters ginger ale

1   (12 ounce) can frozen orange juice concentrate

1   (12 ounce) can frozen lemonade juice concentrate

1   (12 ounce) can frozen pineapple juice concentrate

1   (12 ounce) can frozen limeade juice concentrate

1   (12 ounce) can frozen grapefruit juice concentrate

1   (4 ounce) can frozen cranberry juice concentrate

◢ Thaw concentrate and mix all ingredients well. Add a lot of ice. If ice is not melting add an additional 1½ liters of ginger ale.

BOURBON SLUSH

Serves 12

Easy, must be made ahead

A backyard swing kind of drink.

4 tea bags

2 cups boiling water

2 cups sugar

1 (12 ounce) can frozen orange juice concentrate

1 (6 ounce) can frozen lemonade concentrate

6½ cups cold water

1½ cups bourbon

Steep tea bags in boiling water for 5 minutes. Remove tea bags and mix together with remaining ingredients. Put into zip lock bags and freeze. Mix in blender before serving in large wine glasses.

My aunt lived in a big Victorian home with an old-fashioned rambling garden. I loved playing there and remember summer afternoons scented with flowers and picking mint from the patch by the back door to put in my iced tea.

CHAMPAGNE PUNCH WITH BRANDIED STRAWBERRIES

Serves 30

Average, must be made ahead

This punch makes an elegant presentation.

1   pound clean fresh strawberries

7   ounces caster sugar or super fine sugar

1   cup kirsch or brandy

2   bottles cold Chablis or chardonnay

1   liter soda water

1   bottle champagne

◢ Combine strawberries, sugar and brandy in a punch bowl several hours before serving at room temperature. Before serving, add remaining ingredients.

You can substitute caster sugar by putting granulated sugar in a blender until it is a finer texture.

69

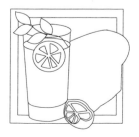

RASPBERRY ROSÉ PUNCH

Serves 12 - 15

Easy, can be made ahead

This is so simple and has a beautiful rose color.

1   large bottle chilled
    Rosé wine

1   (6 ounce) can frozen
    lemonade

1   large bottle chilled
    ginger ale

1   package frozen
    raspberries (slightly
    thawed)

Mix wine and lemonade. Just before serving add ginger ale and raspberries.

70

ROMAN RUM PUNCH

Serves 20

Average, can prepare ahead

Great for a summer barbecue.

2   cups crushed pineapple

½   cup grenadine syrup

½   cup lemon juice

½   cup orange juice

1½   cups unsweetened pineapple juice

1⅓   cups peach brandy

1   (750 ml) bottle light rum

1   (750 ml) bottle dark rum

1   ice block, prepared ahead

2   large bottles cold club soda

1   pint strawberries, washed and hulled

◢ In a large container mix pineapple, grenadine, lemon juice, orange juice, pineapple juice, peach brandy, light rum, and dark rum. Stir well. Chill for 2 hours.

◢ Pour mixture over a block of ice in a bowl. Add two bottles of club soda and stir gently. Float 1 pint of strawberries in the mixture.

71

Early Risers

SANGRIA

Makes 2 large pitchers

Easy

Try diced nectarines or pomegranates for new flavor.

2 bottles dry red wine

2 quarts of orange juice

1 cup lemon juice

1 liter of bitter lemon

½ cup sugar dissolved in 1 cup of boiling water

½ cup brandy

¾ cup of triple sec

lemons, oranges, or other fruit, sliced

▲ Mix all ingredients into a large bowl and chill. Serve over ice.

This recipe was given to us by a bartender in Cordoba, Spain. It is the best sangria we've ever tasted!

72

SCARLETT O'HARAS

Serve 4 - 6

Easy

Serve this tempting drink instead of mimosas.

1 (32 ounce) bottle cranberry juice cocktail, chilled

2 cups chilled champagne

1 ounce triple sec

4-6 lime slices

▲ Combine the juice, champagne, and triple sec. Rub the edge of the champagne glass with the lime slice and place the lime on the glass edge. Pour drinks into glasses and serve immediately.

IRISH CREAM LIQUEUR

Makes 5 cups

Average, can make ahead

Serve after dinner with chocolate mints.

1½   cups Irish whiskey liqueur

1   (14 ounce) can sweetened condensed milk

1   cup whipping cream

4   eggs

2   tablespoons chocolate syrup

2   teaspoons instant coffee

1   teaspoon vanilla extract

½   teaspoon almond extract

◢ Combine all ingredients in blender. Blend until smooth. Store in refrigerator. Shake well before serving, garnish with cinnamon sticks.

◢ Bourbon, rye or brandy can be substituted for whiskey.

73

FRUIT WASSAIL

Makes 3 quarts

Average, can be made ahead

Children and adults will both love this winter drink.

2 quarts apple juice

2¼ cups pineapple juice

2 cups orange juice

1 cup lemon juice

½ cup sugar

1 stick cinnamon, approximately 3 inches

1 teaspoon whole cloves

4-square inch piece of cheesecloth

◢ Combine all of the juices in a large pot. Add sugar and stir.

◢ Put cinnamon and cloves in the cheesecloth and tie securely. Add to juice mixture.

◢ Bring to a boil. Cover, reduce heat and simmer for 15 minutes. Discard the cheesecloth and serve hot.

HOSPITALITY SPICE TEA

Serves 12 - 15

Average, can be made ahead

Keep this aromatic warm drink on hand in case a friend stops by.

1   stick cinnamon

1   tablespoon whole cloves

1   cup sugar

4   cups water

3   tea bags

4   cups boiling water

1   (6 ounce) can frozen orange juice concentrate

2-3 cups pineapple juice

     juice of 2 lemons

◢ Tie cloves and cinnamon in a small cheesecloth bag.

◢ In a large saucepan, combine spices, sugar and 4 cups water. Boil for 5 minutes. In a separate container, steep tea bags in 4 cups boiling water for 5 minutes.

◢ Strain tea into spice mixture along with juices. Remove spice bag. Heat to serve but do not boil.

◢ Store in the refrigerator up to two weeks. Heat and serve as desired.

75

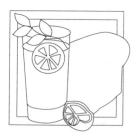

CRANBERRY TEA

Serves 10 - 12

Average, can be made ahead

A tempting blend of fruit and spice.

5	cups boiling water
½	teaspoon nutmeg
½	teaspoon cinnamon
½	teaspoon allspice
3	tea bags
1½	cups sugar
1	cup orange juice
½	cup lemon juice
1	quart cranberry juice
3	cinnamon sticks
1	cup rum (optional)

▲ Add spices, tea bags, sugar and juices to boiling water. Heat together on medium high burner with three cinnamon sticks simmering in the mixture.

▲ Discard teabags and serve. If alcohol is desired, add before removing from heat.

For winter parties, serve a warm punch in a big earthen crock on the hearth before the fire.

HOT MULLED WINE

Serves 18

Easy, can be made ahead

Savor the delightful aroma and mellow taste.

4   cups sugar

1   tablespoon ground cinnamon or 6 medium cinnamon sticks

1   teaspoon ground cloves or whole cloves

2   cups boiling water

3   medium oranges, thinly sliced

1   medium lemon, thinly sliced

1   gallon dry red wine

In an 8 quart sauce pot, combine sugar, cinnamon, cloves and water. Add orange and lemon slices to mixture. Heat over high heat; boil 5 minutes, stirring occasionally.

Reduce heat to medium; add wine; heat until piping hot but not boiling, stirring occasionally.

Carefully ladle individual servings of hot wine into punch cups or heat safe glasses.

77

HOT BUTTERED RUM

Serves 24

Average, must be made ahead

The make-ahead batter makes this perfect for fixing a quick delicious drink to warm your chilled crew.

1   pound softened butter

1   pound dark brown sugar

1   pound powdered sugar

1   quart vanilla ice cream (softened)

1   teaspoon nutmeg

2   teaspoons cinnamon

1   teaspoon allspice

Brandy

Rum

cinnamon sticks

▲ Heat all ingredients slowly, stirring until mixture resembles cake batter.

▲ In one mug, spoon 1 to 2 teaspoons of batter (depending on mug size). Add 1 jigger of rum and 1 jigger of brandy. Brandy and rum amounts can be adjusted for taste and potency. Fill rest of mug with boiling water. Put a stick of cinnamon in each mug and sprinkle top with freshly grated nutmeg.

▲ Store batter in freezer, scooping out portions when necessary. Batter will keep for 6 months or so stored in an airtight freezer container. No need to melt batter once it is frozen.

SHERRY WASSAIL

Serves 15

Average, can prepare ahead
Greet your guests warmly!

1	cup sugar
4	cinnamon sticks
3	lemon slices, ½" thick
2	cups pineapple juice
2	cups orange juice
6	cups red wine
½	cup lemon juice
1½	cups dry sherry

Boil sugar, cinnamon sticks, and lemon slices in ½ cup water. Add remaining ingredients and simmer until warm. Remove lemon slices and cinnamon sticks before serving.

London Town Publik House and Gardens is the only remaining building of the colonial settlement of London. The elegant Georgian house and gardens commands a knoll overlooking the South River. It was one of a series of ferry crossings between Annapolis and Williamsburg.

79

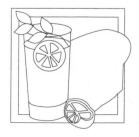

G L O G G

Serves 10

*Gourmet, must prepare one
day ahead*

A classic for the holidays.

2   teaspoons dried orange
    peel

1   teaspoon whole cloves

4   whole cardamom,
    cracked

3   short cinnamon sticks

1   cup dark seedless
    raisins

1   (8 ounce) package
    dried apricots

2   (⅘ quart) bottles or 6½
    cups burgundy wine

1   (⅘ quart) bottle vodka
    or gin

¾   cup sugar

1   cup whole blanched
    almonds

    cheesecloth

▲ Place orange peel and spices in
piece of cheesecloth and tie with a
string to form a bag.

▲ In a covered 4 quart saucepan over
medium low heat, simmer raisins,
apricots, spice bag and one bottle
of burgundy wine for 30 minutes.
Remove from heat and discard
spice bag.

▲ Stir in vodka, sugar and remaining
burgundy wine. Cover mixture and
let stand overnight at room temperature.

▲ To serve: heat mixture over high
heat until piping hot but not boiling, stirring occasionally.

▲ Ignite mixture with long match and
let burn a few seconds. Cover pan
to extinguish flame.

▲ Add almonds and pour into heated
punch bowl or serving cups.

CHOCOLATE RASPBERRY TRUFFLE COFFEE

Serves 4

Average, can be made ahead partially

A decadent finish for dinner.

½ pound chocolate raspberry truffle coffee beans

1 cup raspberry flavored liqueur, divided

3 tablespoons sugar

1 cup heavy cream, whipped

1 tablespoon powdered sugar

   chocolate shavings for garnish

Grind coffee beans to desired consistency. Make coffee according to directions for your coffee maker.

Meanwhile, create sugar coated cup rims by dipping each coffee cup or mug into the raspberry flavored liqueur followed by sugar.

Whip the heavy cream until soft peaks form. Add powdered sugar and continue beating until sugar is incorporated and the cream is whipped.

Pour 2 tablespoons of raspberry flavored liqueur into each mug and fill remaining with the freshly brewed coffee. Top with a scoop of whipped cream. Garnish with chocolate shavings. Serve immediately.

81

SAILOR'S COFFEE

Makes an 8 - 10 cup coffee pot

Average

A specialty for boating or camping.

1   tablespoon coffee per cup of water

½   teaspoon cinnamon

½   teaspoon nutmeg

¼   teaspoon ground clove

pinch salt

 Place water in coffee pot and bring to boil. Take off heat, put a filter in the percolator basket and place coffee and seasonings in the basket. Place the pot back on the stove, bring water to a simmer.

 Let the coffee perk for 8 to 10 minutes or until it has reached the strength you enjoy. Never let the coffee boil. Works in an electric percolator as well.

A sailor on one of the tall ships passed along this recipe for making coffee on board a boat to me. Its aroma always brings pleasant memories of mornings anchored in quiet coves, watching ducks and geese flying overhead.

TANGY LEMON NUT BREAD

Makes one loaf

Easy
Perfect for an afternoon tea.

½   cup butter

1   cup sugar

2   eggs

1⅔ cups flour

½   teaspoon salt

1   teaspoon baking
     powder

½   cup milk

½   cup finely chopped
     nuts

2   lemons: grate zest;
     reserve juice for glaze

Glaze

¼   cup powdered sugar

     reserved lemon juice

▲ Preheat oven to 350°. Cream butter and sugar, add eggs, and beat mixture until fluffy.

▲ Sift flour, add baking powder and salt; sift again.

▲ Alternately add flour mixture and milk to butter mixture, mixing constantly. Fold in nuts and lemon peel.

▲ Bake in a greased and floured 9"x5"x3" loaf pan for 55-65 minutes.

▲ For glaze, combine lemon juice and powdered sugar in a small bowl. Prick hot bread with a toothpick, pour on glaze. Let cool in pan for 15 -20 minutes before removing.

▲ The lemon glaze makes the bread moist, do not omit.

83

Use toasted grape-nut cereal as a low-fat alternative to nuts for baking.

CRANBERRY-ORANGE LOAF

Makes one loaf

Average, may be frozen

Great at Thanksgiving and for gift giving.

2 cups all purpose flour

1½ teaspoons baking powder

½ teaspoon baking soda

½ teaspoon salt

1 cup sugar

1 tablespoon oil

2 egg whites

1 tablespoon grated orange rind

½ teaspoon almond extract

1½ cups cranberries, coarsely chopped

Preheat oven to 350°. Combine flour, baking powder, baking soda, salt, and sugar; set aside. Combine oil, egg whites, orange rind and almond extract; stir well.

Add orange mixture to flour mixture, stirring only until dry ingredients are moistened. Fold in cranberries.

Spoon batter into a greased and floured 8½"x4½"x3" loaf pan. Bake for 60 minutes or until bread tests done with a toothpick. Cool in pan for 10 minutes, remove and cool completely before serving.

PEAR BREAD

Makes one loaf

Easy

A real treat when served with soft cream cheese.

½   cup butter or margarine, softened

1   cup sugar

2   eggs

2   cups flour

½   teaspoon salt

½   teaspoon baking soda

1   teaspoon baking powder

¼   teaspoon nutmeg

¼   cup vanilla yogurt or buttermilk

1   cup very ripe pears, coarsely chopped and cored

1   teaspoon vanilla extract

◣ Preheat oven to 350°. Cream butter and gradually beat in sugar. Beat in eggs one at a time.

◣ Combine dry ingredients; add to egg mixture alternating with yogurt. Stir in pears and vanilla.

◣ Pour into a buttered 9"x5"x3" loaf pan. Bake for one hour. Cool in pan for 15 minutes. Remove from pan and serve.

Different-flavor extracts can be successfully substituted for vanilla extract in most baking recipes to create different flavors. Use your imagination!

85

APRICOT-ALMOND BREAD

Makes one loaf

Gourmet, can be made ahead

*A tradition at our family's
Christmas brunch.
Wonderful when toasted!*

2   cups chopped dried
    apricots

1   cup orange juice,
    boiling

4   tablespoons butter or
    margarine

1   cup sugar

½   cup packed brown
    sugar

2   eggs

½   teaspoon allspice

3   cups sifted all-purpose
    flour

2   tablespoons baking
    powder

½   teaspoon salt

1   cup chopped toasted
    almonds

    sliced almonds for
    garnish

▲ Preheat oven to 375° and grease
and flour one 9"x5"x3" loaf pan.
Combine apricots with boiling juice
and let stand for 10 to 15 minutes.

▲ Cream butter and sugars, add the
eggs and the apricot mixture.
Gradually add the dry ingredients.
Fold in the chopped almonds and
pour into the prepared loaf pan.
Decorate the top with sliced almonds.

▲ Cover the pan with foil and bake
for 35 minutes. Uncover the pan
and bake for another 15 - 20 minutes, or until a toothpick placed in
the center comes out clean. If the
edges are getting too brown, edge
the pan with strips of aluminum
foil.

*For the holidays,
decorate the loaf by
placing the almonds in
the shape of a tree or a
star on top.*

86

ZUCCHINI-CARROT BREAD

Makes two loaves

Easy

A heavenly blend of spices make this bread special.

3 cups all-purpose flour

1 teaspoon baking powder

1 teaspoon baking soda

½ teaspoon salt

1 teaspoon ground cinnamon

1 teaspoon ground nutmeg

1 cup chopped pecans or walnuts

2 eggs, slightly beaten

1½ cups granulated sugar

¾ cup vegetable oil

½ cup honey

2 teaspoons vanilla extract

1 cup shredded unpeeled zucchini

1 cup shredded carrots

◢ Preheat oven to 350°. Grease and flour two 9"x5"x3" loaf pans.

◢ Combine flour, baking powder, baking soda, salt, cinnamon, nutmeg and nuts; set aside.

◢ In another bowl, combine eggs, oil, sugar, honey and vanilla. Add liquid mixture alternately with zucchini and carrots to flour mixture and mix well.

◢ Pour into two loaf pans and bake for 65 minutes or until a toothpick inserted in the center comes out clean.

◢ Cool in pans for 10 minutes and remove to wire racks to cool completely.

87

Reduce oil by 1/2 and substitute the same amount of fruit purée or yogurt for moisture when baking quick breads. You can use bananas, applesauce, baby food, or strained prunes. Depending on the sweetness of the fruit, also reduce sugar by 1/2.

CHUTNEY BREAD

Makes one loaf

Easy

Delightful served with a lemon cream cheese spread.

2½   cups flour

½   cup sugar

½   cup brown sugar

1¼   cups milk

3   tablespoons vegetable oil

2   tablespoons grated orange peel

1   teaspoon salt

3½   teaspoons baking powder

1   egg

1   cup chopped nuts

¾   cup mild chutney, chopped

88

◢ Preheat oven to 350°, grease a 9"x5"x3" loaf pan.

◢ Mix flour, sugars, milk, oil, orange peel, salt, baking powder and egg. Beat on low until moist.

◢ Fold in nuts and chutney. Pour into prepared loaf pan and bake for 60 minutes.

◢ Cool in pan for 10 minutes and remove.

POPPY SEED MUFFINS

Makes 2 dozen

Easy

Orange juice makes these muffins moist and delicious.

3⅓ cups flour

4 teaspoons baking powder

1 teaspoon salt

6 tablespoons poppyseeds

1 cup vegetable oil

1¼ cups sugar

¾ cup milk

¾ cup orange juice

1 teaspoon vanilla extract

½ teaspoon almond extract

3 eggs

1 tablespoon grated orange peel

◢ Preheat oven to 375°. Coat two 12 cup muffin tins with cooking spray or use muffin wrappers.

◢ Combine flour, baking powder, salt and poppyseeds; set aside. In a large bowl combine oil and sugar, add milk, orange juice, vanilla and almond extracts. Mix well.

◢ In a separate bowl beat eggs with a fork and add to sugar mixture. Add grated orange peel and mix well.

◢ Gradually add flour mixture to sugar mixture, mixing well. Pour mixture into muffin tins, filling ⅔ cup full. Bake for 13 - 18 minutes until muffin edges turn golden brown. Cool in pan for 10 minutes.

89

Early Risers

GRANNY APPLE MUFFINS

Makes 2 dozen

Average

A great breakfast treat which can be frozen and microwaved when ready to eat.

2½   cups flour

2   teaspoons baking soda

1   teaspoon cinnamon

1½   cups sugar

1   cup canola oil

3   egg whites

¼   cup lemon juice

1   teaspoon lemon peel

2   teaspoons vanilla extract

2   cups grated Granny Smith apples

1   cup chopped nuts (walnuts or pecans)

▲ Preheat oven to 350°. Line two 12 cup muffin pans with paper muffin cups.

▲ Sift flour, baking soda and cinnamon into a bowl and set aside. In another large bowl combine sugar, oil, egg whites, lemon juice, lemon peel and vanilla. Whisk to blend and mix in dry ingredients. Fold in apples and nuts.

▲ Fill each muffin cup ⅓ full and bake for 35 minutes. Cool in pan for 5 minutes and serve warm.

Twelve or more people, including the minister, routinely came to Sunday brunch at my parents' house. The sideboard was crowded with tempting dishes. I raced sailboats then, and Sunday brunch was my secret energy source!

GINGERBREAD MUFFINS

Makes 4 dozen

Average
Good and Spicy!

1	cup softened butter or vegetable shortening
1	cup sugar
4	eggs
1	cup molasses
1	cup buttermilk
4	cups flour
2	teaspoons baking soda
½	teaspoon cinnamon
½	teaspoon allspice
2	teaspoons ginger
½	cup raisins
½	cup chopped pecans

◢ Preheat oven to 350° and spray four 12 cup muffin pans with non-stick cooking spray.

◢ In a large bowl, cream together butter and sugar until smooth. Beat in eggs one at a time. Add molasses and buttermilk. Set aside.

◢ In a separate bowl, sift together flour, baking soda, and spices. Add to butter mixture. Add raisins and pecans.

◢ Fill each muffin pan ⅔ cup full and bake for 15 minutes. Cool in pan for 5 minutes and serve warm.

91

BLUEBERRY STREUSEL MUFFINS

Makes 1 dozen

Gourmet

Beautiful muffins, worth the extra effort!

1½ cups unbleached all-purpose flour

¼ cup granulated sugar

¼ cup packed brown sugar

2 teaspoons baking powder

¼ teaspoon salt

1 teaspoon ground cinnamon

1 egg, slightly beaten

½ cup unsalted butter, melted

½ cup milk

1-1¼ cups blueberries, fresh or frozen and defrosted

1 teaspoon grated lemon zest

Streusel Topping

½ cup chopped pecans

½ cup brown sugar

¼ cup flour

1 teaspoon ground cinnamon

1 teaspoon grated lemon zest

2 tablespoons unsalted butter, melted

Glaze

½ cup powdered sugar

1 tablespoon fresh lemon juice

◢ Preheat oven to 350° and place paper liners in one 12 cup muffin pan.

◢ In a large bowl, sift together flour, sugar, brown sugar, baking powder, salt and 1 teaspoon cinnamon. Make a well in the center. Place egg, ½ cup melted butter and milk in the well. Stir until combined. Gently stir in blueberries and 1 teaspoon of the lemon zest.

◢ Fill each muffin cup ¾ full with batter.

◢ Make streusel topping by combining pecans, brown sugar, flour, cinnamon and lemon zest with a fork. Pour in melted butter and stir to combine. Sprinkle topping over each muffin.

◢ Bake for 20 - 25 minutes until muffins are browned and firm.

◢ Make glaze by mixing powdered sugar and lemon juice. Use a teaspoon to drizzle glaze over warm muffins. Serve immediately.

BLUE CHEESE BISCUITS

Serves 6 - 8

Easy

An effortless dinner party roll.

1   package refrigerator dough biscuits (10-12)

3   tablespoons blue cheese, crumbled

½   cup butter

▲ Preheat oven to 400°. Cut biscuits into quarters and place in a greased (12 cup) muffin tin.

▲ Melt together butter and blue cheese; pour mixture over biscuits. Bake for 10 - 15 minutes or until golden brown. Serve hot.

HERB CHEESE BREAD

Makes one loaf

Average

A nice compliment to soups and salads.

2   cups flour

2   teaspoons baking powder

1   tablespoon sugar

½   teaspoon salt

¼   cup butter, cut into 4 pieces

1   cup grated sharp cheddar cheese

1   tablespoon grated onion

1½   teaspoons dried dill weed

¾   cup milk

1   egg, slightly beaten

▲ Preheat oven to 350°. Mix flour, baking powder, salt and sugar in a large bowl. Cut in butter until coarse crumbs result. Stir in cheese, onion and dill weed; mix well.

▲ Combine milk and beaten egg. Pour into flour mixture all at once. Stir quickly with a fork to moisten flour. Do not overbeat.

▲ Pour into a greased 9"x5"x3" loaf pan and bake for 40 - 50 minutes. Cool in the pan for 10 minutes prior to serving. Serve warm.

ANGEL BISCUITS

Makes 12 biscuits

Easy

Good even if you think you can't make biscuits!

1 package active dry yeast

¼ cup warm water (105°-115°F)

2 tablespoons sugar

3 cups unsifted all-purpose flour

1 tablespoon baking powder

½ teaspoon salt

½ cup margarine or butter

¼ cup milk

 In a small bowl, sprinkle yeast over water. Stir in sugar and set aside until mixture is foamy, about 10 minutes.

 In a medium size bowl, combine flour, baking powder, and salt. With pastry blender or 2 knives cut in butter until mixture resembles coarse crumbs. Add yeast mixture and milk; mix lightly with fork until well combined.

 Cover dough with clean cloth and let rise in warm place away from drafts. Let dough double in size, about 30 minutes.

 Grease large baking sheet. On lightly floured surface, roll out dough to ½ inch thickness. With 3" round cutter, cut out 12 biscuits, re-rolling dough if necessary.

 Place biscuits on greased baking sheet. With tines of fork, pierce biscuits lightly a few times. Let biscuits rise for 45 minutes.

 Preheat oven to 375°. Bake biscuits 15 - 18 minutes or until golden brown. Serve warm.

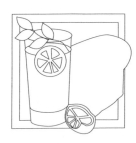

COTTAGE DILL ROLLS

Makes 12 large rolls

Easy

A delightful roll with a flavor similar to sourdough bread.

1 pound small curd cottage cheese

2½ tablespoons sugar

1 tablespoon finely chopped onion

2 tablespoons butter, softened

1 teaspoon salt

1 teaspoon finely chopped fresh dill

½ teaspoon baking soda

1 egg

1 tablespoon horseradish

1½ ounce cake yeast (or ¾ ounce active dry yeast)

½ cup water

3½ cups bread flour

2 tablespoons butter, melted

◢ Preheat oven to 350°.

◢ Mix cottage cheese, sugar, onion, butter, salt, dill, soda, egg, and horseradish together in a mixer with the paddle attachment or at slow speed with a regular mixer.

◢ Add remaining ingredients and mix with a dough hook until well mixed, or knead by hand for 10 minutes. Add any additional flour as needed to prevent sticking.

◢ No rising is required. Shape into rolls, place on a greased cookie sheet and bake for 30 minutes or until golden brown. Rolls should sound hollow when tapped. Brush with melted butter when done. Serve immediately.

HONEY WHEAT ROLLS

Makes 24 rolls

Average, can be made ahead

A family favorite!

4½ cups all-purpose flour

2½ cups whole wheat flour

2   packages dry active yeast

1   tablespoon salt

⅓   cup honey

3   tablespoons butter or margarine

2½ cups hot tap water

▲ Grease two 12 cup muffin pans.

▲ In a large bowl, combine yeast, salt, and 2 cups of the all-purpose flour. Add honey, butter, and hot tap water. Beat with an electric mixer for 2 minutes at medium speed. Add 1 cup of all-purpose flour and ½ cup whole wheat flour. Beat 1 minute more. Add 2 cups whole wheat flour and 1½ cups all-purpose flour until dough is soft and sticky.

▲ Turn dough out onto floured surface and knead 5 - 10 minutes, adding more flour as needed until smooth and elastic. Cover with plastic wrap and towel and let rest 20 minutes on counter top.

▲ Punch dough down, divide into 24 pieces, and divide again into thirds. Place 3 small balls in each muffin cup. Brush lightly with oil, cover with plastic wrap, and refrigerate 2 - 24 hours.

▲ Remove from refrigerator 10 minutes before baking and remove plastic wrap. Bake for 15 minutes in a preheated 400° oven.

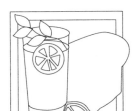

COOL RISE WHITE BREAD

Makes two loaves

Gourmet

Make the night before your dinner party.

7¾-8¾ cups unsifted white flour

3 tablespoons sugar

4½ teaspoons salt

3 packages active dry yeast

⅓ cup softened margarine

⅔ cup very warm tap water

vegetable oil

In a large bowl thoroughly mix 3 cups of flour, sugar, salt and undissolved yeast. Add margarine and gradually add tap water to dry ingredients and beat two minutes at medium speed of an electric mixer, scraping bowl occasionally.

Add ⅓ cup of flour and beat at high speed for an additional two minutes. Continue to stir in enough additional flour to make a stiff dough.

Turn the dough out onto a lightly floured board; knead until smooth and elastic, about 10 - 12 minutes. Cover with plastic wrap, then a towel. Let rest for 20 minutes.

97

Divide dough in half. Roll each half into a 14 x 9 inch rectangle. Shape into loaves by rolling tightly from narrow end. Seal loaves and fold under. Place in two greased 9"x5"x3" loaf pans. Brush with oil. Cover tightly with plastic wrap. Refrigerate 2 to 12 hours.

When ready to bake, remove from refrigerator. Uncover the dough carefully and let stand at room temperature for 10 minutes. Preheat oven to 400°. Puncture any gas bubbles which may have formed with a greased toothpick or a metal skewer. Bake for 30 to 40 minutes or until done. Remove from baking pans and cool on wire racks.

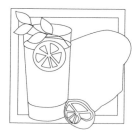

Early Risers

JALAPEÑO CORNBREAD

Serves 8

Easy

This moist flavorful cornbread is great with chili!

1½ cups self-rising cornmeal

1¼ cups milk

¼ cup oil

2 eggs

1 teaspoon sugar

½ cup creamed corn

¼ cup chopped jalapeño peppers

¼ cup shredded sharp cheddar cheese

1 small finely chopped onion

◢ Preheat oven to 400°. Grease two 8"x8"x2" pans or one 13"x9"x2" pan.

◢ In a medium bowl, stir milk into cornmeal. Add remaining ingredients and mix together.

◢ Pour into prepared pans and bake for 25 minutes until lightly brown and bread pulls away from the side of the pan.

YORKSHIRE PUDDING

Serves 4

Easy

A must with roast beef!

¼ teaspoon salt

1 cup milk

1 cup flour

2 eggs

¼ cup melted butter or hot beef drippings

◢ Preheat oven to 450°. Mix salt and flour, gradually add milk and beat into a smooth paste. Add eggs and beat for two minutes.

◢ Cover the bottom of a 8"x1¼" shallow baking dish or 12 cup muffin tins with melted butter or beef drippings. Pour egg mixture in pan and bake for 20 minutes. Keep oven door closed while baking.

◢ Cut into squares and serve immediately.

MOM'S BEST CINNAMON ROLLS

Makes 3 dozen

Gourmet

A special treat for family reunions.

Sweet Roll Dough

2	packages dry yeast
½	cup warm water
2½	cups milk
½	cup margarine or butter
⅔	cup sugar
2	teaspoons salt
4	eggs
9	cups flour

Cinnamon Filling

½	cup margarine or butter, melted
1	cup brown sugar
4	teaspoons cinnamon
½	cup chopped pecans or walnuts
½	cup raisins or currants

Icing

1	cup sifted powdered sugar
¼	teaspoon vanilla
1½	teaspoons milk
1	teaspoon lemon juice

◢ Dissolve the 2 packages of yeast in warm water; set aside.

◢ Preheat oven to 375°. Combine the milk, margarine, sugar and salt in a medium sauce pan and heat until margarine is just melted. Remove from heat and let cool.

◢ In a large mixing bowl, beat the eggs with a fork until completely mixed. Add the yeast mixture to the eggs and then add the egg mixture to the cooled milk mixture.

◢ Add the flour gradually to the liquid mixture until it becomes a soft dough. If you have a mixer with a dough hook you can use it here. The dough will be soft, do not knead it.

◢ Let the dough rise until it is double in size. Punch down and roll out one third of the dough into a 12"x8" rectangle. Repeat with remaining two-thirds of dough. Brush rectangles with melted butter.

◢ Mix together remaining butter, brown sugar, cinnamon, nuts and raisins for filling. Cover the rectangles with the filling mixture.

◢ Roll the rectangle into a jelly roll and slice into individual rolls. Place in a greased 13"x9"x2" baking dish, cover and let rise until double, about 30 minutes.

◢ Bake for 18 to 20 minutes until lightly browned. Remove to wire rack and cool slightly.

◢ For icing combine powdered sugar, vanilla, milk, and lemon juice, mixing with a fork just enough to make it drizzle consistency. If the mixture is too thick add more milk, or if too thin add more powdered sugar.

◢ Drizzle icing over warm rolls and serve.

SOUR CREAM ALMOND COFFEE CAKE

Serves 8

Average, can be made ahead
Grand for Sunday Brunch!

½ cup butter

1 cup sugar

2 eggs

1 teaspoon vanilla extract

½ teaspoon almond extract

2 cups flour

½ teaspoon baking soda

1 teaspoon baking powder

1 cup sour cream

Filling

⅔ cup almond paste

½ cup sugar

1 teaspoon cinnamon

▲ Preheat oven to 375°. Cream butter and sugar. Add eggs, vanilla and almond extracts; set aside. Mix dry ingredients and add to egg mixture, alternating with sour cream. Set aside.

▲ In a separate bowl, mix together almond paste, sugar and cinnamon to make the filling; set aside.

▲ Grease and flour a 9"x3" tube pan. Alternate pouring the batter and filling into the pan by thirds.

▲ Bake for 35 minutes, remove from pan and cool. Do not be concerned if the cake drops.

BREAKFAST BUBBLE BREAD

Serves 8 - 10

Average

Children and adults both love this classic.

1   (3 ounce) package vanilla pudding

1   cup brown sugar

1   cup white sugar

1   teaspoon cinnamon

½   cup melted butter or margarine

1   cup chopped pecans

1   package Rich's frozen rolls

◢ Mix together dry pudding mix, brown sugar, white sugar and cinnamon; set aside.

◢ Grease a 9"x3" bundt pan and place chopped pecans in the bottom. Place frozen rolls in bundt pan on top of pecans. Pour pudding mixture on top of rolls and cover with melted butter.

◢ Cover and let rise overnight or at least 8 hours. Bake 25 to 30 minutes at 350°.

101

CASHEW COFFEE BISCOTTI

Makes 24 Biscotti

Gourmet

An elegant after dinner treat with espresso.

1½ cups unsalted cashews

1¾ cups all-purpose flour

½ teaspoon salt

½ teaspoon baking powder

⅔ cup sugar

4 tablespoons cold unsalted butter, cut into small cubes

2 tablespoons instant coffee granules

2 large eggs

½ teaspoon vanilla extract

◢ Preheat oven to 350°. Spread cashews on a large baking sheet and toast in the oven for 10 to 12 minutes until golden brown. Transfer to a medium bowl and cool.

◢ In a food processor combine flour, baking powder, salt and ⅔ cup of the sugar. Add the diced butter and pulse until the mixture resembles a coarse meal.

◢ Add the flour mixture to the cashews and toss. Mix in coffee granules.

◢ Using a fork lightly beat the eggs with the vanilla. Stir the egg mixture into the flour mixture and mix with your hands until just blended. Pat into a disk.

◢ On a lightly floured work surface, quarter the disk into 4 equal wedges. Using your hands, roll each wedge into an 8 inch log. Place the two logs 2 inches apart on a lightly buttered baking sheet and flatten with the heel of your hand to a width of 2 inches. Sprinkle the tops with sugar and bake for 20 minutes or until golden brown.

◢ Using two metal spatulas, carefully transfer the logs to a rack to cool slightly (5 to 10 minutes).

◢ Once cool, place the logs on a work surface and using a sharp knife in a quick motion, slice each log on the diagonal ½ inch thick.

◢ Place the biscotti cut side down on the baking sheet and bake for 5 to 7 minutes, just until they begin to color. Transfer to the rack and cool completely.

DOUBLE DECKER FRENCH TOAST

Serves 2

Easy

Children will love this special breakfast treat. Add a teaspoon of liqueur or fruit preserves to the cream cheese for breakfast when the kids are away.

4	slices whole wheat bread
2	ounces softened cream cheese
2	eggs
1	tablespoon milk
1	teaspoon vanilla extract
¼	teaspoon ground cinnamon
3	tablespoons butter or margarine

◢ Spread each slice of the bread with 1 ounce of the softened cream cheese. Top each slice with another slice of bread.

◢ Beat the eggs until frothy in a flat soup plate or pie plate. Beat in the milk, cinnamon and vanilla.

◢ Melt the butter on a griddle or in a large frying pan. While the butter is melting, soak each of the sandwiches on both sides in the egg mixture until well saturated.

◢ Place the soaked sandwiches on the griddle and cook, turning once until golden brown on both sides. Serve at once sprinkled with additional cinnamon or dribbled with maple syrup.

103

BAKED CINNAMON PANCAKE

Serves 2

Easy

Easy gourmet breakfast for two on a Sunday morning!

4	tablespoons butter or margarine
½	cup flour
½	cup milk
2	eggs
¼	teaspoon vanilla extract
	dash of cinnamon
	syrup

▲ Preheat oven to 425°. Melt butter in oven-proof 8"x1¼" round shallow ceramic baking dish.

▲ Mix flour, milk, eggs and vanilla in a small bowl. Add cinnamon. Pour mixture into the baking dish. Bake for 30 minutes.

▲ Serve immediately with syrup.

My college roommates and I gave our first brunch before a football game. We had too many guests, the kitchen was a disaster, but we laid out our best hand-me-down linens and confidently served that reliable dish, breakfast casserole. Everyone had a wonderful time! A good recipe for egg casserole is a must for the novice hostess.

BUFFET BREAKFAST CASSEROLE

Serves 20

Average

Lots of relatives in for the holidays? Keep breakfast easy with this wonderful dish.

1	large loaf day old French bread, torn into pieces
6	tablespoons melted butter
½	pound chopped ham
¾	pound shredded Swiss cheese
½	pound shredded Monterey Jack cheese
16	eggs
3	cups milk
¾	cup dry white wine
4	green onions, thinly sliced
¼	teaspoon red pepper
1½	tablespoons spicy mustard
1½	cups sour cream
¾	cup Parmesan cheese

Grease two 13"x9"x2" casserole dishes. Spread bread pieces in each pan and drizzle with butter. Sprinkle with ham, Swiss and Monterey jack cheeses.

Mix eggs, milk, wine, green onions, mustard and pepper and beat until foamy. Pour half over each casserole and refrigerate several hours or overnight.

Remove from refrigerator 30 minutes before baking. Preheat oven to 325°, cover and bake for 1 hour.

Remove from oven, spread with sour cream and sprinkle tops with Parmesan cheese. Bake uncovered for an additional 10 minutes or until lightly browned.

105

EXTRAORDINARY CRAB QUICHE

Serves 4 - 6

Easy

A classic for breakfast overlooking the water.

1	10 inch pie shell
½	cup mayonnaise
2	tablespoons flour
2	eggs, beaten
½	cup dry white wine
½	pound crab meat
⅓	cup sliced celery
8	ounces grated Swiss cheese
¼	cup diced onion
¼	cup diced green pepper or sweet red pepper
¼	teaspoon white ground pepper
2	teaspoons sherry

106

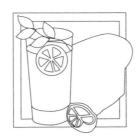

▲ Preheat oven to 350°. Prick pie shell and bake for 5 minutes.

▲ Combine mayonnaise, flour, eggs, and wine and mix well. Add lumped crab, celery, onion, white pepper, sherry and cheese. Mix well and pour into pie shell. Bake for 45 minutes or until surface is firm.

▲ To reheat, bake at 200° for 35 minutes.

CRÊPES DE VOLAILLE

Serves 5

Gourmet

Impress your guests!

Crêpes

1   cup flour

    dash of salt

1   egg

    dash of nutmeg

1½ cups milk

1   teaspoon melted butter

Velouté Sauce

⅓   cup butter

3½ tablespoons flour

1   cup chicken broth

Filling

¼   pound mushrooms, cubed

1   tablespoon sherry

2   teaspoons chopped green onions

½   teaspoon salt

2   drops hot pepper sauce

1   cup cubed, cooked chicken

Topping

1   cup Velouté sauce

¼   cup light cream

¼   cup butter

¼   cup whipped cream

1   egg yolk, beaten

3   tablespoons Parmesan cheese

◢ Combine crêpe ingredients and beat thoroughly in a blender. Strain out lumps. Heat and lightly butter a 7" skillet. Measure ¼ cup batter into skillet and tip gently to spread batter to nearly cover pan; flipping once. Separate crêpes with plastic wrap and store in zip lock bags (can be made a day ahead or frozen).

◢ For the Velouté sauce, melt butter, whisk in flour, cooking until just golden. Gradually add chicken broth and stir until thickened.

◢ For the filling, brown mushrooms lightly in butter and add sherry, onion, salt, hot pepper sauce and chicken. Add about 2 tablespoons velouté sauce to moisten.

◢ For the topping, place remaining velouté sauce in a pan and add light cream and stir until smooth. Add yolk and butter. Heat thoroughly, stirring constantly, but do not boil. Remove from heat and stir in whipped cream.

◢ To assemble, put filling across the center of each crêpe and roll. Place edges down in a shallow baking dish. Cover with topping and sprinkle lightly with Parmesan cheese. Broil until top is golden brown.

MEXICAN CHEESE SOUFFLÉ

Serves 6 - 8

Easy

A brunch dish with zip!

1	pound shredded cheddar cheese
1	pound shredded Monterey jack cheese
4	ounces chopped green chilies (can double or half to taste)
4	eggs, separated
⅔	cup milk
2	sliced tomatoes

108

▲ Preheat oven to 325°. Mix cheeses and chilies together. Place in a greased 13"x9"x2" pan.

▲ Beat egg whites until soft peaks form. Mix yolks with milk. Fold yolk/milk mixture into egg whites. Pour over cheese mixture and mix gently.

▲ Bake for 30 minutes.

▲ Remove from oven and place sliced tomatoes in a single layer on top and bake approximately 30 minutes more or until knife inserted in the center comes out clean.

Egg-based casseroles and quiches are just as tasty cooked with egg substitutes and low-fat milk, or try two egg whites for each whole egg.

PESTO AND PROSCIUTTO
BREAKFAST STRATA

Serves 6

Average

For Sunday breakfast during the summer.

1   cup milk

½   cup dry white wine

1   loaf day old French or peasant bread, cut into ½" slices

8   ounces prosciutto or ham, thinly sliced

1   cup fresh dill, snipped

3   tablespoons olive oil

1   pound smoked Gouda cheese, grated

3   sliced ripe tomatoes

½   cup basil pesto

6   eggs beaten

     salt and pepper to taste

1   cup whipping cream

One day before serving, mix the milk and wine in a shallow bowl. Dip 1 or 2 slices of bread in milk mixture and gently squeeze as much liquid as possible from the bread without tearing it. Place bread in a 13"x9"x2" glass baking dish sprayed with cooking spray.

Cover bread with prosciutto and snipped dill. Drizzle with olive oil, add grated cheese and a few tomato slices. Drizzle sparingly with pesto. Repeat the layering, overlapping the bread slices until the dish is filled.

Beat the eggs with salt and pepper to taste and pour evenly over the layers in the dish. Cover with plastic wrap and refrigerate overnight.

Remove from the refrigerator the next day and let warm to room temperature. Preheat oven to 350°. Drizzle top with cream and bake until puffy and browned, about 45 minutes to one hour. Serve immediately.

If using long, narrow baguette-type loaf, cut the slices on a 45° angle to allow for slightly bigger slices.

109

HERBED SAUSAGE PUFFS

Serves 6 - 8

Easy

Versatile as an appetizer or side dish.

2 (12 ounce) packages bulk sausage, 1 regular and 1 hot

1 cup Swiss cheese, grated

1 tablespoon grated Parmesan cheese

3 eggs, well beaten

1 tablespoon dried or fresh parsley flakes

1 tablespoon dried or fresh basil leaves, crushed

1 teaspoon garlic powder

salt and pepper to taste

1 (17¾ ounce) package frozen puff pastry, thawed

Sauce

½ cup Dijon mustard

2 tablespoons honey

▲ Preheat oven to 350°. Brown sausage in large skillet, drain and set aside to cool.

▲ Add cheeses, eggs (reserve 2 tablespoons) and seasoning to sausage and stir gently.

▲ Keep pastry very cold until ready to use. Roll out one sheet of pastry to a 12"x17" rectangle. Place half of sausage mixture along one side of the rectangle. Bring sides together by rolling oven and pinch ends tightly. Repeat with remaining pastry and sausage.

▲ Place on cookie sheet and form a semi-circle. Brush with reserved egg and bake at 350° for 30 to 40 minutes or until golden brown. Remove from the oven and cool 10 minutes. Slice into 1½" slices.

▲ Combine mustard and honey and serve with puffs.

This can be frozen once formed. Remove from freezer and let thaw before baking.

ITALIAN TORTA

Serves 8 - 10

Gourmet, must be made a day ahead.

A hearty main dish for a tailgate party or brunch.

3   sheets puff pastry dough

2   (10 ounce) packages frozen spinach, thawed and well-drained

¼   teaspoon nutmeg

1   clove crushed garlic

2   tablespoons olive oil or butter

15 ounces ricotta cheese

¼   cup chopped parsley

2   eggs

16 ounces shredded mozzarella cheese

1   pound ham, proscuitto, or cooked bacon

2   sliced roasted red peppers

1   small can sliced black olives

1   small jar artichoke hearts, drained and sliced

1   sliced ripe tomato

◢ Preheat oven to 400°. Gently unfold 2 sheets of pastry dough and roll to ⅛ inch thickness. Spray 9½"x 2½" springform pan with cooking spray.

◢ Line pan with the rolled pastry dough so that the dough overlaps and edges go over side of pan. Press together gently.

◢ Sauté spinach, olive oil, and garlic together in a saucepan until liquid evaporates. Add nutmeg and remove from heat.

◢ In a bowl combine ricotta, parsley, eggs and mozzarella. If using ham, chop into bite size pieces and combine with peppers and olives. Otherwise, combine pepper and olives.

111

◢ In pan layer spinach mixture, cheese, ham mixture or layer of proscuitto or bacon and pepper/olive mixture. Place layer of sliced artichoke hearts on top, followed by tomatoes. Repeat spinach, cheese, and meat layers.

◢ Place last sheet of pastry dough on top. Trim and press together edges. Cut slits in top. Brush with beaten egg if desired. Bake for 30 - 35 minutes until golden brown.

◢ Chill overnight. Remove from springform pan just before serving. Serve cold or at room temperature.

VEGETABLE FRITTATA

Serves 6 - 8

Average, can be served hot or cold

This baked omelette is good for leftovers too.

2	tablespoons olive oil
1	thinly sliced yellow onion
2	small sliced cooked potatoes
1	small sliced zucchini
1	small sliced red pepper
1	small sliced green pepper
½	cup chopped ham
¼	cup grated Gruyère or Monterey jack cheese
1	tablespoon chopped parsley
6	eggs, slightly beaten
	salt and pepper to taste

112

Preheat oven to 450°. Pour olive oil in a 8"x1¼" pie plate or oven proof ceramic quiche dish. Arrange onion slices in the bottom of the dish and bake for 5 minutes while preparing the other ingredients.

Remove baking dish from the oven, the onion should be slightly cooked. Arrange the potatoes, zucchini, red and green pepper and ham on top of the onion. Sprinkle with cheese and parsley. Season to taste with salt and pepper.

Reduce oven to temperature to 400°. Pour eggs over vegetables and cheese. Bake for approximately 20 minutes, until the eggs have puffed and the center of the frittata is set. Be careful not to overcook. Slice into wedges.

VIDALIA ONION TORTE

Serves 6

Average, can make ahead

The sweet onions and nutmeg give this dish a mellow flavor.

¼ cup white wine

10 slices of bacon, cut into 1 inch pieces

5 medium Vidalia onions, sliced thinly

6 tablespoons butter or margarine

1 tablespoon flour

1 cup light cream

1 teaspoon salt

¼ teaspoon pepper

½ teaspoon nutmeg

4 eggs, slightly beaten

1 (9"x1½") unbaked pastry shell

◢ Boil white wine until reduced by half. Cook bacon until crisp and drain.

◢ Cook onions over low heat in butter until tender and clear. Use a whisk to stir in flour, then add cream gradually, whisking constantly, until mixture thickens. Add the reduced wine, salt, pepper and nutmeg to the mixture. Cook for two minutes more, then remove from heat and let cool.

◢ Add eggs and bacon to the mixture. Put in the pastry shell. Bake in a 400° oven for 20 minutes or until a knife inserted halfway between the outside and the center comes clean. Let stand for 10 minutes and serve.

HONEY BUTTER

1 1/4 cups

Easy, will keep up to 1 month

Serve with warm fresh bread.

1 stick (½ cup) sweet butter, softened

⅔ cup honey

⅓ cup sifted light brown sugar

◢ In a bowl, with an electric mixer or with a food processor blend butter, honey, and sugar.

◢ Place contents in a crock and chill thoroughly until firm but spreading consistency.

PINEAPPLE CREAM CHEESE

1 cup

Easy, will keep up to 2 weeks

Wonderful with breakfast breads, you can substitute other fruits with great results.

▲ Beat cream cheese until creamy. Add remaining ingredients and mix well. Store covered in the refrigerator.

4	ounces softened cream cheese
4	tablespoons drained unsweetened crushed pineapple
1½	teaspoons sugar
	dash of vanilla extract

FRUIT BUTTER

1 1/2 cups

Easy, will keep up to 2 weeks

Try different fruits such as strawberries, peaches, and even blueberries. Serve on bread, pancakes or waffles.

▲ Combine all ingredients in a mixer or food processor until creamy. Store in the refrigerator.

1	cup softened sweet butter
½	cup drained, chopped fruit
¼	cup powdered sugar (or light brown sugar for a heartier texture)

Fresh Starts

SOUPS & SALADS

The Capital City

During the course of her existence, Annapolis has had to play many different roles; roles that reflect the tumultuous history of a growing nation. No function has been as closely identified with her as the seat of government — local, state and federal.

By the time of the American Revolution, Annapolis had been a colonial capital for 80 years. Maryland patriots had propelled the movement toward revolution in Annapolis's clubs and taverns, on the campus greens, and in the colonial legislature. From these vigorous efforts, Annapolis assumed a brief but central position in the founding of the new nation. It was here that the Continental Congress ratified the Treaty of Paris which ended the war. The State House was the home of the first peace-time capital of the United States from November 26, 1783 to August 13, 1784. The Annapolis Convention of 1786 set in motion progress toward abolishing the Articles of Confederation and convening the Constitutional Convention in Philadelphia the next year.

For ninety calendar days beginning the second Wednesday in January, Annapolis assumes her long-standing role as the state capital. Maryland's state legislature meets in the oldest state capitol building still in continuous legislative use. In the beautiful pillared brick building senators and delegates dash past the Old Senate Chamber where General George Washington resigned his commission as commander-in-chief of the Continental Army. Eager young aides race down the marble Grand Staircase on their way to deliver information on pending legislation. Annapolitans grow used to seeing the lawmakers huddled in earnest conversation at a local restaurant or the governor walking down the street listening to a constituent.

At the local level, Annapolis is the county seat for Anne Arundel County. County council members meet weekly to map out solutions to concerns facing a relatively rural area sandwiched between two cities. Annapolis city council members struggle to preserve the integrity of Annapolis's lifestyle while confronting challenges common to a more urban setting.

The vibrant exchange of ideas and the commitment to public service continues despite changes in the three hundred years since Annapolis was first designated the capital of Maryland. Politics is as much an integral part of her life today as it was yesterday and will be tomorrow.

CHESAPEAKE CLAM CHOWDER

Serves 8 - 10

Easy, can be made ahead.

This makes a delicious dinner on a winter night.

3   ounces shelled clams (save juice)

3   cups clam broth

4   slices bacon

4   tablespoons butter

4   cups whipping cream

2   tablespoons flour

2   medium chopped onions

2½ cups diced raw potatoes

¼   teaspoon white pepper

    salt to taste

▲ Drain all juice from clams and strain a couple of times. Grind clam meat.

▲ Cut bacon into 2" pieces and fry with onions until browned. Drain grease and place ground clams into a large soup pot; add enough water to cook potatoes and clams.

▲ When done, add clam juice, cream, bacon-onion mixture and seasonings. Add flour and butter to thicken, if necessary. Simmer gently until ready to serve. Garnish with chopped chives.

MANHATTAN CLAM CHOWDER

Serves 8

Easy, can be made ahead and frozen

Serve with cornbread.

3 tablespoons butter

2 cups chopped yellow onion

1 cup chopped celery

5 cups chicken broth

2 teaspoons ground thyme

2 bay leaves

2 (28 ounce) cans Italian plum tomatoes

4 boiled potatoes, peeled and chopped

6 carrots, peeled and chopped

½ teaspoon ground white pepper

5 (6½ ounce) cans chopped clams

salt and pepper to taste

◢ Melt butter in soup pan. Add celery and onion and cook until onion is transparent, about 10 minutes.

◢ Add other ingredients, except clams, and simmer for 30-40 minutes or until potatoes and carrots are tender.

◢ Add clams and heat thoroughly.

118

CRAB AND ASPARAGUS CHOWDER

Serves 8-10

Gourmet, can be made ahead

A delectable blend of tastes with a touch of basil.

¼ cup butter

1 medium chopped onion

2 stalks diced celery

1 pound chopped potatoes

1 pound asparagus, cut in 1" chunks

½ cup white wine

4 tablespoons clam juice

½ teaspoon pepper

1 teaspoon celery salt

1½ teaspoons onion salt

2 cups milk, divided

½ cup flour

2 cups half and half

½ cup scallions, thinly sliced

1½ tablespoons dried basil or ⅓ cup fresh chopped basil

1 pound crabmeat, picked to remove shell

◢ Melt butter. Sauté onion and celery 10 minutes over medium heat. Add potatoes, asparagus, wine, clam juice, pepper, celery salt, and onion salt. Bring to a boil and simmer vigorously until vegetables are tender.

◢ In a small bowl combine 1 cup of milk with flour. Mix until smooth. Add to soup and mix well. Reduce to gentle simmer.

◢ Add 1 cup milk, 2 cups half and half, scallions, basil, and crabmeat. Simmer until hot. Do not boil. Garnish each bowl with a lemon slice.

119

CRAB BISQUE

Serves 8 - 10

Easy, can be made ahead

A classic cream of crab soup.

2   cups crab meat, picked
    and cleaned

2   cans condensed cream
    of mushroom soup

2   cans condensed cream
    of asparagus soup

2   cups half and half

2½ cups whole milk

1   teaspoon
    Worcestershire sauce

¼   teaspoon Tabasco
    sauce or ½ teaspoon
    seafood seasoning

⅓-⅔ cup dry sherry,
    divided

120

◢ Pour soups, cream and milk into blender and blend well.

◢ Pour into saucepan and add remaining ingredients. Heat until hot, not boiling. Add remaining sherry to taste.

If I had to leave Annapolis, I would take cream of crab soup with me to remember it by. I love its velvety rich texture with the sweet lumps of crab and fragrant hint of sherry. So simple, but so perfect.

COLD CRAB GUMBO

Serves 6-8

Average, must be made ahead

Wonderful Maryland mix of ingredients.

½ cup chopped celery

½ cup chopped onion

¼ cup chopped green pepper

3 tablespoons butter

1¾ cups sliced fresh okra

8 cups chicken broth

1¾ cups canned Italian plum tomatoes

½ cup white long grain rice

1¼ cups lump crab meat, shell and cartilage removed

salt and pepper to taste

▲ Sauté celery, onion and green pepper in butter until vegetables are soft.

▲ Add okra, chicken broth, tomatoes and rice.

▲ Bring to a boil and simmer for 1 hour. Cool and refrigerate.

▲ Stir in crab meat. Season with salt and pepper to taste.

▲ Serve well chilled.

121

CRAB AND CHEDDAR SOUP

Serves 4-6

Easy, can be made ahead

Your children will devour this rich soup.

2　tablespoons butter

2　tablespoons flour

½　teaspoon salt

1　teaspoon white pepper

4　cups milk

½　pound grated cheddar cheese

　dash Tabasco sauce or 1 teaspoon prepared brown mustard

2　cups crab meat, shell and cartilage removed

　chopped chives

　Chesapeake-style seafood seasoning to taste

 In saucepan melt butter and blend in salt, pepper, and flour. Gradually add milk, stirring constantly, until thickened.

 Add cheese, stirring over low heat until cheese melts.

 Add crabmeat and heat very slowly. Garnish with chives and seafood seasoning.

 To make 10-12 servings, triple the recipe, using 3 cups crab meat. Reheat soup on very low microwave setting. Seasonings can be adjusted widely to taste.

Make croutons for soups or salads in fancy shapes using small cookie cutters. Sprinkle the croutons with dried garlic or herbs and toast on a cookie sheet.

CREAM OF TOMATO AND MUSSEL BISQUE

Serves 6

Gourmet

*An elegant and hearty
dinner for a snowy night.*

3   cups water

3   chicken bouillon cubes

1   cup white wine

1   clove crushed garlic

½   teaspoon red pepper

1   medium diced onion

¼   cup chopped fresh
     parsley

1   (12 ounce) can
     tomatoes

½   teaspoon dried basil

½   teaspoon dried chives

½   teaspoon dried thyme

30-36 fresh or canned
     cultured mussels

⅔   cup heavy cream

⅔   cup milk

2   egg yolks

2   minced scallions

▲ Mussels will have a small beard hanging from the shell. Clip this off, then rinse the mussels well under running cold water, shaking the colander frequently. Drain the mussels.

▲ Combine the water, bouillon, wine, garlic, pepper, onions, parsley, basil, chives, and thyme in a stock pot. Bring to a low boil. Add mussels and cook 5 to 6 minutes with the cover on until the mussels open. Agitate the pot to move the mussels around.

▲ Remove from heat. With a slotted spoon, remove the mussels to a bowl. Discard any mussels which did not open. Gently strain the liquid into a bowl through a strainer lined with double cheesecloth. The herbs will remain on the bottom of the pot. Do not strain the herbs.

▲ Place the tomatoes and the herb mixture in a food processor or blender and purée. Put back in stock pot, add the strained reserved liquid, bring to a boil, and reduce by half (about 20 minutes.) Beat egg yolks, cream, and milk. Stir into tomato mixture and cook for five minutes more over medium heat.

▲ Arrange 5 or 6 mussels in the bottom of a shallow soup bowl. Ladle the soup mixture over the mussels until the shells are two thirds covered. Garnish lightly with chopped parsley and scallions. Serve with an herb bread or french rolls.

CARIBBEAN SHRIMP SOUP

Serves 6 - 8

Gourmet

Serve this on your boat and sail to the tropics for lunch!

2   green bananas, peeled and sliced in rounds

1   teaspoon salt

3   pounds fresh shrimp (unshelled, with heads if possible)

     pinch of salt

1   large sliced onion

2   tablespoons olive oil

2   large cloves crushed garlic

3   medium chopped tomatoes

2   chili peppers, chopped or crushed, or 1 teaspoon cayenne pepper

4   medium potatoes, cut into chunks

▲ Dissolve the salt in enough water to cover the banana pieces. Soak them in the salt water for about 10-15 minutes to draw out the flavor of the fruit.

▲ Wash the shrimp in cold water, but don't shell or remove the heads. Cook in two cups of boiling water for 6-8 minutes, then peel off shells and remove heads. Save heads and cooking water.

▲ In a large heavy skillet or stew pot, sauté the onion in oil over moderate heat until golden. Stir in garlic, tomatoes, and pepper. Add shrimp.

▲ If you have the shrimp heads, push them through a sieve. Stir into the pot along with the water in which they cooked. Drain bananas and add them, with the potatoes, and cook until tender, about 20 minutes. Add water if necessary.

CHESAPEAKE BAY SEAFOOD GAZPACHO

Serves 8-10

Average, must make ahead

A new twist on gazpacho.

½ pound regular crab meat, shell and cartilage removed

½ pound small shrimp, peeled and cooked

1 medium cucumber, peeled, seeded, and diced

2 large ripe tomatoes, seeded and diced

1 medium green pepper, finely chopped

1 medium red onion (to taste), finely chopped

2 tablespoons chopped parsley

2 quarts canned tomato juice, chilled

3 hard boiled eggs

3 cloves garlic, minced

2 tablespoons whole grain mustard

¼ cup olive oil

1 tablespoon Worcestershire sauce

½ cup lemon juice

1 teaspoon salt

Tabasco sauce to taste

◢ Pick crab meat and put in a large bowl. Add cooked shrimp. Add tomato, cucumber, green pepper, onion, and parsley. Pour in the tomato juice and chill soup base while preparing the seasonings.

◢ Separate hard boiled egg yolks from whites, saving the whites. Put yolks in blender; add the remaining ingredients and blend well.

◢ Stir the blended seasonings into the soup and correct seasoning. Serve very cold; garnish with chopped egg whites.

CLASSIC OYSTER STEW

Serves 4

Easy, cannot be made ahead
A Chesapeake Bay tradition.

1   pint oysters, undrained

½   cup sherry

½   cup butter

2   cups half and half

 Heat undrained oysters over medium heat just until edges curl.

 In separate pan combine butter, sherry, and half and half; heat until butter is melted. Do not boil.

 Add oysters, and salt and pepper to taste. Garnish with chives, parsley, or croutons.

CARROT SOUP

Serves 6

Easy, can be made ahead
Carrots never tasted so good!

2   tablespoons butter

¾   cup finely chopped onion

3   cups finely chopped carrots

1   quart chicken broth

2   teaspoons tomato paste

2   tablespoons rice

½   cup heavy cream

    salt and pepper

    carrot curls

1   teaspoon butter, softened (do not substitute)

In a large saucepan, melt butter over medium heat. Stir in onions; cook for 5 minutes or until soft but not brown. Add carrots, broth, tomato paste, rice and simmer uncovered for 30 minutes.

Purée soup in blender and pour into a saucepan. Season with salt and pepper. Stir in cream and heat until warm; do not boil.

Prior to serving, stir in teaspoon soft butter; garnish with carrot curls.

127

Cream soups lend themselves to a variety of garnishes. Try a combination of cheese and toasted nuts, crumbled bacon, sunflower or toasted pumpkin seeds, a swirl of sour cream, or chopped herbs.

CHILLED CUCUMBER SOUP

Serves 6

Average

One of our favorites.

2   medium chopped onions

¼   cup olive oil

4   cucumbers, peeled and seeded

1   pound white potatoes, peeled and sliced

1   cup chicken stock

1   cup water

1   cup buttermilk

½   cup of peeled chopped cucumbers

2   tablespoons snipped fresh chives; extra for garnish

     salt and pepper to taste

 In a large skillet sauté the onion in olive oil until golden. Add cucumbers and sauté 5 minutes. Add the potatoes, chicken stock and water. Simmer the mixture over low heat for 30 minutes.

 Purée the soup in the blender and pour the mixture into a bowl. Add the buttermilk, diced cucumbers, and snipped chives. Taste for the seasoning; add salt and pepper to taste.

 Chill soup at least 6 hours. Serve and garnish with chopped chives.

For an elegant touch serve cold soups in a shallow champagne glass, a parfait glass, or a pewter cup.

RED POTATO, LEEK, AND CORN CHOWDER

Makes 6 quarts

Gourmet

Sweet tasting with a hot bite!

4   unpeeled diced potatoes

2   sticks butter, divided

4   tablespoons flour

2½ quarts half and half

½   cup chopped parsley

1-2 teaspoons honey

¼   teaspoon black pepper

¼   teaspoon salt

¼   teaspoon nutmeg

1   bay leaf

1   large Spanish onion, minced

4   cloves garlic, minced

1   leek, (white part only) sliced

3   scallions, white and green parts, chopped

¾   teaspoon dry mustard

½   teaspoon cayenne pepper

6   stalks diced celery

4   (20 ounce) boxes frozen whole kernel corn

1½ teaspoon ground thyme

3   vegetable bouillon cubes

◢ Parboil potatoes in water to cover for 7-8 minutes. Drain and reserve.

◢ To make sauce, in heavy saucepan, melt ½ stick butter. Add flour and a pinch of salt. Cook over low flame for 10 minutes.

◢ Add half and half, stirring constantly for 10 minutes. Add parsley, honey, bay leaf, pepper, and nutmeg.

◢ To make sauce, sauté onions, garlic, leeks, and scallions for 20-25 minutes in remaining butter. Season with mustard, cayenne, and salt to taste. Raise the heat and add celery. Cook 3-4 minutes.

◢ Add corn and bouillon cubes. Cook 3-4 minutes more.

◢ To combine, add the potatoes to the sauce and season with thyme. Taste and add salt if necessary. Serve piping hot!

129

GAZPACHO

Serves 6

Easy, must be made ahead

Stop by your local produce stand for fresh tomatoes.

2   tomatoes, seeded and finely chopped

1   cup chopped celery

1   green pepper, seeded and chopped

1   cucumber, peeled, seeded, and chopped

¼   cup chopped onion

¼   cup olive oil

2   tablespoons lemon juice

2   cups tomato or vegetable juice

1   cup chicken broth

    Tabasco to taste

⅛   teaspoon pepper

½   teaspoon salt

    fresh chopped cilantro for garnish

▲ Finely mince tomatoes, celery, green pepper, cucumber, and onion in food processor, saving some for garnish.

▲ Stir in olive oil, lemon juice, tomato juice, and chicken broth. Season with salt, pepper, and Tabasco. Chill for 2-3 hours. Garnish with cilantro and serve cold.

▲ Guests can individualize their gazpacho by selecting their garnish from an assortment of chopped green pepper, cucumber and onion.

Chill or warm soup bowls before serving to retain temperature.

MULLIGATAWNY SOUP

Serves 10

Average, can be made ahead

Autumn tastes for a football tailgate party!

½ cup celery, finely chopped

1 cup onion, finely chopped

3 tablespoons butter

½ cup flour

1½ tablespoons curry powder

2 quarts chicken broth

½ cup tomato purée

2 apples, peeled and diced

1 cup eggplant, peeled and diced

½ cup shredded coconut

½ cup whipping cream

In soup kettle sauté onions and celery in 3 tablespoons butter over medium heat until clear. Stir in flour, slowly making a roux. Add curry powder.

Gradually whisk in the broth being careful to avoid lumps.

Add tomato purée, apples, eggplant, and coconut. Simmer 30 minutes. Season with salt and pepper to taste.

Remove to blender (add about 1½-2 cups at a time) and purée until smooth. Gradually purée entire soup until smooth.

Add cream; heat before serving; and season as necessary.

131

MINESTRONE

Makes about 3 quarts

Average
Terrific next day too!

1	pound boneless beef, cubed
½	cup flour
3	tablespoons oil
¼	cup diced onion
1	cup diced zucchini (1" pieces)
1	cup cauliflower (1" pieces)
½	cup diced carrots
1	clove garlic, pressed
1	(16 ounce) can tomatoes, undrained
1	(6 ounce) can tomato paste
1	(8 ounce) can tomato sauce
1	tablespoon Worcestershire sauce
1	teaspoon parsley
2	quarts beef broth
½	teaspoon ground thyme
½	teaspoon pepper
1	teaspoon salt
1	cup minestrone pasta or barley

132

◢ Heat oil in skillet. Dredge beef in flour and brown in oil. Add onions and cook until beef is brown and onions are clear.

◢ Transfer to soup pot and add all other ingredients. Bring to a boil on stove top, stirring frequently.

◢ Simmer, stir occasionally until mixture thickens.

Sometimes it is not only the weather's chill that a good thick soup vanquishes. A steaming bowl with thick crusty bread and a sympathetic Mom sitting alongside has done more to soothe playground heartaches and adolescent dilemmas than any psychologist. Keep some "first aid for the soul" ready in your freezer.

PUMPKIN AND APPLE BISQUE

Serves 10-12

Gourmet

Try this for Thanksgiving Dinner.

6   cups pumpkin purée

8   tablespoons butter

1   medium onion, finely chopped

5   Granny Smith apples, peeled and quartered

2   tablespoons lemon juice

2   teaspoons salt

1   teaspoon white pepper

1½   cups apple juice or apple liquor (apple schnapps or brandy)

1   pinch cayenne pepper

1   cup heavy cream or half and half

4   quarts chicken broth

1   cup flour

1   cup butter

     chopped chives and/or toasted pumpkin seeds for garnish

Heat 8 tablespoons butter in a stock pot. Sauté onions until tender. Add apples and cook until soft.

Deglaze pan with apple juice or liquor (flambé if using liquor.) When the flames are gone, add the pumpkin purée and sauté for 10 minutes.

Pour in the chicken broth and lemon juice and simmer covered about 15-20 minutes. Add seasonings and heavy cream.

In a separate skillet, melt the remaining butter and add the flour. Stir constantly for 2 minutes until lightly brown. Remove from heat and slowly add to the soup while continuing to stir.

133

Bring soup to a simmer and remove from heat.

Place soup in batches in the blender and purée until smooth. Pour back into the soup pot and keep on warm.

Garnish with chopped chives or toasted pumpkin seeds.

SWEET RED PEPPER AND CURRY BISQUE

Serves 4

Average

A hearty, flavorful soup for winter.

3	large sweet red peppers, seeded and thinly sliced
2	tablespoons olive oil
4	tablespoons butter
¼	cup finely chopped onion
2	tablespoons flour
2	cups chicken broth
2	cups milk or half and half
1½	teaspoons curry powder
½	teaspoon white pepper
½	cup bourbon or sherry
	chopped fresh parsley

Sauté peppers in olive oil until softened. Set aside 8 slices of red pepper on a paper towel. Drain oil, then purée peppers in a food processor.

Melt butter in a 10" skillet. Add onion and sauté over low to medium heat until clear. Stir in flour. Gradually add the chicken broth, stirring to keep the soup smooth.

Stir in half and half, curry, pepper, red pepper purée, and bourbon or sherry. Simmer over low heat for 20 minutes or until thickened.

To serve, sprinkle fresh parsley on top and garnish with two thin slices of sautéed red pepper. A dollop of sherry can be added as well.

For extra flavor, use roasted red peppers.

HERBED SWEET PEPPER SOUP

Serves 6

Average

A heavenly medley of tastes.

¼ cup olive oil

2 cups chopped red onion

1½ pounds chopped sweet red peppers

1 tablespoon minced garlic

1½ pounds ripe tomatoes, peeled, seeded and chopped

1¼ teaspoons each of dried rosemary, thyme and marjoram

½ teaspoon dried basil

2 bay leaves

2 cups canned chicken broth diluted with 2 cups water

1 teaspoon ground cumin

1¼ tablespoons fresh ginger, peeled and minced

fresh ground pepper and salt to taste

◢ Heat oil in a large pot. Add the onion, sweet red pepper and garlic and coat with olive oil. Reduce heat and cover, stir occasionally until onion and pepper are soft, about 30 minutes.

◢ Remove the cover and stir in tomatoes, herbs, bay leaves, chicken broth, cumin, ginger, salt, and pepper. Increase heat and bring to a boil, then simmer on low heat for 30 minutes.

◢ Remove from heat and cool for 20 minutes, then transfer to a blender and purée. After cooling, may be refrigerated for up to 2 days. Reheat over low heat.

135

MUSHROOM BISQUE

Serves 8

Average

An elegant first course.

1 pound fresh firm mushrooms, washed and sliced

⅔ cup minced shallots

2 garlic cloves, minced

4 tablespoons unsalted butter

2 tablespoons flour

½ teaspoon tarragon, dried

3 cups chicken broth

3 cups heavy cream

6 sliced raw mushrooms for garnish

 In a large skillet, sauté mushrooms, shallots, and garlic in butter until translucent.

 Stir in flour and tarragon and cook 3 minutes stirring constantly.

 Remove pan from the heat and slowly add the chicken stock, stirring after each addition.

 In a blender blend the mixture until smooth and return it to a clean saucepan. Add the cream slowly, stirring well. Heat the mixture, stirring constantly. Do not boil.

 Garnish soup with thinly sliced raw mushrooms.

S T R A W B E R R Y   S O U P

Serves 6

Easy, must be made ahead

A surprising start for a spring brunch.

2   pints fresh strawberries

½   cup sugar

¾   cup sour cream

½   cup half and half

1½ cups dry white wine

2-3 strawberries for garnish

◢ Purée strawberries and sugar in electric blender. Pour into large bowl, whisk in sour cream, half and half, and wine. Mix well, chill thoroughly.

◢ Serve in well chilled glasses.

137

A U T U M N   S A I L   T O M A T O   B I S Q U E

Serves 4

Easy, can be made ahead

Warm and place in large thermos to take sailing.

1   (28 ounce) can crushed tomatoes, undrained

2   cups water

2   tablespoons sugar

1   tablespoon pepper

1   tablespoon basil

1   tablespoon oregano

1   whole bunch scallions, chopped

1   cup milk

1   cup half and half

◢ Combine all ingredients except half and half and milk and cook for 30-45 minutes at medium low heat to reduce liquid.

◢ Add milk and half and half and heat to just below boiling point.

CHILLED TOMATO AND YOGURT BISQUE

Serves 4-6

Easy, can be made ahead
Good for summertime.

1 cucumber, peeled and seeded

1 sweet red pepper, seeded and chopped

1 chopped scallion

1 clove crushed garlic

1 teaspoon honey

4 cups tomato juice

1 cup plain yogurt or sour cream

½ teaspoon dill

¼ teaspoon pepper

pinch salt

138

In blender or food processor, purée cucumber, sweet pepper, scallion and garlic.

Add honey, tomato juice, and yogurt. Blend well. Add seasoning.

Chill thoroughly. Garnish with croutons and fresh dill sprigs.

VEGETABLE BEEF SOUP

Serves 8

Easy, can be prepared ahead and frozen

Save for when the cook is out of town!

1 pound lean ground beef

1 medium onion, finely chopped

1 cup sliced celery

1 cup thinly sliced carrots

1 cup peeled, diced potatoes

1 bay leaf

½ teaspoon basil

2 teaspoons salt

1 cup shredded cabbage

1 (16 ounce) can tomatoes, undrained

3 cups hot water

1 cup tomato juice

◢ Brown beef in soup kettle and drain.

◢ Stir in onion, celery, carrots, potatoes, bay leaf, basil, salt, cabbage, tomatoes, hot water, and tomato juice. Bring to a boil.

◢ Reduce heat and simmer 40-45 minutes until vegetables are tender.

Float a paper towel on top of hot soup to absorb any grease.

139

CHICKEN AND GRUYÈRE BISQUE

Serves 6

Easy, can be made ahead

An elegant use for leftover chicken.

4 tablespoons butter

½ cup finely chopped onion

1 stalk finely chopped celery

2 peeled and grated carrots

2 pints half and half, divided

8 ounces Gruyère cheese in cubes

1-2 cups cooked chicken in small pieces

white wine or 1 teaspoon tarragon, optional

 In soup pan, melt butter and sauté vegetables until soft. Remove from heat.

In another saucepan, heat 1 cup of half and half; add cheese and stir constantly until melted.

Add remaining half and half and heat thoroughly. Add vegetables and chicken. Stir well.

Add dash of white wine or tarragon, if desired.

ARUGULA, EGG, AND TOMATO SALAD

Serves 4

Easy

Beautiful color and goes well with grilled seafood or meat.

¾ pound arugula

4 ripe plum tomatoes

2 hard boiled eggs, peeled and quartered

1 medium size red onion, cut into thin slices

2 teaspoons finely chopped garlic

2 tablespoons red wine vinegar

6 tablespoons olive oil

4 tablespoons coarsely chopped parsley

▲ Pick over arugula, discarding any tough stems. Rinse well and shake off excess moisture.

▲ Core tomatoes and cut into cubes.

▲ Put all ingredients in salad bowl, toss well before serving.

141

ARTICHOKE, TOMATO, AND RICE SALAD

Serves 4

Easy, can be made ahead

Simple, but bursting with flavor. Serve in a glass bowl to show off the color.

3 cups cooked rice

1 tablespoon fresh chopped parsley

1 (2 ounce) can black pitted, sliced olives

1 jar marinated artichoke hearts

2 large diced tomatoes

2 tablespoons diced green pepper

¼-½ cup mayonnaise

▲ Add other ingredients to chilled rice.

▲ Add enough mayonnaise to hold it together. Refrigerate. Tastes best when refrigerated about 2 hours.

AVOCADO AND PINE NUT SALAD

Serves 6

Average

Excellent first course for an Italian meal.

1	head green leaf lettuce
1	avocado, peeled and chopped
⅓	cup pine nuts, toasted
¼	cup alfalfa sprouts
¼	cup minced red onion
¼	cup grated mozzarella cheese
2	tablespoons white wine vinegar
1½	tablespoons Dijon mustard
6	tablespoons olive oil
	salt and pepper to taste

◢ Tear lettuce into large bowl.

◢ Add avocado, tomato, pine nuts, alfalfa sprouts, red onion, and mozzarella cheese.

◢ In a separate bowl, whisk vinegar and mustard. Gradually whisk in oil. Season with salt and pepper.

◢ Pour ⅓ cup dressing over salad and toss.

◢ Serve, passing remaining dressing.

143

GREEK SALAD

Serves 6-8

Average

Good with grilled lamb.

1	head romaine lettuce
1	head red tip lettuce
⅔	cup crumbled feta cheese
4	sliced scallions
1	small green pepper, sliced in rings
2	chopped tomatoes
1	sliced cucumber
2	teaspoons chopped parsley
1	sliced celery stalk
6	sliced black olives
1	can quartered artichoke hearts

Dressing

¼	cup olive oil
⅓	cup red wine vinegar
1	lemon, juiced
¼	teaspoon oregano
1	medium clove garlic, crushed
	ground pepper

 Whisk dressing ingredients together.

 Combine salad ingredients in large salad bowl. Toss with dressing and serve.

GRUYÈRE AND MIXED GREENS SALAD

Serves 6

Easy

An appealing alternative for a side salad.

1   head chicory (curly endive)

1   bunch watercress, stemmed

1   head red leaf lettuce

½   cup homemade garlic croutons

½   cup shredded Gruyère cheese

⅓   cup virgin olive oil

¼   cup red wine vinegar

½   teaspoon Dijon mustard

1   clove crushed garlic

    salt and pepper to taste

▲ To make dressing, combine olive oil, wine vinegar, mustard, garlic, salt, and pepper. Blend well.

▲ Trim and clean thoroughly endive and red leaf lettuce. Rinse in cold water and spin dry in a salad spinner.

▲ Stem the watercress, rinse and dry.

▲ In a large bowl, place greens. At serving time, add dressing and toss. Add croutons and shredded cheese and toss again.

145

HEARTS OF PALM SALAD WITH AVOCADO AND GRAPEFRUIT

Serves 4

Easy, can be made ahead, partially

A refreshing citrus taste.

1½ tablespoons lime juice

1½ tablespoons Dijon mustard

½ teaspoon salt

freshly ground pepper to taste

⅓ cup olive oil or salad oil

1 (14 ounce) can hearts of palm, drained and cut into 1" pieces

bibb lettuce

mixed greens

avocado slices

½ fresh pink grapefruit, cut into sections

▲ In a small bowl, combine lime juice, mustard, salt and pepper. Whisk.

▲ Add oil in a stream, whisking constantly until dressing is thick.

▲ Add hearts of palm and marinate several hours or overnight.

▲ To serve, toss with lettuce and avocado slices. Decorate with grapefruit slices.

146

PARSLEY SALAD

Serves 6

Easy, can be made ahead

Vibrant texture and taste. A nice contrast to strongly flavored dishes.

3   bunches parsley

3   tomatoes

1   onion

2   tablespoons lemon juice

2   tablespoons olive oil

salt and pepper to taste

▲ Wash parsley well. With scissors, snip parsley, but do not include stems.

▲ Mince tomatoes and onions in bowl; add parsley. Add salt, pepper, lemon juice, and oil and toss.

147

MARINATED VEGETABLE SALAD

Serves 6-8

Average, must be made ahead

This salad is a snap to prepare! Expect rave reviews!

2   cucumbers, peeled and sliced

1   onion, thinly sliced

1   green pepper, thinly sliced

1   red pepper, thinly sliced

3   carrots, peeled and thinly sliced

2   sliced zucchini

2   cups broccoli florets

1   (6 ounce) can sliced black olives

½   cup freshly grated Parmesan cheese

1   teaspoon minced fresh parsley

½   teaspoon dried basil

1   (12 ounce) basket cherry tomatoes

     salt and pepper to taste

▲ Combine ingredients for dressing in blender until smooth. Add blue cheese.

▲ Pour over vegetables and toss to blend. Cover and refrigerate at least 2 hours.

▲ Add cherry tomatoes and serve.

Continued on next page

MARINATED VEGETABLE SALAD

(c o n t i n u e d)

Blue Cheese Vinaigrette

½   cup olive oil

⅓   cup red wine vinegar

¼   cup finely chopped parsley

2   medium cloves garlic

1   tablespoon Dijon mustard

1   tablespoon honey

½   tablespoon crushed basil

¼   tablespoon salt

⅛   tablespoon freshly ground pepper

¼   cup crumbled blue cheese

Parsley always looked like a miniature tree to my three year old eyes. I would hide this "treasure" garnishing my plate in my mother's purse when we went out for Sunday breakfast and then forget it. My baffled mother was constantly finding dried parsley in her handbag.

GRILLED THREE PEPPER AND MOZZARELLA SALAD

Serves 8

Average, must make ahead

Spectacular color and perfect for entertaining.

2   large green peppers

2   large sweet yellow peppers

2   large sweet red peppers

1   large Bermuda onion

1   pound whole mozzarella cheese

1   (8 ounce) can medium black olives

Spanish Vinaigrette

⅓   cup red wine vinegar

2   tablespoons lemon juice

⅔   cup olive oil

1   teaspoon dried or 1 tablespoon fresh chopped basil leaves

2   tablespoons whole grain Dijon mustard

½   teaspoon red pepper

½   teaspoon garlic powder

◢ Cut the peppers into 1" chunks and place on skewers.

◢ Grill or broil, turning occasionally, until the edges of the peppers have browned.

◢ Remove from heat, take off skewers, and place in a bowl.

◢ Slice Bermuda onion into long thin pieces and add to pepper mixture.

◢ Drain olives and slice in half. Cut the mozzarella into bite size chunks. Add olives and cheese to the salad. Chill.

◢ Combine dressing ingredients in a shaker or food processor. Just before serving, add the dressing to the salad and toss.

SWEET PEPPER SALAD WITH NIÇOISE SAUCE

Serves 6

Gourmet, can prepare ahead partially

A delectable first course.

6   roasted red peppers

1   tablespoon olive oil

2   tablespoons red wine vinegar

2   tablespoons sugar

3   cubes instant beef bouillon

Sauce

½   teaspoon dry mustard

1   clove garlic

1   teaspoon salt

3   tablespoons lemon juice

½   cup and 1 tablespoon olive oil

1   (6½ ounce) can chunk white tuna packed in water

◢ Cut the roasted peppers into 1" pieces.

◢ Sauté in olive oil over medium heat. Reduce heat to low and add vinegar and sugar.

◢ When juice has rendered from peppers, add and dissolve bouillon. Cook over medium heat until liquid has almost evaporated.

◢ Put garlic, salt, and mustard into food processor and grind together in on/off turns. Add lemon juice.

◢ With food processor running, gradually add olive oil (can be prepared ahead to this point.)

◢ Add tuna a little at a time until sauce is smooth.

◢ Arrange peppers on a plate. Place the nicoise sauce over the peppers.

◢ Best served at room temperature. Peppers can be prepared a day or so ahead of time; nicoise sauce finished at the last minute.

151

Roast red or yellow peppers by placing on a hot grill or under preheated broiler on the top rack. Rotate one quarter around every 5 minutes until brown and wrinkled. Remove from heat, place in a paper bag for 20 minutes to absorb moisture. Rinse under cold water, peel skin and remove seeds.

CREAMY POTATO SALAD

Serves 12

Average, must be made ahead

Serve for a Fourth of July Barbecue and watch it disappear.

9   medium red potatoes

3   hard boiled eggs

⅔   cup mayonnaise

1   teaspoon prepared mustard

¾   cup sour cream

¼   cup Italian dressing (optional)

1   teaspoon salt

¼   teaspoon pepper

11   slices bacon, cooked crisp and crumbled

¼   cup chopped onion

½   cup chopped celery

Boil potatoes in salted water until tender. Drain and cool slightly. Peel and cut potatoes into ¾" cubes.

Remove yolks from eggs and mash them. Set whites aside.

Stir mayonnaise, mustard, sour cream, salt and pepper into yolks and set aside.

Chop egg whites, add bacon, potatoes, onion, celery, and Italian dressing. Fold in mayonnaise mixture.

Chill at least 2 hours.

DILL AND ARTICHOKE POTATO SALAD

Serves 16

Average, must be prepared ahead

A winner for picnics! Garnish with fresh dill.

3 pounds whole tiny new potatoes

1 cup mayonnaise

2 tablespoons red wine vinegar

2 tablespoons Dijon mustard

1 tablespoon lemon-pepper seasoning, or to taste

1 tablespoon fresh dill or 3 teaspoons dried dill

4 hard cooked eggs, chopped

12 ounces marinated artichoke hearts, drained and sliced

¾ cup chopped onion

2 tablespoons chopped dill pickle

Scrub potatoes with a brush. In Dutch oven, cook unpeeled potatoes covered in slightly boiling water for 20 minutes or until tender. Drain; cool; cut into bite size pieces.

In a very large bowl, stir together mayonnaise, vinegar, mustard, lemon-pepper seasoning, and dill.

Gently fold in potatoes, eggs, artichoke hearts, onion and pickle.

Cover and chill for 24 hours. Stir gently before serving.

153

STRAWBERRY AND SPINACH SALAD

Serves 8

Easy

The jewel-like red and green of this salad is a showstopper for a buffet. Toasted nuts can be added, too.

1   pound fresh spinach, washed, dried and broken into pieces.

1   pint strawberries, washed, hulled, and sliced

Sweet French Dressing

⅓   cup sugar

½   cup vegetable oil

¼   cup white vinegar

¼   teaspoon salt

¼   cup catsup

½   tablespoon Worcestershire sauce

▲ Prepare spinach and strawberries and return to refrigerator to chill.

▲ Make dressing and chill.

▲ Just prior to serving, toss spinach, strawberries, and dressing.

154

CURRIED CHICKEN SALAD WITH CANTALOUPE AND CHUTNEY

Serves 4

Easy, can be made ahead
Perfect for a summer day.

3   cups cubed cooked chicken

1   cup sliced green grapes

2   cups chopped celery

½   cantaloupe, cut in chunks

1   cup mayonnaise

⅓   cup mango chutney

1   teaspoon curry powder

2   tablespoons cream

Mix chicken, grapes, celery, and cantaloupe.

Blend in mayonnaise, chutney, curry powder, and cream.

Put over salad. Toss just before serving.

155

WILD RICE AND RED APPLE CHICKEN SALAD

Serves 4

Easy, can be made ahead

Delicious for a luncheon. Try using grilled chicken.

1   pound boneless chicken breast

½   cup prepared long grain and wild rice mix

¼   cup mayonnaise

¼   cup sour cream

½   teaspoon curry powder

    black pepper to taste

    dash Worcestershire sauce

2   tablespoons sliced almonds

1   diced cooking apple

    lettuce for garnish

▲ Place chicken in shallow baking dish filled with ¼" water. Cover and bake in 350° oven until done, about 30 minutes.

▲ While cooking chicken, prepare rice according to package directions.

▲ Allow chicken and rice to cool. Cut chicken into cubes.

▲ In bowl, combine sour cream, mayonnaise, Worcestershire sauce, curry powder, and pepper.

▲ In a large bowl, combine chicken, rice, almonds, apple pieces and sauce.

▲ Serve chilled on a bed of lettuce.

156

SHRIMP AND STRAW MUSHROOM SALAD WITH GINGER DRESSING

Serves 8

Average, must prepare ahead

A delightful first course.

2   pounds shrimp, cooked, peeled and cleaned

2½ cups blanched snow peas

1   (8 ounce) can straw mushrooms, drained

Dressing

3   tablespoons white wine vinegar

2   tablespoons fresh ginger, peeled and minced

2   tablespoons lemon juice

2   tablespoons lite soy sauce

2   tablespoons Dijon mustard

6   tablespoons vegetable oil

½   cup sesame oil

1   clove garlic

2   tablespoons chives, snipped

    salt and pepper to taste

◢ Combine vinegar, ginger, lemon juice, soy sauce, salt, and pepper. Add oils in a stream until creamy. Whisk in garlic and chives.

◢ Marinate shrimp in dressing overnight (2 nights, if possible.)

◢ Add peas and mushrooms at least one hour before serving.

157

SWEET AND TANGY GRILLED SHRIMP SALAD

Serves 4

Gourmet, can be made ahead, partially

A crisp shrimp dish with wonderful sweet and sour flavor. Take on a boat for grilling in the evening!

Barbecue Sauce

¼   cup vinegar

½   cup water

¼   cup butter or margarine

½   cup catsup

¼   cup brown sugar

1   tablespoon prepared mustard

¼   teaspoon ground pepper

⅛   teaspoon Tabasco sauce

1   sliced thick lemon

1   sliced medium onion

▲   Combine ingredients in a medium saucepan, simmer uncovered until thick (about 2 hours.) Strain and place in jar.

▲   Either can or place in refrigerator for storage. Will keep up to six months. Makes 1 pint. This barbecue sauce is particularly good with shrimp.

Continued on next page

158

SWEET AND TANGY GRILLED SHRIMP SALAD (Continued)

Salad

28   medium shrimp

10   slices of trimmed lean bacon (or regular bacon partially cooked)

2   cucumbers

1   can water chestnuts

barbecue sauce

⅓   cup red wine vinegar

⅔   cup olive oil

1   clove garlic, minced

1   teaspoon celery seed

1   teaspoon grated onion

1   teaspoon paprika

1   teaspoon pepper

◢ Peel cucumbers. Cut cucumber lengthwise in half, and scoop out seeds. Slice in ¼" thick slices.

◢ Combine vinegar, olive oil, garlic, celery seed, onion, paprika, and pepper. Add cucumbers, cover and marinate in refrigerator for 2 hours.

◢ Peel shrimp. Cut bacon strips in thirds, and wrap one slice around each shrimp.

◢ Place on skewer by putting skewer through the shrimp near the tail and again near the top. The dish can be made ahead up to this point.

◢ Baste shrimp with barbecue sauce and grill, basting occasionally until shrimp is done (about 8 minutes.)

159

◢ Stir in water chestnuts with cucumbers. With a slotted spoon to drain off excess dressing, place a bed of cucumber salad on each plate. Remove shrimp from skewers and place on cucumber. Brush with barbecue sauce.

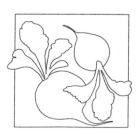

STEAK SALAD

Serves 4-6 as an entree

Easy, can be prepared ahead and transported

Flavorful use for leftover grilled steak.

2   pounds cubed grilled steak

½   pound sliced fresh mushrooms

1   (13 ounce) jar of artichoke hearts, quartered

1   bunch thinly sliced scallions

2   tablespoons chives

2   tablespoons parsley

2   tablespoons olive oil

⅛   teaspoon salt

⅛   teaspoon pepper

2   medium tomatoes, wedged

1   bunch romaine lettuce

Dressing

2   tablespoons tarragon vinegar

1½   teaspoons lemon juice

1   teaspoon salt

1   egg

1   teaspoon Dijon mustard

1   teaspoon honey

⅓   cup oil

▲ Mix the first 9 ingredients together in a salad bowl.

▲ Blend all of the dressing ingredients together in a blender, adding the oil slowly while blending.

▲ Prepare each plate with a bed of Romaine lettuce.

▲ Toss the first 9 ingredients with the salad dressing, then arrange the mixture on top of the Romaine lettuce on each plate. Garnish with tomato wedges.

HERBED VINAIGRETTE

Makes 1 cup

Easy

Use this wonderful dressing over greens or in seafood salads.

3	tablespoons wine vinegar
½	teaspoon Dijon mustard
½	cup olive oil
1	clove garlic, minced
½	teaspoon fresh parsley
½	teaspoon fresh tarragon
½	teaspoon fresh chervil
½	teaspoon fresh chives
	salt and pepper to taste

▲ In a blender, combine all ingredients and blend at medium speed. Add salt and pepper to taste.

Parsley's bright green color, fresh taste, and adaptability as a flavor enhancer makes it a universal favorite for cooks. Place in salads or chop and add generously to cooked dishes. Put it in at the end of the cooking time to avoid overwhelming the delicate flavor.

161

ORIENTAL DRESSING

Makes 1 1/2 cups

Easy, can be made ahead
Try with chicken, seafood, or vegetable salads.

2 tablespoons thick soy sauce

4 tablespoons olive oil

1 tablespoon sherry

1 teaspoon sugar

1 clove garlic

2 teaspoons ginger

black milled pepper

◢ Place ingredients in blender or food processor until well blended.

GARLIC MUSTARD DRESSING

Makes 3 cups

Easy
This is for garlic lovers.
Serve with grilled meat or a substantial salad.

1 egg

⅓ cup Dijon mustard

⅔ cup red wine vinegar

salt and pepper to taste

4-6 cloves garlic

2 cups best quality olive oil

◢ Combine egg, mustard, and vinegar in a food processor. Season with salt and pepper. Drop garlic cloves through tube.

◢ Dribble in olive oil in slow steady stream.

◢ Transfer to storage container and refrigerate until ready to use.

SWEET DIJON MUSTARD DRESSING

Makes 1 cup

Easy
Versatile and Popular.

1	clove garlic, minced
¾	cup oil
½	large egg yolk
2	tablespoons Dijon mustard
2	tablespoons sugar
1	teaspoon salt
1	teaspoon pepper
1½	tablespoons lemon juice
1	tablespoon white vinegar

◢ To make dressing, in a large bowl mix garlic, oil, yolk, Dijon, sugar, salt, and pepper.

◢ Slowly drizzle in lemon juice and vinegar. Mix until smooth. Keep refrigerated.

Use different salad greens to give color and interest to a tossed salad. Try combinations of spinach, romaine, watercress, parsley in addition to Bibb or iceberg.

163

RED ROQUEFORT DRESSING

Makes 2 cups

Average, can make ahead

A nice sweet and sour taste popular with guests.

½   cup brown sugar

½   cup vinegar

1   cup salad oil

½   cup catsup

½   teaspoon garlic powder

¾   tablespoon onion juice

    juice of ½ lemon

½   teaspoon salt

¼   teaspoon pepper

½   cup water

1   package Roquefort cheese, crumbled

▲ Mix all together, not in blender.

▲ Allow to stand at least 3 hours with Roquefort in it.

▲ Will store for 3 months in refrigerator.

Add dressings at the last minute to keep the vegetables' color bright. Toss salads to reduce the amount of dressing used.

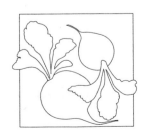

First Mates

VEGETABLES & ACCOMPANIMENTS

Maryland Agriculture

For hundreds of years the Chesapeake Bay has enriched the land surrounding it, allowing local farmers and the enthusiastic home gardener to grow an abundance of fresh fruits and vegetables. Captain John Smith, the principal discoverer of the Bay, described "a faire Bay compassed but for the mouth with fruitful and delightsome land....Heaven and earth never agreed better to frame a place for man's habitation."

In this congenial land the Native Americans and the colonists found the plentiful harvests essential to their cooking. Early recipes pay homage to the sweet corn and berries, crisp ripe apples and peaches, fresh beans and other vegetables. Combined with the fish and shellfish of the Bay, the colonists were provided with a healthy diet.

Modern cooks in Anne Arundel County still plan many of their meals around the seasonal availability of local produce. Small pick-your-own farms and produce stands dot the back roads. Frequent stops at them are an essential part of grocery shopping during the long growing season. Even the tiniest kindergartner knows to pick the strawberries that are red and ripe on the vine, and few can resist placing the juiciest berries in their mouths rather than in the bucket. Equally tantalizing are the mounds of luscious ripe tomatoes and peaches that occupy the stands all summer. Devotees of the sweet white corn, Silver Queen, wait impatiently for July, when the farmers deliver truckfuls of plump ears to the stands. Newcomers to Annapolis are constantly astounded at the local appetite for this sweet corn. Hostesses know to plan on cooking three ears for guests, and a few bold souls will admit to routinely polishing off up to six ears at home.

The local produce is so tasty that dishes made from these ingredients tend to be very light, relying more on the natural freshness than on heavy sauces. Herbs and spices are used to enhance the flavor and add piquancy to dishes. Mouths water at the sight of fresh sliced tomatoes topped with chopped basil and drizzled with a light vinaigrette or sweet garden peas mixed with mint and a touch of butter. Captain Smith's "delightsome land" still provides a flavorful harvest for the table.

OLD MARYLAND BAKED APPLES

Serves 6

Easy

Delightful with pork chops or duck.

6   cooking apples

6   teaspoons brown sugar

1   teaspoon lemon zest

¼   cup chopped raisins

¼   cup chopped dates

1   cup Marsala wine

◢ Core apples and place in a buttered baking dish. Can peel if desired.

◢ In a small bowl, mix together sugar, lemon zest, raisins and dates. Fill apples with this mixture. Pour Marsala wine over apples.

◢ Bake at 375° until apples are soft, about 40 minutes, basting frequently with wine. Serve from the pan with warm sauce over apples.

167

GLAZED ASPARAGUS

Serves 4

Average, can be partially made ahead

The simple but elegant glaze is also good with snowpeas.

16   stalks fresh asparagus, rinsed and peeled, if desired

2   tablespoons soy sauce

2   tablespoons lemon juice

2   tablespoons butter or margarine

◢ Break white parts off of asparagus. Place in rapidly boiling water and cook until tender but crisp; about 5-7 minutes. Remove from heat and drain.

◢ Before serving, combine soy sauce, lemon juice and butter in a large skillet. Over medium heat, reduce by one half or until sauce becomes syrupy.

◢ Add asparagus and warm for 1 minute, shaking asparagus until well coated. Serve immediately.

Cut vegetables in even sizes to achieve evenly cooked pieces.

BAKED BEANS WITH ORANGE

Serves 6-8

Average,can be made ahead

The only baked bean recipe you'll ever need.

4 bacon slices

1 onion, chopped

1 (28 ounce) can baked beans

1 teaspoon dry mustard

1 tablespoon brown sugar

1 tablespoon molasses

2 oranges, peeled, sliced, and seeded

⅓ cup orange curaçao or liqueur

▲ In skillet, sauté bacon until crisp. Remove and crumble. Reserve 1 tablespoon drippings. Sauté onion until soft.

▲ Combine ingredients except oranges into 1½ - 2 quart casserole. Place oranges on top of beans. Bake uncovered at 350° for 2 hours.

BROCCOLI IN LIME BUTTER

Serves 6

Easy

A piquant sauce to spruce up broccoli.

2   heads broccoli

½   cup butter or margarine

¼   cup lime juice

2   tablespoons rough grain Dijon mustard

1   tablespoon horseradish

◢ Cut broccoli into bite size florets If you use the stem, peel off the outer skin. Cook in boiling water until tender to taste. Make sure that the water covers the florets or else the broccoli may turn yellow. Remove and drain.

◢ Combine remaining ingredients in a small saucepan over low heat, until the butter is melted. Just before serving, pour over broccoli and toss.

169

Use lemon juice, lime juice, salsa or vinaigrette as low fat alternatives to butter.

BROCCOLI CHEDDAR PIE IN POTATO CRUST

Serves 6

Gourmet

A perfectly delicious side dish that is also good with cauliflower.

Crust

2 cups packed, grated raw potato

½ teaspoon salt

1 egg

¼ cup grated onion

Filling

1½ cups packed, grated cheddar cheese

1 medium head broccoli, broken into florets

1 medium clove of pressed garlic

1 cup chopped yellow onion

3 tablespoons butter

Dash thyme

½ teaspoon basil

½ teaspoon salt

2 eggs, beaten together

¼ cup milk

1 tablespoon oil

Black pepper to taste

Paprika

▲ Crust: Heat over to 400°. Salt the grated potato and drain for 10 minutes in a colander over a bowl. Squeeze out excess water and add to remaining ingredients.

▲ Pat it into a greased 9 inch pie pan, building the sides of the crust with lightly floured fingers. Bake for 40-45 minutes, until browned. After the first 30 minutes, brush the crust with a little oil to crispen it.

▲ Filling: Turn oven down to 375°. Sauté onions and garlic, lightly salted in butter for 5 minutes. Add herbs and broccoli and cook, covered 10 minutes, stirring occasionally.

▲ Spread half the cheese into the baked crust, then the sauté, then the rest of the cheese. Beat eggs, milk and oil together. Pour custard over and dust with paprika. Bake 35-40 minutes, until set.

HONEY GLAZED GREEN BEANS ALMANDINE

Serves 6

Easy, can be made ahead

Nutmeg adds a mellow flavor.

4   cups fresh green beans

1   tablespoon butter or margarine

1   tablespoon honey

¼   teaspoon ground nutmeg

½   cup toasted almond slivers

   salt and pepper to taste

▲ Prepare green beans by slicing ends at an angle. Boil or steam until tender. Drain and place on serving dish.

▲ Melt butter over low heat and add honey, nutmeg, salt, and pepper. Stir into green beans. Garnish with toasted almond slivers.

171

GREEN BEANS VINAIGRETTE

Serves 10-12

Average, can be made ahead

A classic summer picnic dish.

3 pounds fresh green beans

1 large red onion, thinly sliced

½ cup olive oil

3 tablespoons red wine vinegar

1 teaspoon Dijon mustard

½ teaspoon salt

¼ teaspoon ground pepper

▲ Steam green beans 7-8 minutes or to taste. Drain and pat dry. In a large bowl, mix remaining ingredients, except onions, into a vinaigrette.

▲ Add red onion slices. Add beans and toss to coat. Serve immediately or refrigerate and serve cold.

GINGER-ORANGE GLAZED CARROTS

Serves 8

Average, can be made ahead

Children and guests both love these tangy carrots.

2   pounds carrots

2   tablespoons sugar

2   teaspoons cornstarch

½   teaspoon salt

½   teaspoon ground ginger

½   cup orange juice

2   tablespoons margarine

◢ Slice carrots and cook in boiling water for 8 minutes or until tender. Drain. Keep warm.

◢ In saucepan, combine sugar, cornstarch, salt, and ginger. Slowly add orange juice. Stir well. Bring to a boil and boil for 1 minute, stirring constantly.

◢ Stir in butter. Pour mixture over carrots and serve.

173

Ginger's zesty flavor and smell is an essential part of many oriental dishes. It goes well with fruit, especially citrus, and is delicious in vegetable sauces.

BROILED CAULIFLOWER WITH ROSEMARY

Serves 4

Easy

Perfect with beef or lamb. Also try the dressing with roasted new potatoes.

1   head fresh cauliflower, cut into even sized pieces

1   teaspoon crushed, dried rosemary

2   tablespoons olive oil

     salt and pepper to taste

▲ Place cauliflower pieces in boiling water and cook until just barely tender. Drain. Combine olive oil and rosemary in a large bowl.

▲ Toss cauliflower in dressing until evenly covered. Place cauliflower on a baking sheet and broil for 15 minutes until evenly browned. Serve immediately.

CHESAPEAKE GRILLED CORN

Serves 6-8

Easy, can prepare ahead and refrigerate

Take this favorite to a cookout.

6-8 ears of corn, shucked

6-8 tablespoons butter or margarine, melted

Chesapeake-style seafood seasoning to taste

salt and pepper to taste

6-8 square pieces aluminum foil (approximately 12 inch x 12 inch)

◢ Lay each ear of corn in center of a piece of foil. Pour melted butter over each ear to coat.

◢ Generously sprinkle seafood seasoning, salt and pepper and roll corn in mixture. Seal foil tightly and place on hot grill. Cook for 10-15 minutes on each side.

I love to see my daughter perched on Grandma's counter, right where I used to sit, talking to my mother while she cooks dinner. She always gets a preview taste from Grandma's spoon too!

SUMMERTIME CORN MEDLEY

2 cups

Average

Serve with fresh tomatoes and grilled chicken for an easy meal.

1   cup uncooked corn kernels

⅔   cup white wine vinegar

½   cup chopped red pepper

½   cup chopped green pepper

½   cup sugar

⅓   cup chopped celery

⅓   cup chopped onion

1   tablespoon mustard seed

2   teaspoons celery seed

2   teaspoons salt

▲ Combine all ingredients in a saucepan and simmer the mixture for 15 minutes.

▲ Serve warm or chilled. For canning purposes, pack medley in sterilized jars and seal.

EGGPLANT PARMIGIANA

Serves 6

*Gourmet, can be made ahead
and reheated*

*A mellow blend of
vegetables, herbs and
cheeses.*

3   small eggplants, peeled
and sliced in ½" slices

3   tablespoons olive oil

1   chopped onion

3   cloves minced garlic

3   large cubed tomatoes

2   (8 ounce) cans tomato
sauce

½   teaspoon ground
thyme

1   tablespoon sugar

½   teaspoon black pepper

2   cups grated mozzarella
cheese

⅓   cup grated Parmesan
cheese

▲ Sprinkle eggplant with salt and let sit for 30 minutes. Sauté onion and garlic in olive oil. Add tomatoes and simmer uncovered for ten minutes.

▲ Add tomato sauce, thyme and sugar. Add pepper to taste, and continue simmering for 20 more minutes. Stir regularly.

▲ Layer eggplant, mozzarella cheese and sauce in a 9 inch x 13 inch x 2 inch baking dish. Top with Parmesan cheese. Bake uncovered for 30 minutes at 350°.

177

GARLIC NEW POTATOES

Serves 4-6

Easy

Delicious with beef.

16　small new potatoes

¼　cup melted butter or margarine

1　clove crushed garlic or ½ teaspoon garlic powder

½　cup chopped parsley

1　teaspoon salt

◢ In a large covered pot, boil potatoes for 5 minutes. Drain. Sauté potatoes in butter and garlic over medium heat until tender or golden. Shake frequently.

◢ Add parsley and salt and serve at once.

178

PARMESAN POTATOES

Serves 4

Easy

Simple and satisfying.

1　pound red skin potatoes, thickly sliced

1　tablespoon olive oil

½　teaspoon salt

¼　teaspoon pepper

3　tablespoons grated Parmesan cheese

◢ Preheat oven to 425°. Combine potatoes, olive oil, salt and pepper in a 13 inch x 9 inch x 2 inch baking dish.

◢ Sprinkle with Parmesan cheese. Cover with foil. Bake 30 minutes until tender.

SWEET POTATO-TANGERINE SOUFFLÉ

Serves 6-8

Gourmet, can be made ahead

A pleasant and light accompaniment for roasted poultry.

3   pounds peeled sweet potatoes

5   tablespoons melted butter

8   tablespoons brown sugar

¼   cup dark rum

¼   teaspoon nutmeg

½   teaspoon salt

5   tangerines

3   tablespoons chopped pecans

◢ Preheat oven to 350°. Boil and mash sweet potatoes. Add 3 tablespoons butter, 6 tablespoons sugar, rum, nutmeg, and salt. Blend together until smooth.

◢ Peel tangerines and remove white membranes. Cut the sections from 3 of the tangerines in half. Remove the seeds. Fold tangerines into the sweet potato mixture. Purée in blender. Pour mixture into a greased 2 quart casserole dish.

◢ Puncture the centers of the remaining tangerines to remove the seeds. Arrange them on top of the pudding. Combine the remaining sugar and butter with the pecans. Sprinkle over top of souffle and bake for 30 minutes.

179

SPINACH-ONION SQUARES

Serves 16-20

Easy, can be prepared ahead

A popular side for buffets.

10 ounces frozen chopped spinach

5 eggs

1 cup grated cheddar cheese

1 cup grated Swiss cheese

½ cup flour

1 cup milk

4 ounces chopped mushrooms

2 ounces sliced pimentos (optional)

½ teaspoon basil

⅛ teaspoon salt

6 ounces french fried onions

▲ Thaw and drain spinach. Mix ingredients, except onions. Spread into a 9 inch x 13 inch buttered pan. Sprinkle onions on top.

▲ Bake at 350° for 30 minutes or until firm. Cut into squares, serve warm.

To cut fat use chicken broth to sauté vegetables instead of butter or oil. Onions can be sautéed in white wine as well.

CHEDDAR SQUASH BAKE

Serves 6

Average

A great way to cook the squash from the garden.

1   pound yellow squash

1   large onion

2   beaten eggs

1   cup milk

1   cup grated cheddar cheese

2   teaspoons butter

1   cup toasted bread crumbs

½   cup sour cream

½   stick butter or margarine

▲ Cook squash and onion in salted water until tender. Drain. Mix together squash, onion, beaten eggs and milk. Add the sour cream, ½ of the bread crumbs, and ½ of the grated cheese.

▲ Pour into greased casserole dish. Dot with butter or margarine. Top with remaining cheese and crumbs.

▲ Bake at 350° for 20-30 minutes until slightly brown.

181

THANKSGIVING SAUERKRAUT

Serves 12

Easy

A Maryland tradition with Thanksgiving turkey.

3   (27 ounce) cans sauerkraut

3   pork chops or country-style spareribs

▲ Approximately 24 hours before serving time, layer pork, then sauerkraut in a crock pot. Cook on low for 24 hours.

▲ Before serving, remove bones and chop pork. Stir to distribute pork through the sauerkraut.

SAUTÉED ZUCCHINI IN HERBED TOMATO SAUCE

Serves 6

Average

A celebration of summer's fresh vegetables and herbs.

6   medium zucchini, sliced ¼" thick

1   small thinly sliced onion

6   tablespoons olive oil

1   teaspoon chopped garlic

¼   cup chopped fresh parsley or 1 tablespoon dried parsley

1   tablespoon fresh basil or 1 teaspoon dried basil

1   tablespoon fresh marjoram or 1 teaspoon dried marjoram

1   (8 ounce) can tomato sauce

1   fresh tomato, chopped

½   teaspoon sugar

    salt and pepper to taste

 In a large skillet, sauté onions in olive oil until clear. Add garlic and zucchini. Sauté over medium heat for 10 minutes.

 Stir in remaining ingredients, turn to low heat and simmer for 10 minutes. Serve warm.

CARROT BROWN RICE

Serves 4

Easy, can be made ahead

A flavorful and colorful rice.

2⅓ cups chicken broth

1 cup brown rice

½ pound carrots, peeled and chopped or julienned

2 medium onions, sliced

1 tablespoon butter

½ teaspoon salt

◢ Bring broth to a boil. Add rice, carrots, onion, butter and salt; stir. Cover tightly and cook over low heat until all liquid is absorbed, about 50 minutes.

183

BAKED LEMON RICE

Serves 8

Average

A perfect accompaniment for seafood.

⅓ cup butter

½ cup chopped onion

2½ cups packaged long grain rice

1 (16-ounce) jar clam juice

¼ cup lemon juice

1½ teaspoons salt

water

lemon peel cut into fine slivers

◢ In a 2 quart casserole dish melt butter over low heat. Add onion; increase heat and sauté until translucent, about 5 minutes; remove from heat.

◢ Combine clam juice, lemon juice and enough water to equal total liquid called for on rice package. Add liquids to rice with salt; cover tightly. Can prepare ahead and let stand at room temperature for up to 4 hours.

◢ Preheat oven to 400°. Bake until liquid is absorbed, about 60 minutes. Remove from oven; let stand for 5 minutes. Toss in lemon peel; serve.

SPINACH MUSHROOM GAME RICE

Serves 8-10

Gourmet, can be made ahead and frozen

A great side dish with venison, goose, and other game.

1   (6 ounce) package long grain wild rice

4   ounces diced mushrooms

½   teaspoon salt

2   teaspoons Dijon mustard

2¼ cups water

10 ounces frozen spinach, thawed and drained

¾   cup chopped onion

1   tablespoon butter

1   (8 ounce) package cream cheese, softened

¼   cup shredded cheddar cheese

¼   cup dry sherry

▲ Place rice, mushrooms, salt, and mustard in a 2 quart casserole. Combine water, spinach, onion, and butter in sauce pan. Bring to boil. Pour over rice mixture, stir.

▲ Cover tightly, bake for 30 minutes at 375°. Uncover, stir in cream cheese and sherry. Can be frozen at this point.

▲ Bring to room temperature if frozen and add cheddar cheese on top and bake uncovered for 10-15 minutes.

184

HERBED CRANBERRY STUFFING

Serves 8-10

Easy

A delicious stuffing for turkey, cornish hens, and pork loin.

1   medium red onion

2   tablespoons butter or margarine

2   cups fresh cranberries

2   tablespoons brown sugar

2   teaspoons rosemary

½   teaspoon sage

     salt and pepper to taste

7   cups dried, cubed orange/raisin bread crumbs

½   cup orange juice

◢ Dice onion, cook in butter in large skillet over low heat. Add cranberries, brown sugar, rosemary, sage, salt and pepper. Stir until warm.

◢ Transfer mixture to large bowl. Mix in remaining ingredients, blending thoroughly. Stuff into main course.

Sage is a pungent herb that is best used with strongly flavored meats and cheeses. It is often used in poultry stuffing. Dried sage should not be kept for longer than 3 months or else it will develop a musty taste.

185

SKIPJACK OYSTER DRESSING

Serves 6

Easy, can be made a day ahead

A classic Maryland recipe.

¼   pound butter or margarine

4   tablespoons finely chopped onion

4   tablespoons finely chopped celery

4   cups dry bread crumbs

¼   teaspoon ground pepper

    salt, to taste

2   cups oysters in bite size pieces

2   tablespoons fresh parsley

▲ Melt butter or margarine in skillet. Stir in onion, celery, and oysters reserving ¼ cup of oyster liquid. Mix oyster liquid with dry bread crumbs and set aside.

▲ Cook primary mixture over low heat until onion is soft. Add mixture to crumbs and liquid. Toss lightly with salt, pepper, and parsley.

Thanksgiving day began with the sounds and smells of my mother preparing stuffing. Bowls of dry bread would be on the counter, and she would brown the onions and celery in bacon drippings. It smelled so good!

Prime Thyme

ENTREES

Colonial Preservation

Any city that is approximately 300 years old faces the delicate balance of combining historical preservation with modern day living. Annapolis is no exception. As early as 1769, William Eddis wrote the following description of Annapolis to a correspondent in England: "At present, this city has more the appearance of an agreeable village than the metropolis of an opulent province, as it contains within its limits a number of small fields, which are intended for future erections. But in a few years it will probably be one of the best built cities in America, as a spirit of improvement is predominant and the situation is allowed to be equally healthy and pleasant with any on this side of the Atlantic."

Since that time the preservation of Annapolis has been an ongoing battle waged primarily by an extraordinary group of individuals — none of great wealth but all of great concern for the town. During the 1920s and 1930s efforts to retain the colonial flavor of the city advanced when St. John's College purchased buildings and furniture made in Annapolis as a basis for courses studying the colonial period. Dr. James Bordley was instrumental in dissuading Henry Ford from moving the William Buckland-designed mansion, the Hammond-Harwood House, to Detroit after the College was forced to sell it during the Great Depression. His intervention allowed the College enough time to find a local buyer in a group of determined citizens who formed the Hammond-Harwood House Association. This group still operates the house as a museum.

In 1952 the preservation of Annapolis was renewed with the founding of Historic Annapolis, Inc. The remarkable persistence and foresight of these volunteers resulted with Annapolis being declared a National Historic Landmark district in 1966. Historic Annapolis combined public and private funds to preserve the historic quality of the city while encouraging economic stability. Their notable achievements include the restoration of the Customs House, the rescue of the Charles Carroll the Barrister house, and the elegant restoration of the William Paca House and Gardens.

Dr. Eddis's "spirit of improvement" continues with today's preservation efforts. A tour of the restored buildings or a visit through the lively historic district gives the visitor perspective into Annapolis's heritage and appreciation for her future.

GINGER FRIED CHICKEN

Serves 6

Average, can be made ahead

Refreshing flavor to classic fried chicken.

2½ pound cut up frying chicken

¼ cup soy sauce

¼ cup sake

2 teaspoons peeled fresh minced ginger root

2 fresh minced garlic cloves

⅓ cup flour

⅓ cup cornstarch

¼ teaspoon salt

½ teaspoon fresh ground pepper

1½ cups vegetable oil

lemon wedges

◢ Place chicken in a glass dish large enough to hold chicken in one layer. Combine soy sauce, sake, ginger and garlic; add the mixture to the poultry. Marinate the chicken for one hour, turning and basting often.

◢ In a flat pan, combine the flour, cornstarch, salt and pepper. Dredge the chicken pieces in the mixture and shake off the excess. Transfer the chicken to a tray. Let the chicken stand for 15 minutes.

◢ In a large, deep skillet heat the oil. Fry the chicken in batches until golden brown. Drain and cool the pieces on paper towels. Serve hot or at room temperature with lemon wedges.

189

CURRIED CHICKEN ROLLS WITH APPLE AND RAISIN STUFFING

Serves 8

Average, can be made ahead and frozen

A hostess's dream, a make ahead dish that everyone will like!

8-10 boneless chicken breasts

¼ cup chopped onion

¼ cup butter

1 small chopped apple

½ cup raisins or currants

¼ teaspoon ground ginger

2 teaspoons curry

¼ teaspoon cinnamon

¼ teaspoon allspice

1½ cups cooked rice

½ cup toasted slivered almonds

To baste chicken rolls

2 tablespoons butter

¼ teaspoon cinnamon

¼ teaspoon allspice

◢ Melt butter in saucepan. Sauté apples and onions until clear. Remove from heat and stir in remaining ingredients for rolls.

◢ Spray a 9x12 inch casserole with cooking spray. Pound or roll chicken breasts until they are ¼ inch thick. Place a heaping tablespoon (more for larger breasts) of stuffing in the center of each breast. Fold edges together to form a packet and place them in the dish with folded edges down.

◢ Melt butter with the spices and baste the chicken generously. Cover with foil and bake for one hour at 350°. Chicken rolls can be frozen at this point if making ahead.

Continued on next page

190

Entrees

CURRIED CHICKEN ROLLS WITH APPLE
AND RAISIN STUFFING (Continued)

For the sauce

4   tablespoons butter

3   tablespoons flour

¼   cup white wine

2   cups half-and-half or milk

1½   teaspoons curry powder

½   teaspoon allspice

⅓   cup chutney

◢ While chicken breasts are baking, make sauce. Melt butter in a skillet over medium heat. Whisk in flour, then gradually add white wine and milk whisking constantly. Stir in spices and chutney, cook for 5 minutes, stirring frequently.

◢ If chicken rolls were made ahead, defrost them, place in casserole and cover with sauce. If chicken rolls are cooking, remove foil after 1 hour, add sauce to casserole and cook for 30 minutes.

191

BROILED CHICKEN PROVENÇAL

Serves 6 to 8

Easy, can be made ahead

Tasty as a dinner and a delicious cold picnic chicken.

⅓   cup melted butter

½   teaspoon salt

½   teaspoon pepper

1   teaspoon dried thyme

1   teaspoon marjoram

½   teaspoon rosemary

2   (2 to 2½ pound) cut up chickens

2   tablespoons fresh chopped parsley

◢ Combine melted butter and all herbs except parsley. Baste chicken with butter mix and place chicken skin side down in pan with no rack.

◢ Broil 5 to 7 inches from heat for 20 minutes. Baste chicken, turn, broil 15 to 20 minutes.

◢ Sprinkle with fresh parsley before serving.

HERBED CHICKEN IN WINE

Serves 4

Easy, can be made ahead

A speedy and savory family meal.

4 or 5 boneless and skinless chicken breasts

½   cup flour

4   tablespoons salad oil

2   cups dry, white wine

2   cups fresh sliced mushrooms

2   teaspoons salt

1½ teaspoons ground tarragon

1½ teaspoons ground thyme leaves

2   teaspoons chives

½   teaspoon ground black pepper

In plastic bag, coat chicken breasts with flour. Heat oil in heavy skillet over medium heat. Brown chicken on both sides in oil. Drain oil.

Add mushrooms and wine. Sprinkle with herbs and spices. Bring to a boil, reduce heat to low, cover and simmer 30 minutes. Serve immediately over hot rice.

My mother combined a passion for historic houses with a passion for their gardens, where she would find a favorite herb and crush a little sprig between her fingers, enjoying its fragrance as she toured the grounds.

Entrees

HONEY MUSTARD GRILLED CHICKEN

Serves 4

Easy, must make ahead, partially

This chicken is a real crowd pleaser and is easily doubled or tripled.

¼   cup olive oil

¼   cup vegetable oil

½   cup Dijon mustard

¼   cup whole grain mustard

¼   cup honey

3   teaspoons white wine vinegar

4   split chicken breasts

▲ Combine all ingredients. Marinate chicken in sauce for 6 to 8 hours.

▲ Grill chicken, basting occasionally with sauce, for approximately 35 minutes.

▲ Leftover chicken is delicious in grilled chicken salads.

Remove meats from grill to baste to prevent fire flareups.

193

ORANGE ALMOND CHICKEN

Serves 4

Easy

An exceptional low fat meal.

4   skinless and boneless chicken breasts

1   teaspoon nutmeg

½   teaspoon salt

⅛   teaspoon pepper

1½ cups orange juice

½   cup honey

½   cup raisins (or less to taste)

1   tablespoon cornstarch

2   tablespoons water

¼   cup toasted almond slices

▲ Lightly flatten chicken breasts. Sprinkle both sides with nutmeg, salt and pepper. Combine orange juice, honey and raisins in large skillet. Heat sauce and add chicken. Cover and simmer 15-20 minutes or until chicken is tender.

▲ Remove chicken from sauce. Dissolve cornstarch in water. Stir into juice mixture. Cook until thickened stirring constantly.

▲ Return chicken to the skillet. Stir in almonds. Serve over rice or a pilaf dish.

Entrees

CHICKEN ITALIANO

Serves 4

Easy

Need to fix a quick meal before the kids go to sports practice? Try this children's favorite.

½ cup grated Parmesan

2 tablespoons fresh parsley

1 teaspoon Italian seasoning

1 minced garlic clove

1 teaspoon pepper

4 boneless chicken breasts

3 tablespoons melted butter

◢ Combine Parmesan, parsley, seasoning, garlic and pepper.

◢ Dip chicken in melted butter, then in cheese mixture.

◢ Place in shallow baking dish, drizzle with remaining butter and cheese mixture.

◢ Bake at 375° for 25 minutes or until tender.

Try non-fat yogurt instead of butter or oil to hold breading or seasonings on baked chicken.

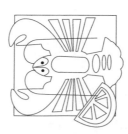

CHICKEN WITH RED AND YELLOW PEPPERS IN CAPERS SAUCE

Serves 2

Average, can be made ahead

A colorful and zesty chicken, perfect for a romantic dinner.

2   skinless and boneless chicken breasts

     dash of salt and pepper

2   teaspoons olive oil

1   minced garlic clove

¼   cup chopped onion

2   tablespoons dry white wine

1   jar of rinsed drained capers

2   teaspoons lemon juice

1½   teaspoons butter

     chopped parsley

1   sliced red pepper

1   sliced yellow pepper

     paprika for garnish

◢ Sprinkle chicken with salt and pepper. In a 9 inch skillet, heat oil and add chicken. Cook until lightly browned, about 3 minutes on each side. Set aside and keep warm.

◢ Add garlic and onion to oil, stirring constantly for about 30 seconds. Add wine, capers and lemon juice and bring to a boil. Turn off the heat and add butter. Stir.

◢ Slice chicken diagonally on plate and top with caper sauce. Serve over rice and garnish with red and yellow pepper slices, paprika and chopped parsley.

◢ Chicken can be prepared ahead and reheated. Sauce can be prepared ahead and heated when preparing to eat.

Entrees

LEMON AND ROSEMARY CHICKEN

Serves 6

Average

The tangy sauce makes this a family favorite.

4   boneless and skinless chicken breasts

1½ teaspoons rosemary leaves (fresh or dried)

4   tablespoons olive oil

⅓   cup dry white wine

⅔   cup lemon juice

¼   cup bread crumbs

   parsley and lemon slices for garnish

Rosemary, the herb of remembrance, gives a smoky flavor to meats. Crush dried leaves and rub over meat before grilling or browning. Place a sprig of fresh rosemary inside chickens before roasting.

◢ Place chicken breasts between two pieces of wax paper. Pound each breast to ¼ inch thickness with a meat mallet. Cut the flattened pieces into halves or thirds. Coat each piece with bread crumbs.

◢ Heat the olive oil over medium heat in a 10 inch frying pan. When oil is hot, place half of the chicken pieces in oil in the pan and sprinkle half of the rosemary leaves over the chicken pieces. Brown the chicken breasts until a light golden brown. Remove and drain on a paper towel. Repeat with the other half of the chicken and rosemary leaves.

◢ Pour off the excess oil from the frying pan, being careful not to remove the browned rosemary leaves and chicken left on the bottom of the pan. Return immediately to the heat and add lemon juice and wine to the pan. Stir with a whisk to loosen the leavings on the bottom of the pan. Cook over medium heat until the sauce is reduced by one-third.

◢ Place the chicken on a platter and pour ⅓ of the sauce over the chicken pieces. Pour the remaining sauce into a pitcher and serve alongside. Garnish with lemon slices and parsley.

◢ Excellent served with rice.

BAKED LIME CHICKEN

Serves 6

Easy

A delectable summer dish.

2-4 limes

3½ pounds broiler fryer parts or breasts

3 tablespoons butter

¼ cup flour

1¼ teaspoons salt

½ teaspoon pepper

2 tablespoons brown sugar

1 (14 ounce) can chicken broth

1 tablespoon grated lime peel

▲ Preheat oven to 400°. Grate lime peel. Squeeze 2 tablespoons lime juice and toss juice with chicken pieces. In 9x13 inch roasting pan, melt butter in oven. Mix flour, salt and pepper. Dip chicken pieces in flour and then dip in butter. Arrange chicken skin side down in pan.

▲ Mix lime peel and brown sugar and sprinkle over chicken.

▲ Pour broth and remaining lime juice into pan and bake uncovered for 50 minutes, basting occasionally. Use one-half can of broth for boneless breasts. Can add more lime juice if desired.

Sauté chicken in chicken broth or white wine to reduce fat.

198

Entrees

ONE-DISH CHICKEN LO MEIN

Serves 4

Average

A low calorie, low fat and low energy dinner!

1   tablespoon dark sesame oil

1   pound boneless and skinless chicken breasts, cut into strips

1   (14 ounce) can low salt chicken broth

1   cup water

½   teaspoon ginger

¼   teaspoon crushed red pepper flakes

3   tablespoons teriyaki sauce

1   (8 ounce) package spaghetti

1   package (1 pound) frozen broccoli, carrot, red pepper and water chestnut combination

2   sliced green onions

◢ In skillet, heat oil over medium-high heat; brown chicken, about 3 minutes. Remove to plate.

◢ In same pan, bring broth, water, ginger, pepper flakes and teriyaki sauce to a boil; add spaghetti. Simmer, covered, 8 minutes, stirring often.

◢ Stir in vegetables and chicken. Bring to a boil; simmer, covered, 4 minutes. Stir in onions. Remove from heat and serve.

199

CHAMPAGNE MUSTARD CHICKEN WITH MUSHROOMS

Serves 4

Average

Delicious with rice or pasta.

2	tablespoons olive oil
8	peeled shallots
4	boneless chicken breasts
1¼	cups chicken broth
2½	tablespoons champagne mustard
2	teaspoons ground thyme
2	cups small mushrooms
1	cup grated Jarlsburg cheese
	flour seasoned with salt, pepper and thyme
	fresh thyme for garnish

◢ Heat ½ oil in large skillet, add mushrooms and shallots, sauté until golden. Remove from pan, add rest of oil to pan.

◢ Lightly dust each breast with seasoned flour, sauté until golden brown.

◢ Add chicken broth, mustard, thyme, salt and pepper to taste. Cover and simmer 10 minutes.

◢ Sprinkle each breast with cheese, add shallots and mushrooms. Cover and simmer for 7 minutes.

◢ Garnish with fresh thyme and serve.

S W E E T   N '   S O U R   C H I C K E N

Serves 4-6

Easy, can be made ahead

A cup of pineapple, mandarin oranges and water chestnuts can add variety to this great weekday dinner.

1	cut up chicken or assorted chicken pieces
3	tablespoons oil
1	medium chopped onion
1	medium chopped green pepper
1	medium chopped red pepper
1	minced garlic clove
¾	cup ketchup
½	cup water
¾	cup sugar
⅓	cup lemon juice
4	tablespoons Worcestershire sauce
2	tablespoons prepared mustard
	salt (to taste)
	pepper (to taste)

▲ Place chicken in baking dish.

▲ Heat oil in frying pan. Sauté onion, peppers and garlic until soft.

▲ Combine rest of ingredients. Mix thoroughly. (Food processor works well with plastic blade). Pour into frying pan and bring to boil. Sauce may also be done in the microwave.

▲ Pour over chicken and bake at 350° uncovered until done. Time depends on type of chicken used - 45 minutes for boneless chicken pieces or 1 hour 20 minutes for cut up chicken parts.

▲ Serve over rice. Fruit can be added 5 minutes before serving.

Whenever we travel, I try to bring back a regional recipe from our vacation spot. I make it the night we get our pictures back from the photo developer. My family tells favorite vacation stories, and we get to extend the vacation one more night.

TARRAGON CHICKEN IN PHYLLO

Serves 8-10

Gourmet, can be made ahead

An elegant and easy dish. Makes a beautiful presentation for dinner parties.

1½ cups mayonnaise

1 cup chopped green onions

⅓ cup lemon juice

1 teaspoon dry tarragon

2 minced garlic cloves

12 boned and skinned halved chicken breasts

24 sheets phyllo dough

1⅓ cups melted butter

⅓ cup grated Parmesan

salt and pepper

◢ Combine first 5 ingredients to make sauce.

◢ Lightly sprinkle chicken pieces with salt and pepper.

◢ Place one sheet of phyllo on working surface and quickly brush with 2 teaspoons melted butter.

◢ Place second sheet over this and again brush with butter. Spread 1½ teaspoons of sauce on each side of breast.

◢ Place a chicken breast in one corner of the phyllo. Fold corner, then fold sides and roll sheet to form a package. Place in an ungreased baking dish or on a cookie sheet.

◢ Repeat until all chicken is used.

◢ Brush with remaining butter and sprinkle with Parmesan cheese. Bake at 375° for 20-25 minutes until golden brown.

This dish may be converted to an appetizer by cutting chicken to bite size bundles and tying with green onion stems.

HERBED CHICKEN POT PIE

Serves 5-6

Average, can be made ahead

Fragrant and welcoming on a winter evening.

1	tablespoon butter or margarine
2	tablespoons oil
2	cups carrots (¼" thick)
2	cups diced onions
2	cups diced potatoes
2	cups cleaned snow peas
2	cups chicken broth
2	cups cooked chicken
1	teaspoon cornstarch
½	teaspoon powdered ginger
¼	teaspoon chopped dill
1	egg yolk, mixed with 1 tablespoon of water
1	batch dough
	salt and pepper (to taste)

Dough

½	teaspoon salt
1½	teaspoons baking powder
1	teaspoon sugar
5	tablespoons butter
¾	cup buttermilk
2	cups flour
¼	teaspoon chopped dill

▲ Sauté carrots, onions and potatoes over low heat for 15 minutes. Fold in chicken.

▲ Mix cornstarch and ginger with whisk. Add 1 cup chicken broth, mix until smooth. Add to vegetable mixture.

▲ Add snow peas. Stir, cook 5 minutes. Season with salt, pepper and dill. Remove from heat. Spoon into greased 2 quart dish.

▲ Preheat oven to 350°.

▲ Melt butter with oil in a saucepan.

▲ In medium bowl, combine flour, baking powder, sugar and salt. Add butter and cut until mixture looks like fine crumbs.

▲ Add buttermilk and dill and stir. Gather dough into ball.

▲ On lightly floured surface, roll out dough to ¼ inch thickness.

▲ Drape dough over vegetable/chicken mixture, pinch edges; brush with egg water mixture.

▲ Bake 30 minutes, or until top is lightly browned.

Every family has a "welcome home dish," a favorite that says "we're glad you're safe and with us." It never tastes as good as it does when Mom or Dad cooks it. Love must be the secret ingredient.

203

CITRUS CHICKEN WITH AVOCADO AND MACADAMIA NUTS

Serves 6

Average

Take your family to the islands for supper.

1   brown-in bag

6   chicken breast halves

1   (6 ounce) can frozen pineapple-orange juice concentrate, thawed

1   teaspoon fresh or crystallized finely diced ginger

1   teaspoon soy sauce

2   tablespoons butter or margarine

1   peeled and sliced avocado

1   tablespoon lime juice

4   cups cooked rice

½   cup chopped macadamia nuts (optional)

▲ Preheat oven to 350°.

▲ Put fruit juice concentrate, chicken breasts, ginger, soy sauce and butter in brown-in bag.

▲ Cook for 50 minutes.

▲ Cook rice according to package directions.

▲ Brush avocado with lime juice.

▲ Arrange chicken and avocado on rice and sprinkle with nuts. Pour remaining sauce over chicken and serve.

204

Entrees

TROPICAL CHICKEN BOAT CASSEROLE

Serves 6

Average, can be prepared ahead and frozen

The secret boat recipe from an enthusiastic sailing family.

2   (7 ounce) packages seasoned wild and long grain rice

1   (8½ ounce) can chopped and drained artichoke hearts

1   (10½ ounce) can drained mandarin oranges

1   cup tropical trail mix

6   cooked chicken breasts

2   tablespoons curry powder

    salt and pepper to taste

½   cup chopped onion

1   cup cooked and chopped green beans

¼   cup Dijon mustard

2   cups half-and-half

◢ Cook rice and place in the bottom of a 9"x13" greased casserole dish.

◢ Place the chicken on top of the rice, then mix the remaining ingredients (except the mustard and half-and-half) and spread over casserole.

◢ Mix mustard and half-and-half and pour over the casserole.

◢ Bake uncovered at 350° for 30 minutes.

◢ If being prepared for a boat trip, check the size of the boat's oven to change pan size if necessary.

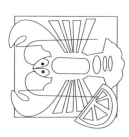

WHITE CHILI

Serves 6

Easy

Cinnamon gives this chili a hearty flavor.

1	tablespoon salad oil
1	medium onion
1	clove garlic
1	teaspoon cumin
¼	teaspoon cinnamon
1½	cups water
2	large whole chicken breasts, cut into bite size pieces
1	can drained white kidney beans
1	can drained garbanzo beans
1	can drained white corn
2	(4 ounce) cans green chopped chilies
2	chicken bouillon cubes

 Sauté first four ingredients.

 Combine next eight ingredients.

 Cover and bake at 350° for 50-60 minutes.

 Serve topped with Monterey Jack cheese and fresh tomatoes.

Broil meat instead of browning it to reduce fat in casseroles and stews.

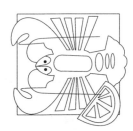

ROCK CORNISH HENS WITH PINEAPPLE WALNUT STUFFING

Serves 4

Average, can be made ahead partially

The dressing is a delicious accompaniment to the glazed hen.

4   Rock cornish hens

Honey-Lemon Glaze

¼   cup lemon juice

½   cup honey

¼   cup grenadine syrup

½   cup soft butter

½   teaspoon horseradish (optional)

Pineapple-Walnut Stuffing

½   cup water or pineapple juice

¼   cup butter

½   package bread stuffing mix (4 ounce)

1   slightly beaten egg

½   cup crushed and drained pineapple

¼   cup finely chopped walnuts

◣ Heat water or pineapple juice and add butter. Heat until butter is melted. Stir in remaining ingredients for stuffing.

◣ Stuff hens with dressing.

◣ Combine lemon juice, honey, horseradish and grenadine. Set aside ½ cup for basting; blend remainder with butter. Spread over surface of birds. Roast at 350° for about an hour or until done. Brush occasionally with honey mixture while cooking.

207

Seal the juices in roast chicken or turkey by warming the oven to 450 then reducing the heat to 350 when you put the bird in the oven.

ROAST DUCKLING IN GREEN PEPPERCORN SAUCE

Serves 4

Gourmet

Try this marvelous sauce with pheasant or other game.

2   (5 pound) domestic ducklings

½   cup water

1   teaspoon salt

⅓   cup butter

1   cup Madeira

3   tablespoons drained green peppercorns packed in brine

1   cup whipping cream

     salt and pepper to taste

▲ Remove all fat from ducklings and discard. Dry ducklings thoroughly and prick them all over with a long tonged fork. Sprinkle them all over including cavities with salt and pepper.

▲ Place ducks in a roasting pan on a wire rack and pour water in the bottom of pan. Place the birds in a preheated 425° oven and roast them for 45 minutes.

▲ Pour off all accumulated fat. Combine the Madeira and butter and pour over duckling and roast birds for an additional 20 minutes. Transfer the ducklings to a serving platter.

▲ Pour drained peppercorns into small saucepan. Add accumulated drippings from the roasting pan and simmer for 5 minutes. Add whipping cream and cook an additional 5 minutes-do not boil. Cut ducks in half and spoon some sauce over them and serve the rest on the side.

208

Entrees

PROVIDENCETOWN HOLIDAY TURKEY

Serves 8-10

Average, can be made ahead

The rich brown color and mellow flavor of this roasted turkey is truly something to be thankful for! It is particularly good when roasted in a kettle grill. Good with roast chicken also.

1 (15 to 17 pound) turkey

½ cup olive oil

½ cup Chesapeake seafood seasoning

1 stick butter

2 sliced oranges

½ cup bourbon or sherry

1 tablespoon rosemary

◢ Preheat oven to 325° or arrange banks of very hot coals on lower grill around a 9x12 inch aluminum drip pan.

◢ Remove neck and giblets from defrosted turkey and rinse cavity. Pat skin dry with paper towel. Using hands, rub turkey skin with olive oil and then rub in seafood seasoning, coating top of turkey evenly.

◢ Place butter, oranges, bourbon or sherry and rosemary in cavity. Put bird in roasting pan and cover tightly with lid or aluminum foil or place on top grill and cover with kettle lid. Roast until meat thermometer registers 185°. Time will vary depending on size of bird and heat of coals. If roasting in oven, baste occasionally after first hour.

I prepared my first turkey the year after my mother died. My father came into the kitchen as I triumphantly yanked the neck out after a maddening hour's struggle. He said through his laughter, "Honey, your mama always called me to do that." Some kitchen secrets mamas just don't pass on.

ELEGANT LIGHT BEEF WELLINGTON

Serves 8 to 10

Gourmet

Don't let the "Light" scare you! Perfect for putting on the Ritz!

3   cups all purpose flour

¼   teaspoon salt

½   cup safflower margarine

7   tablespoons water

1   pound finely minced mushrooms

1   seeded and finely minced red bell pepper

1   seeded and finely minced green bell pepper

3   large peeled and finely minced shallots

1   large peeled and finely minced garlic clove

2   tablespoons finely minced parsley

¾   teaspoon crushed dried thyme

¾   teaspoon crushed dried savory

1¼   cups beef broth, divided

1   cup plus 2 tablespoons Madeira

1   (2½ pound) beef tenderloin roast

In large bowl, combine flour and salt. Cut in margarine until small flakes are formed. Add 7 tablespoons water, a few at a time, stir with fork until dough holds together. Wrap in waxed paper and set aside.

In large skillet, combine mushrooms, red and green bell peppers, shallots, garlic, parsley, ½ teaspoon each savory and thyme, ¼ cup beef broth and 2 tablespoons Madeira. Bring to boil then reduce heat to medium high and cook mixture until liquid starts to evaporate, about 10 minutes. Reduce heat to medium and continue cooking 30 minutes, stirring often until mixture starts to thicken. Lower heat to keep from scorching, if necessary. Remove duxelles from pan and cool completely. The duxelles can be made ahead and refrigerated until ready to use.

Trim excess fat from meat. Sear meat on all sides in non stick skillet over medium heat. Cool beef 1 hour.

On floured surface, roll dough to 13x13 inch square. Pat cooled duxelles over surface of meat and center on dough. Gently wrap dough over meat and tuck under the ends. Place on lightly greased baking sheet and brush with egg whites.

Bake at 375° for 50 minutes or until the meat registers 150° on the thermometer. Remove meat from baking sheet and let it rest for 10 minutes.

Continued on next page

210

Entrees

1 lightly beaten egg white

½ peeled and chopped onion

2 peeled and minced garlic cloves

2 coarsely chopped tomatoes

¼ teaspoon freshly ground black pepper

1 tablespoon arrowroot

1 tablespoon water

▲ In saucepan, combine remaining 1 cup each of beef broth and Madeira, tomatoes, onion, pepper and remaining ¼ teaspoon each thyme and savory. Bring to boil then reduce heat and simmer 25 minutes. Strain and return to pan. Combine arrowroot and 1 tablespoon water. Return liquid in pan to boil then whisk in arrowroot mixture. Simmer until thickened (about 2 minutes).

▲ When meat is finished cooking, add any cooking juices to the sauce (over low heat if necessary).

211

▲ To serve, carve needed number of slices off beef Wellington with electric knife to minimize cracking of pastry. Pour some sauce over the meat and offer remaining meat and sauce on the side.

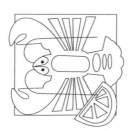

BEEF BURGUNDY

Serves 6-8

Easy, can be made ahead

Delicious the day after too. Your family will love the fragrance of the dish simmering.

1	tablespoon oil
2	pounds cubed round steak
2	sliced medium onions, separated into rings
6½	tablespoons flour
½	teaspoon ground rosemary
¼	teaspoon ground thyme
1	teaspoon salt
¼	teaspoon pepper
1½	cups burgundy
⅓	cup brandy
½	cup beef broth
4	bay leaves
2	finely chopped garlic cloves
½	teaspoon sugar
½	teaspoon dried thyme
½	teaspoon dried marjoram
½	pound fresh sliced mushrooms
1-2	tablespoons poppy seeds (optional)

◢ Season flour with rosemary and thyme. Dredge beef in flour and brown in deep skillet or frying pan in oil.

◢ Add all ingredients except the mushrooms, stir, and simmer over low heat for 1 hour. Add mushrooms, stir and simmer for 15 more minutes.

◢ Serve over fluffy rice, egg noodles or mashed potatoes.

◢ Goes well with sautéed cherry tomatoes or baked tomatoes and steamed fresh broccoli.

Thyme adds a savory taste to beef dishes. It works well in long-simmering dishes. Wrap thyme, parsley and bay in cheesecloth to make a bouquet garni for stews.

212

Entrees

MARINATED STEAK WITH BRANDY MUSTARD SAUCE

Serves 4

Average, must be made ahead partially

Delightful for fall or spring home entertaining.

1   flank or 4 sirloin steaks

1   cup brandy

1   thinly sliced green onion

1   tablespoon mustard

1   tablespoon Worcestershire sauce

1   teaspoon fresh ground pepper

½   cup cream

1   tablespoon mustard

◢ Marinate steak in ingredients 2 through 6, for 2 hours.

◢ Grill steak to the desired level, reserving the marinade.

◢ Pour marinade in a medium saucepan and cook over medium heat until it is reduced by one third. Strain marinade and return to heat. Add cream and the second tablespoon of mustard and cook for 3 more minutes.

◢ Slice the steak with the grain and drizzle mustard sauce over the steak. Serve immediately.

SPICY BEEF TENDERLOIN

Serves 10 to 12 as entree

Gourmet, must prepare at least 8 hours ahead to chill and marinate beef.

Excellent for large winter dinner parties.

1   cup port wine

1   cup soy sauce

½   cup olive oil

1   teaspoon pepper

1   teaspoon dried whole thyme

½   teaspoon hot sauce

4   crushed garlic cloves

1   crumbled bay leaf

5-6 pounds beef tenderloin, trimmed of fat

     watercress as garnish

10-12 tomato roses as garnish

▲ Combine first 8 ingredients and mix well.

▲ Place tenderloin in large shallow dish, pour the mixture in step one over the top and cover tightly. Refrigerate for 8 hours turning the beef occasionally.

▲ Uncover the beef and strain and reserve the marinade. Place beef on cooking rack and insert meat thermometer. Bake at 425° for 55 to 60 minutes or until thermometer reads 150° for medium rare or 160° for medium.

▲ Heat the reserved marinade over low heat adding the juice of the tenderloin from cooking and ½ cup of water. Season the marinade with salt and pepper to taste. Use this as an optional "light sauce" to be served on the side.

▲ Slice beef and garnish with watercress and tomatoes. Serve warm.

Entrees

STUFFED TENDERLOIN

Serves 8-10

Average

Hearty and sophisticated.

1   (3-4 pound) beef tenderloin (with pocket cut in center for stuffing)

6   tablespoons butter or margarine

½   cup chopped yellow onion

½   cup chopped celery

1   cup chopped fresh mushrooms

1   cup sliced fresh mushrooms

3   cups herb-seasoned stuffing mix

8   slices bacon

½   teaspoon bottled brown bouquet sauce

1   teaspoon Worcestershire sauce

¼   cup water

▲ Sauté onion, celery and chopped mushrooms in butter. Preheat oven to 450°.

▲ Mix the above from step one with bread crumbs and stuff entire mixture into the tenderloin pocket. Secure the stuffing in the pocket with skewers or toothpicks. Top the meat with bacon strips.

▲ Place meat on baking rack and sear in a 450° preheated oven for 10 minutes. Reduce heat to 325° and roast for 1 hour and 15 minutes. Remove roast from oven and reserve all pan drippings.

▲ In a saucepan, place the pan drippings and add the Worcestershire sauce, ¼ cup water and bottled brown bouquet sauce stirring over low heat. Add the sliced mushrooms and heat thoroughly.

▲ Serve the roast and stuffing warm with gravy on the side.

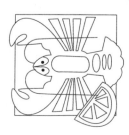

VEAL WITH CRAB OR LOBSTER AND ASPARAGUS

Serves 4

Gourmet, cannot make ahead

Simple and striking. Use either the classic bernaise or the low-fat wine sauce.

24 ounces veal scalloppine

4 tablespoons flour

½ teaspoon salt

½ teaspoon white pepper

4 tablespoons butter

8 ounces lump crab or lobster meat, picked clean

16 fresh white or green asparagus spears

Béarnaise

½ cup dry white wine

2 tablespoons finely chopped green onions

½ teaspoon dried tarragon

½ teaspoon chopped chervil

½ teaspoon chopped parsley

216

◢ Peel the asparagus stems with a potato peeler (optional for thin and tender spears.)

◢ Put ½ inch of water in a 10 inch frying pan. Heat to a slow boil then reduce to simmer, add the asparagus, and cook for 5 to 7 minutes. (Time varies depending on size, test to easily pierce with a fork). Set aside.

◢ Pound veal between two pieces of waxed paper until ¼ inch thick. See light wine-sauce for directions on cooking veal low-fat.

◢ Blend flour, salt and pepper. Dredge veal in the mixture. Melt butter in a 10 inch skillet and sauté veal until it is white. Remove from heat and transfer veal to serving plates.

◢ Melt 1 tablespoon of butter, add lemon juice and sauté crab or lobster meat until warm. Don't overcook!

◢ Place 4 asparagus spears on each portion of veal. Place ¼ of the seafood mixture on top and top with the bernaise or wine sauce. Serve immediately.

◢ Combine wine, onion, tarragon, parsley, and chervil in a small saucepan and bring to a boil. Reduce heat and cook until mixture is reduced by one half.

◢ In a separate heavy saucepan or a double boiler, combine the egg yolks, butter and lemon juice. Cook over low heat, stirring constantly with a whisk in one direction until

Continued on next page

Entrees

6 tablespoons butter

3 egg yolks

1 tablespoon fresh lemon juice

Light Wine Sauce

1 tablespoon safflower margarine

1 peeled and minced shallot

1 tablespoon and 1 teaspoon all-purpose flour

¾ cup low salt chicken broth

¼ cup dry white wine

2 teaspoons tarragon vinegar

1 teaspoon dried crushed tarragon

1 teaspoon Dijon mustard

¼ teaspoon tomato paste

¼ teaspoon freshly ground black pepper

2 teaspoons safflower oil

the sauce thickens to the consistency of custard. Remove from heat and whisk in the wine mixture.

▲ Sauce can be prepared ahead and refrigerated. Warm briefly in microwave at low heat before serving.

▲ Melt margarine in medium size saucepan. Add shallots and sauté for 2 minutes. Add flour and cook 1 minute while stirring. Whisk in chicken broth, wine, vinegar, tarragon, mustard, tomato paste and pepper. Bring to a boil then reduce heat and simmer for 10 minutes.

217

▲ In large skillet, place 1 teaspoon of oil over medium high heat and add veal in 2 batches. Cook veal for 2 minutes on each side, remove and keep warm in oven.

▲ In same skillet with juices reserved from veal, add 1 teaspoon oil and crab or lobster and sauté for 2 minutes. Remove seafood from pan, leaving juices in the pan, and briefly set it aside.

▲ Pour the tarragon sauce into the hot skillet and add to this any juices that may have gathered around the veal and seafood. Simmer 2 minutes.

▲ Boneless chicken may be substituted for the veal.

Tarragon's warm and subtle flavoring is a perfect complement for chicken and delicious in fish sauces. Tarragon is an essential component of fines herbes, along with chervil and parsley, and is used in béarnaise sauce.

VITELLO TONNATO

Serves 6-8

Gourmet, can be made ahead

Can be served hot or cold. A very special dish with unique ingredients that create a savory flavor. Perfect for entertaining at the steeplechase or on the boat.

¼   cup olive oil

1   (3½ pound) boneless rolled leg of veal

1   large sliced yellow onion

2   chopped carrots

2   chopped celery stalks

2   finely minced large garlic cloves

1   (3 ounce) can drained anchovy fillets

1   (6 ounce) can drained tuna

1   cup dry white wine

3   sprigs parsley

2   bay leaves

    pinch thyme

½   teaspoon salt

¼   teaspoon black pepper

1   cup mayonnaise

½   teaspoon lemon juice

1½ cups rice (to be prepared according to package)

1   small drained bottle of capers

▲ Heat olive oil in large heavy kettle or dutch oven with tight fitting cover.

▲ Add veal and brown lightly on all sides.

▲ Add onion, carrots, celery, garlic, anchovies, tuna, wine, parsley, bay leaves, salt and pepper. Cover tightly and cook for 2 hours and 45 minutes.

▲ Remove the veal from the kettle and chill it thoroughly. Reduce the contents of the kettle by half, then purée it in the blender and chill.

▲ When meat is chilled, remove the purée from the refrigerator and blend in the mayonnaise and lemon juice.

▲ Serve the meat sliced cold, on a bed of fluffy cold white rice topped with the puréed sauce. Garnish with capers and chopped parsley. This can easily be served hot with hot white rice and without capers.

Bring meats to room temperature before cooking to prevent undercooking the meat.

218

VEAL FRANCISCO

Serves 4.

Easy

Delightful and easy recipe for the family or for entertaining. Serve with wild rice and steamed broccoli with hollandaise. Can substitute pork chops or boneless chicken.

4	(1½ inch thick) veal steaks
¼	cup flour
3	tablespoons olive oil
3	mashed garlic cloves
¾	cup dry white wine
1	large crumbled bay leaf
1	tablespoon Worcestershire sauce
⅓	cup chopped parsley
½	teaspoon dried crumbled thyme
	grated rind of 1 lemon
4	slices of lemon
1	(8 ounce) package mushrooms, sliced
1	cup sour cream
4	lemon slices as garnish
	paprika as garnish
	fresh parsley as garnish

▲ Dredge veal steaks in flour and brown on both sides in skillet with olive oil. Add garlic and brown it lightly.

▲ Add wine and sprinkle each steak with bay leaf, Worcestershire, parsley, thyme and lemon rind. Top each steak with a slice of lemon, cover the skillet and simmer for one hour until the meat is tender.

▲ When steaks are tender, make sure that there is a layer of liquid in skillet, if not, add a little wine. Add sliced mushrooms and simmer covered for 10 more minutes.

▲ Season with salt and pepper, remove from heat, and gently stir in sour cream.

▲ Remove cooked lemon slices and garnish each steak with paprika, parsley and a fresh slice of lemon and serve immediately.

219

SHEPHERD'S PIE

Serves 8-10 as entree

Average, can be made ahead

Transportable, and beef may be substituted for lamb if so desired. Great for apres-ski.

1   (4 pound) leg of lamb

    olive oil (extra virgin recommended)

    soy sauce

    salt

    garlic powder

    fresh ground pepper

¾   cup diced celery

¼   cup diced yellow onion

2   large diced garlic cloves

¾   pound diced fresh mushrooms

½   teaspoon thyme

1   teaspoon sweet basil

1   teaspoon rosemary

1   teaspoon Worcestershire sauce

¼   teaspoon light salt

½   stick butter

4   large peeled and boiled baking potatoes

2   tablespoons milk

2   tablespoons butter

1½   cups water

220

▲ Preheat oven to 450°. Shave lamb to at very most ¼ inch thickness of fat on equivalent of half of surface of lamb, the rest should be meat without fat on surface. Wash then pat dry lamb and rub all over with olive oil, then soy sauce, then lightly salt, garlic powder and pepper.

▲ Place lamb in roasting pan (no rack and uncovered) and sear in oven at 450° for 15 minutes. Reduce heat to 350° and cook for approximately 1 hour. Lamb should be cooked to medium rare at most. Juices should run pink when removed.

▲ Remove lamb from oven and allow it to cool before carving it into bite-sized pieces. Reserve all juices as you are carving as well as the pan juices.

▲ Sauté onions, celery, garlic cloves and diced mushrooms with basil, thyme, rosemary, salt and Worcestershire until they are soft, in butter. Drain and set aside (do not press on the celery and onions when in the colander, allow some of the butter and as much seasoning as possible to remain).

▲ Boil the potatoes, then mash with milk and butter and set aside.

▲ Boil 1½ cups of water and pour it over the roasting pan, using a spatula to free up pieces of meat and free all juices. Pour all of contents into a medium saucepan and bring to a slow simmer adding both chicken and beef bouillon. Stir until dissolved.

Continued on next page

SHEPHERD'S PIE (Continued)

1 cube beef bouillon

1 cube chicken bouillon

¼ pound sliced fresh mushrooms

¼ cup dry sherry

½ stick butter

▲ Turn heat to low and add sherry and sliced mushrooms. Cook thoroughly over low heat, not allowing mixture to boil.

▲ Put sautéed celery and onion mixture in large mixing bowl and combine it with contents of the saucepan and the cubed lamb.

▲ Carefully spoon this mixture into a 13 inch shallow glass baking dish or individual small casserole serving dishes. Be sure to leave 1½ inches at the top. Also make sure that the juices come just to the top of the meat mixture.

▲ Smooth the mashed potatoes over the entire surface of the meat. Melt ½ stick of butter in microwave and paint it over the surface of the mashed potatoes.

▲ Bake uncovered in oven at 325° for 20 minutes, then broil for 3-5 minutes until the top is lightly golden. Serve immediately.

221

HERB AND MUSTARD GLAZED RACK OF LAMB

Serves 4

Easy

Delightfully different roast lamb. Key for entertaining when time is crucial.

½   cup prepared Dijon mustard

2   tablespoons soy sauce

1   teaspoon dried rosemary

¼   teaspoon ground ginger

1   clove garlic

1   egg

2   tablespoons olive oil

2   pound rack of lamb

◤ Combine the first six ingredients in electric blender and process until smooth. Add oil one drop at a time while blending at low speed, until the mixture is light and creamy.

◤ Place lamb fat side up in a shallow roasting pan. Insert a meat thermometer, being careful to not touch fat or bone. Brush the mustard mixture over the lamb and bake at 325° for 1 hour and 20 to 30 minutes (until the thermometer registers 160°).

◤ Slice and serve warm.

CHALUPA

Serves 4 as an entree, 6 as a side dish, 10-12 as appetizer

Easy, can be made ahead and frozen

Family and friends all love this dish. Children particularly enjoy picking their toppings.

1 pound pinto beans

3 cloves minced garlic

1 teaspoon oregano

1 tablespoon salt

1 tablespoon cumin

1 tablespoon garlic salt

1 (28 ounce) can of tomatoes

1 (4 ounce) can drained and chopped green chilies

3 pound pork loin roast

1 bag (14 ounces) tortilla chips or 1 box soft tortillas

1 cup sour cream

½ pound grated cheddar cheese

½ head shredded iceberg lettuce

2 chopped medium tomatoes

10 chopped green onions

1 chopped avocado

20 chopped olives

◢ Put first 8 ingredients into large pot, cover with water (just) and simmer covered for 2 hours.

◢ Add pork and simmer for 6 more hours, covered.

◢ Remove the pork, allow to cool, then remove all bones and shred the meat.

◢ Return pork to mixture and return to heat, simmering to reduce liquid and thicken (do not cover). Simmer for about 15 minutes.

◢ Serve meat on tortillas and allow guests to dress with condiments as they choose.

223

BAKED SPARE RIBS

Serves 8

Easy

Perfect for the casual guests or family. The flavors meld marvelously.

4	pounds pork spareribs
1	cup catsup
2	tablespoons Worcestershire sauce
2	tablespoons vinegar
1	cup water
2	tablespoons light brown sugar
1	teaspoon chili powder
1	medium chopped yellow onion
3	crushed garlic cloves

◢ Cut spareribs between bones to make individual ribs. Place in single layer in a large baking dish.

◢ Bake in a preheated oven at 350° for 30 minutes.

◢ Meanwhile, combine remaining ingredients in saucepan and simmer for 10 minutes.

◢ Remove ribs from oven and drain the fat from the baking dish. Keeping ribs in the baking dish, pour the hot sauce over the ribs and return to the oven for one hour. Turn and baste the ribs with the sauce at least once.

◢ Serve ribs warm to hot with warm sauce on top.

Entrees

MARINATED PORK TENDERLOIN WITH CREAMY MUSTARD SAUCE

Serves 6 as an entree

Savory tenderloin grand for spring entertaining and excellent served with spinach salad. A dash of ginger added to the marinade can create a delightful oriental touch.

¼ cup soy sauce

¼ cup bourbon

2½ tablespoons brown sugar

2 pound pork tenderloin

Mustard Sauce

⅔ cup sour cream (non-fat)

⅔ cup light mayonnaise

2 tablespoons dry mustard

3 finely chopped green onions

▲ In 11"x7" baking dish combine first 3 ingredients then add the tenderloin. Cover and refrigerate for 2 hours or more turning the meat at least twice.

▲ Remove meat from marinade and place on a rack in a roasting pan. Reserve the marinade for basting, and bake for 45 minutes at 325°, basting the meat occasionally with marinade.

▲ Combine all ingredients for the sauce in a small mixing bowl, cover and chill.

▲ Serve pork either warm or cold with mustard sauce on side.

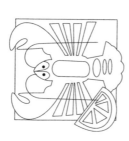

ANNAPOLIS STUFFED PORK ROAST

Serves 6-8

Gourmet

The fruit stuffing is really good and the fragrance is mouthwatering.

1   (3½ pound) boned center loin pork roast

½   teaspoon ground ginger

⅛   teaspoon ground cloves

½   teaspoon fresh ground pepper

½   teaspoon salt

12   large pitted prunes

1½   cups water

⅓   cup dry white bread crumbs

3   tablespoons clarified butter

½   cup heavy cream

2   tablespoons flour

½   teaspoon salt

2   twists fresh ground pepper

◢ Preheat oven to 350°.

◢ Season meat with ginger, cloves, pepper and salt.

◢ In a saucepan, simmer prunes in water, covered over medium heat for 20 minutes. Remove from heat and let stand 15 minutes.

◢ Transfer prunes with slotted spoon to bowl, (reserving the liquid), and combine prunes with the bread crumbs.

◢ Arrange the prune mixture lengthwise in the center of the roast and roll the meat to enclose the filling.

◢ Tie the meat with a kitchen string at 1" intervals, and in an oven proof skillet, brown the roast on all sides in clarified butter over high heat.

◢ Add 1 cup of the reserved prune liquid and bring it to a boil. Transfer the roast to the preheated oven and bake for 1½ hours, uncovered, basting it twice.

◢ Transfer roast to heated platter, remove strings and tent the meat with aluminum foil.

◢ Skim fat from pan juices, add the remaining reserve prune liquid and bring to a boil.

◢ Whisk in heavy cream and flour and simmer 3 minutes. Add salt and pepper.

◢ Spoon a little of the sauce over the meat and slice the roast.

◢ Serve roast warm to hot, with warm sauce on the side.

APPLE RUM PORK CHOPS

Serves 4

Easy

For dinner any time of the year, but the aromas are particularly delightful in the fall.

4   2" center loin well trimmed boneless pork chops

6   tablespoons sweet butter

2   Granny Smith cored and peeled apples, cut into ½" rounds

½   teaspoon ground cinnamon

1   tablespoon sugar

¼   cup dark rum

    salt

    pepper

◢ Sprinkle chops with salt and pepper.

◢ In a large oven proof skillet, brown chops in half of the butter on both sides and transfer to a platter.

◢ Add remainder of butter to pan and add the apple rings. Sauté the apples for 3 minutes on each side then sprinkle them with cinnamon.

◢ Return the chops to the pan placing them carefully on the apple rings. Combine the sugar and rum and pour the mixture over the chops.

227

◢ Cover the skillet with foil and place in a 350° oven and bake for 50 minutes.

◢ Carefully transfer the apples and chops to serving plates or a platter and pour the juices on top of each serving.

BAKED HAM WITH ORANGE-HONEY GLAZE

Serves 12-15

Easy

An old family favorite.

1   (6 ounce) can frozen orange juice concentrate, thawed and undiluted

1¾   cups water

½   cup honey

3   tablespoons cornstarch

1   teaspoon dry mustard

½   teaspoon sage (optional)

½   teaspoon ground nutmeg

1   3" stick of cinnamon

1   (7 to 9 pound) smoked, fully cooked whole boneless ham

10-15 whole cloves

▲ Combine first 3 ingredients in medium saucepan.

▲ Remove ¼ cup of mixture and combine it with cornstarch, stirring until smooth.

▲ Add cornstarch mixture to orange juice and stir until smooth.

▲ Add mustard and next 3 ingredients.

▲ Cook over medium heat, stirring constantly until reaching a boil, then cook 1 minute more. Remove cinnamon stick and remove mixture from heat and set aside.

▲ Score ham in a diamond pattern and stud at corners with cloves. Place ham fat side up in a shallow roaster pan and insert thermometer (do not touch fat).

▲ Bake ham uncovered at 325° for 2 hours until thermometer reads 140°. After the first hour, baste the ham every 15 minutes with sauce.

▲ Ham is excellent served hot or cold. If hot, heat the sauce and serve with the ham on the side.

Entrees

BAVARIAN POT ROAST

Serves 4-6

Average

The perfect fall and winter dish for family gatherings. Serve with roasted potatoes and steamed broccoli.

2   pounds rump roast

1   teaspoon butter

6   medium yellow onions, sliced into rings

1   (6 ounce) bottle of prepared horseradish

¼   cup white wine

2   teaspoons flour

1   pressed garlic clove

1   teaspoon sugar

½   teaspoon salt

¼   teaspoon pepper

◢ In a large skillet, brown the meat quickly in butter and remove it to a platter.

◢ Add the onions to the pan and cook over medium heat for 5 minutes until clear.

◢ To the onion add the flour, horse-radish, garlic, wine, salt, pepper and sugar. Mix thoroughly.

◢ Put the meat back in the skillet, cover and reduce heat to low and cook until tender (approximately 1 hour).

◢ Serve the roast hot with the pan juices on the side.

229

Many German immigrants settled in Baltimore and surrounding areas throughout the 1800s. Maryland cuisine is strongly influenced by this German heritage.

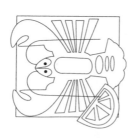

BEER BRAISED VEAL CHOPS WITH CABBAGE

Serves 4

Average

A beautiful presentation and savory blend of tastes.

2	slices bacon
4	center cut well trimmed veal chops
2	tablespoons flour
1	cup finely sliced red cabbage
2	finely chopped shallots
2	tablespoons flour
½	cup beef or veal broth
12	ounces beer (Samuel Adams recommended)
2	sprigs fresh rosemary
1	teaspoon sugar
½	teaspoon pepper
½	cup shelled and chopped chestnuts, pecans or walnuts

▲ Cook bacon in skillet until crisp; remove bacon reserving drippings, and drain and crumble and set aside.

▲ Dredge veal in flour and sear in bacon drippings. Remove veal from skillet and set aside.

▲ Sauté cabbage and shallots in dripping for 2-3 minutes, then add 2 tablespoons of flour and stir well.

▲ Slowly add beef broth and beer, stirring constantly.

▲ Add crumbled bacon and all seasonings and stir. Return veal chops to skillet, ladle juice over them and sprinkle nuts on top. Cook 6-8 minutes uncovered.

▲ Adjust seasonings and serve hot with sauce dribbled over the veal and the cabbage underneath the veal.

Entrees

STUFFED RED CABBAGE

Serves 8

Easy

A very flavorful and colorful dish. Serve with fresh bright green and yellow steamed vegetables, warm bread, and a baked tomato topped with cheese.

1   head red cabbage

1¼   pounds ground beef

½   cup uncooked long grain white rice

1   peeled, cored, and chopped sweet apple

1   can whole cranberry sauce

1   can condensed tomato soup

1   (6 ounce) can frozen lemonade concentrate

1   large chopped yellow onion

Combine meat, rice, apple, 2 tablespoons each of cranberry sauce and tomato soup in large mixing bowl.

Blanch cabbage leaves in boiling water just long enough to make them pliable (about 1 minute each).

Chop ¼ cup of the cabbage and combine with the onion, then add the rest of the soup, cranberry sauce and lemonade to this mixture. Place this sauce in a large deep skillet and slowly heat it.

Roll the meat mixture into each cabbage leaf and use large toothpicks to hold the leaf securely closed. Fill up all remaining cabbage leaves with the meat mixture.

Place the rolled and stuffed cabbage leaves in the sauce and bring it to a simmer. Simmer for ½ hour covered.

Carefully remove the cabbage rolls from the simmering sauce and place them in a glass 9"x12" baking dish. Pour the simmering sauce over the cabbage leaves and bake for 45 minutes at 250° uncovered.

Serve the cabbage leaves warm, with a little simmering sauce dribbled over the top.

LAMB RAGOÛT

Serves 8

Gourmet

Serve as a stew or over rice or pasta. Can substitute beef or pork.

2 tablespoons butter

2 tablespoons olive oil

4 pounds well trimmed and cubed (1½") boneless lamb shoulder

1 teaspoon salt

½ teaspoon thyme

½ teaspoon oregano

½ teaspoon fresh ground black pepper

3 tablespoons flour

2 large chopped yellow onions

1 cup diced, peeled and seeded fresh tomatoes

1½ teaspoons minced fresh garlic

1 teaspoon tomato paste

½ teaspoon salt

½ teaspoon sugar

2 cups beef broth

2 cups chicken broth

1 Bouquet Garni (6 sprigs parsley, 2 sprigs thyme, and 2 bay leaves tied in cheesecloth)

◢ In large deep skillet, melt butter with olive oil. Dry lamb cubes with paper towels and brown cubes in skillet, removing cubes as they are ready to a large oven proof casserole. Reserve butter and oil in skillet.

◢ Add to the casserole salt, thyme, oregano, fresh ground pepper and flour and toss well.

◢ Bake the casserole in a preheated oven at 450° for 20 minutes. When finished, reduce heat to 325°.

◢ Sauté chopped onion in the reserved butter and oil. Add tomato paste, salt and sugar and simmer covered for 10 minutes.

◢ Combine contents of skillet with casserole and add the beef and chicken broth and bouquet garni and mix well. Cover casserole and bake at 325° for 1½ hours.

◢ Place colander over a large bowl and pour the ragoût into the colander, reserving the liquid and transferring it to a skillet. Discard Bouquet Garni. Keep ragoût warm while preparing the next item.

◢ Simmer liquid in skillet and reduce by ⅓, then combine it with the meat mixture.

◢ Sauté mushrooms in butter for 6 minutes, then add them to the ragoût.

◢ Steam all vegetables (peas separately) then toss them in butter and parsley.

Continued on next page

LAMB RAGOÛT (Continued)

½   pound large quartered mushrooms

1   tablespoon butter

20 small white peeled onions

1   pound peeled carrots, cut into fourths

6   white turnips, cut into large cubes

1   pound green beans

2   pounds very small red potatoes

1   pound small french peas

½   cup minced fresh parsley

2   tablespoons butter

Arrange the ragoût in the center of a large platter and scatter the peas over the top of it. Arrange the steamed vegetables around the ragoût and serve immediately.

The Chesapeake Bay Foundation uses a Skipjack for its educational cruises about conserving the endangered resources of the Chesapeake Bay. The Skipjack is a classic Chesapeake boat designed for oyster-dredging under sail.

233

ESTOFADO

Serves 6

Average, can make ahead.
A savory stew that's nice for warming cold fishermen or sailors!

1 pound beef, cut into 2" cubes

1 tablespoon olive oil

1½ cups dry red wine

1 (8 ounce) can tomatoes

1 large Bermuda or Vidalia onion, sliced ¼" thick

1 green pepper, cut into ½" strips

¼ cup raisins

¼ cup chopped dried apricots

2 minced garlic cloves

1½ teaspoons salt

⅛ teaspoon pepper

1 teaspoon dried basil

1 teaspoon dried thyme

1 teaspoon dried tarragon

1 whole bay leaf

8 ounces sliced fresh mushrooms

¼ cup sliced ripe olives

1 tablespoon flour

1 cup cold water

▲ Brown meat in oil in a 10" diameter stewing pot.

▲ Add the next 13 ingredients and simmer covered for 30 minutes.

▲ Add mushrooms and olives and simmer for 15 minutes.

▲ Combine flour and cold water and slowly stir into the stew while simmering.

▲ Cook while stirring constantly until the mixture thickens slightly and bubbles.

▲ Serve immediately over hot rice or egg noodles.

A cherished finale to sailing in the late fall or early spring "frostbite" races is getting out of the wind and cold and warming up with a delicious stew.

234

HENHOUSE BASTING SAUCE

Makes 3/4 cup

Average

Good for chicken or vegetable kebabs.

2 tablespoons lemon juice

1 teaspoon Worcestershire sauce

¼ teaspoon paprika

1 stick butter

¼ cup water

¼ teaspoon pepper

¼ teaspoon salt

¼ teaspoon garlic powder

Melt butter in small saucepan. Add remaining ingredients. Baste regular or skinless chicken with a brush. Continue basting while baking or grilling chicken. Can use as a marinade.

235

GINGER CILANTRO MARINADE

Makes 1/2 cup

Gourmet

A piquant flavor for chicken.

⅓ cup soy sauce

2 tablespoons sesame oil

1 tablespoon rice vinegar

½ inch finely diced ginger root (do not use powder)

1 tablespoon dried cilantro or 3 tablespoons chopped fresh

¼ cup medium diced red onion

1-2 minced garlic cloves

1 pound boneless chicken breast

◢ Mix all ingredients together and marinate chicken in the refrigerator for several hours.

◢ Grill or broil chicken, brushing with marinade.

Leave a little space between food when preparing kebabs for grilling. The food will cook more evenly.

236

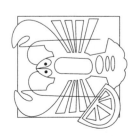

Entrees

HUNT COUNTRY BARBECUE SAUCE

Makes 1 1/3 cups

Easy

An excellent rich barbecue sauce that can be doubled and spiced up with hot pepper sauce if so desired.

½ cup catsup

¼ cup vinegar

¼ cup water

¼ cup finely chopped onion

1½ teaspoons brown sugar

1½ teaspoons Worcestershire sauce

1½ teaspoons prepared mustard

¼ teaspoon salt

⅛ teaspoon pepper

▲ Mix all ingredients well, add hot pepper sauce to taste if desired.

▲ Make early and refrigerate until used.

▲ Baste meat while cooking.

ORANGE BARBECUE SAUCE

Makes 1 1/2 cups

Easy

Deliciously light and fruity. For a milder sauce, eliminate hot pepper sauce. Good for chicken, beef and pork during spring and summer.

¾   cup orange juice concentrate

6   ounces chili sauce

4   tablespoons molasses

3   tablespoons soy sauce

2   tablespoons dry mustard

4   tablespoons cider vinegar

¼   cup chicken broth

2   teaspoons Worcestershire sauce

½   teaspoon ground ginger

1   teaspoon hot pepper sauce

▲ Mix ingredients and baste meat while grilling.

▲ May be used as a dip and served on the side after grilling.

Entrees

TERIYAKI SAUCE

Makes 1 cup

Average

A classic also good with pork.

½ cup olive oil or peanut oil

⅔ cup soy sauce

2   tablespoons grated fresh ginger

2   finely chopped garlic cloves

1   tablespoon grated orange rind

¼ cup cooking sherry

◢ Mix all ingredients together.

◢ Marinate for up to 24 hours and brush mixture over chicken while cooking or marinate beef before cooking.

FLANK STEAK MARINADE

Makes 1 cup

Easy

No-cook marinade with excellent body!

◢ Mix ingredients and marinate flank steak for 8 hours turning at least once.

¼	cup soy sauce
3	tablespoons honey
2	tablespoons cider vinegar
¼	cup lemon juice
1	teaspoon garlic powder
1	teaspoon ground ginger
½	teaspoon ground rosemary
½	teaspoon ground pepper
½	teaspoon dry mustard
¾	cup vegetable oil
1	finely chopped green onion

Entrees

RED WINE MARINADE FOR STEAK

Marinates one 2 pound steak

Easy

Delicious cooked marinade for your favorite guests! Excellent as a sauce for hot or cold steak.

2　whole squeezed lemons (or 4 tablespoons of lemon concentrate)

1　large minced garlic clove

⅓　cup red wine

1　teaspoon Dijon mustard

1　teaspoon seasoned salt

2　teaspoons minced onion

2　tablespoons soy sauce

2　tablespoons ketchup

1　teaspoon dried oregano

2　tablespoons olive oil

1　teaspoon pepper

◢ Combine all ingredients in a small saucepan and cook over medium heat while stirring until well blended.

◢ Allow marinade to cool before pouring over meat, then marinate for at least one hour.

◢ Reserve marinade; may be used as a sauce dribbled over hot meat or as a dip for chilled leftover steak.

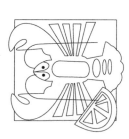

MARINADE AND SAUCE FOR STEAK

Makes 2 cups

Easy

Wonderful recipe for a steak sauce or marinade. May be made ahead and stored in refrigerator for several months.

¼ cup Worcestershire sauce

¼ cup red wine vinegar

½ cup A-1 steak sauce

¼ cup light brown sugar

⅔ cup ketchup

2 teaspoons seasoned salt flavor enhancer (optional)

⅛ teaspoon cayenne pepper

4 sliced fresh mushrooms

½ teaspoon chervil or dried parsley

 Blend all ingredients together in small saucepan and heat slowly over medium heat while stirring.

 If using as a sauce: Prepare ahead and refrigerate before serving.

 If using as a marinade: Allow sauce to cool then pour marinade over filets of beef. Wrap in heavy duty aluminum foil and chill overnight.

HERBED HORSERADISH SAUCE

Yields 3/4 cup

Average
Delicious with tenderloin.

⅓   cup mayonnaise

⅓   cup sour cream

1   tablespoon lemon juice

⅛   teaspoon white pepper

3   drops hot sauce

¼   cup prepared
    horseradish

2   tablespoons chopped
    fresh parsley

½   teaspoon fresh basil
    (optional)

½   teaspoon fresh oregano
    (optional)

◢ Mix all ingredients in mixing bowl together and blend well.

◢ Adjust seasonings to taste and serve.

BLUSTERY BOURBON SAUCE

Makes 1 1/2 cups (hors d'oeuvres for 10)

Easy

Rich and delightfully easy sauce for meatballs. Superb flavors.

1   cup ketchup

1   cup light brown sugar

¼   cup bourbon (sour mash recommended)

244

▲ Mix all ingredients together and warm slowly in a saucepan (do not allow to boil).

▲ Pour over meatballs while hot and serve immediately.

The ship Peggy Stewart was burned in Annapolis Harbor during the American Revolution because it carried tea. The ship's owner, Anthony Stewart, watched it burn from his house on Hanover Street.

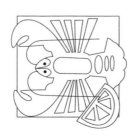

Entrees

CURRANT MAYONNAISE

Makes 2 cups

Gourmet

Serve with game or pork.

2   egg yolks

1   tablespoon hot water

1   teaspoon dry mustard

1   teaspoon white vinegar

½   teaspoon white pepper

½   teaspoon salt

¾   teaspoon walnut oil

¾   teaspoon vegetable oil

¼   cup currant jelly

1   tablespoon lemon juice

    salt and pepper to taste

▲ Place egg yolks in a bowl and mix with hot water.

▲ Add mustard, vinegar, salt and pepper.

▲ Beat on low speed with electric mixer.

▲ Slowly add the walnut oil and vegetable oil a little at a time.

▲ Blend well.

▲ Add the currant jelly and lemon juice.

▲ Correct seasonings to taste.

NECTARINE SALSA

Makes 1 cup

Average

Fruit salsas are a fresh topping for cooked chicken or pork. Try pears too.

1 tablespoon fresh finely chopped cilantro

¼ cup olive oil

5 tablespoons lemon juice

½ teaspoon cinnamon

1 tablespoon red wine vinegar

2 tablespoons brown sugar

2-3 sliced 2-inch diameter nectarines

1 heaping tablespoon chopped scallion greens

▲ Combine cilantro, olive oil, lemon juice, cinnamon, vinegar and brown sugar in food processor until well blended.

▲ Add the nectarines and scallions. Chop on low speed until mixture resembles a coarse relish.

▲ Will keep for 48 hours in the refrigerator.

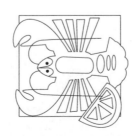

On the Tide

SEAFOOD & A GUIDE TO MARYLAND CRABS

Watermen and the Chesapeake Bay

The Chesapeake Bay has always been a source of enjoyment and sustenance for those who live on her shores. The Bay has a hypnotic quality to her, and those who fall in love with her never tire of her fluctuating moods. On a spring or summer day, she can be deep green and gently rolling under crystal blue skies, or furiously white-capped in the roaring turbulence of a famous Chesapeake Bay thunderstorm. In autumn, she reflects the brilliant changing colors of the shoreline. Thousands of waterfowl— Canadian geese, ducks, doves and pheasants — feed in the surrounding fields and marshland and fill the day and night with their plaintive cries. The Bay in winter is a steely cold lady, abandoned except for the freighters moving in and out of Baltimore harbor, the oystermen dredging their beds, and the occasional hardy sailor.

Of those who have fallen most completely under her spell, the Chesapeake Bay watermen must rank highest. The name waterman, peculiar to the Bay, dates back to the colonial period when those settlers who did not have land turned to the water to earn a living. Many of their descendants still "follow the water." The watermen have a tradition of fierce independence and stern piety, built perhaps on the innate vicissitudes of their profession. It is a hard and unforgiving life, dependent on the rise and fall of the oyster, crab and clam harvests, subject to nature's fierce tempers, and beset by man-made enemies to a fruitful harvest such as pollution.

It is the waterman's nature to persevere, however, and the watermen's associations have fought hard to preserve their way of life and the Bay they love. They know intimately the natures of the crab, the oyster, and other creatures of the Chesapeake. They have developed a single language to describe the habits of the blue crab alone. "Sooks" are mature female crabs. The plump male crab, best for eating, is a "Jimmy". All females "Paint their nails," or have bright red tips on their claws. The soft-shell crab, an epicurean delicacy, is a "Peeler" in the waterman's vocabulary. In enjoying Chesapeake seafood, therefore, remember the men who bring it to your table. Toast their resiliency, their courage, and their love for the Bay and all she nurtures.

On the Tide

A GUIDE TO MARYLAND CRABS

The Maryland Blue Crab is one of the Chesapeake Bay's finest delicacies and an important ingredient for a number of local food specialties. Choosing and preparing crabmeat carefully is important to the quality of the finished dish. This guide is prepared to help you enjoy Maryland crabmeat to the fullest.

Types of Crabmeat

Backfin: Whole lump white meat from the crab's body. Considered the top grade and best for dishes where appearance is important.

Regular: Small pieces of whole meat from the body. Good for soups, crab dips, and crab fillings.

Special: A mixture of backfin and regular. Excellent for crabcakes and crab casseroles.

Claw: The small brownish tinted meat from the claws. Sometimes found on the claw "Finger" which is good for appetizers.

Softshell: Whole live crabs which have shed their shells and have a soft exterior. Considered a gourmet delicacy. See cleaning crabs for further details.

Preparing Crabmeat

Crabmeat should be handled as little as possible so it will not compress and get tough. After purchasing crabmeat run your hands gently through 1/4 cup of the crabmeat at a time and pick out pieces of the cartilage and shell that may be remaining.

Freezing Crabmeat

Cook the crab completely and extract the crabmeat. Pack the meat in plastic containers until three-quarters full. Salt the crab cooking water with 1 teaspoon of salt per quart of water. Fill containers with crab cooking water to the brim and freeze. Thaw in the refrigerator before using.

Crab can get tough if not frozen correctly. For occasional freezing, it is best to make the crab into an uncooked dish to be defrosted and cooked at a later date.

To Clean Hard Crabs

Turn crab onto back
and use a paring knife
to pry off apron flap.
Discard apron flap.

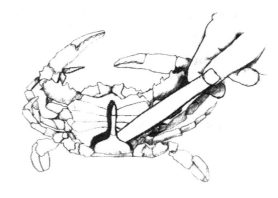

Lift off top. Use knife
to clean out interior of
crab below the apron
down to the hard
transparent membrane
covering the crabmeat.
Discard this residue
and the apron.

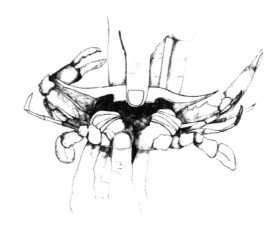

Holding crab at each
side, break it in the
center. Remove legs
by grasping them
firmly and twisting
them out of the body
membrane.

Cut sidewise from center to legs across the membrane and lift out the crab meat. Crack large claws with a mallet or knife to expose leg meat.

To Clean Soft Crabs

Crab should be alive when cleaned. Cut off eye area. Remove apron and remove spongy interior. Rinse in cold water and pat dry. Cook and eat or freeze immediately in individual airtight packets.

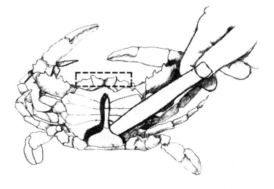

On the Tide

THE ART OF THE CRABFEAST

The crabfeast is the highlight of summer entertaining in Maryland. Picking crabs is a slow task, so the crabfeast has evolved into a leisurely outdoor event spiced with good food and conversation. A crabfeast is perfect entertainment for a crowd. In fact, Annapolis is home to the world's largest crabfeast, the annual Annapolis Rotary Crabfeast which feeds more than 2500 people.

A good crabfeast is an art — a feast of fresh food and a celebration of old and new friendship. Who can be standoffish having once been elbow to elbow at a picnic table surrounded by crabshells?

We are proud to present our version of the classic Annapolis crabfeast.

You Will Need

- 10 good friends or relatives, clad in shorts, dark shirts to hide crab seasoning stains, and boatshoes or bare feet.
- A backyard or deck, preferably overlooking the water.
- A bright sunny day or a twilight sky dotted with fireflies.
- 2 large picnic tables covered with clean brown paper.
- Extra brown paper to clean and reset the table.
- A side table for utensils, condiments, plates and dessert.
- 10 crab mallets, small paring knives, and forks and spoons.
- 2 large bowls for the Annapolis Harbor Boil.
- 2 large pierced serving spoons.
- 20 sturdy paper plates for the Annapolis Harbor Boil.
- 15 paper bowls for dessert.
- 10 or more thick terry hand towels to serve as lap protectors and napkins.
- 30 small paper custard cups for condiments.
- 4 medium bowls filled with cocktail sauce, drawn butter, apple cider vinegar, and Chesapeake-style seafood seasoning.

▲ 4 small ladles for the seasoning.

▲ 2 rolls of paper towels at each table.

▲ 2 large lined and clean trash cans.

▲ 2 clean plastic buckets full of sudsy clean water for hand rinsing.

▲ A handy hooked up hose for greater cleaning emergencies.

▲ 2 large pots, one for crabs and the other for the Annapolis Harbor Boil.

Your Menu Should Include

▲ **Maryland Steamed Crabs**. At least six for each person. Get them steamed at the market or use our recipe.

▲ **Annapolis Harbor Boil**. Our version includes fresh sweet corn, potatoes, steamed shrimp, and savory sausage. The aroma alone is appetizing.

▲ **A huge fresh fruit salad**. The perfect dessert. Make it fresh with whatever is in season at the local produce stand. Serve with Sweet Spice Dip if desired.

▲ **Lots of sodas, ice cold beer, chilled wine or Perfect Party Punch.**

Your Duties as Host Include

▲ Placing cardboard boxes full of hot steamed crabs on each table.

▲ Keeping the bowls full of Annapolis Harbor Boil.

▲ Making sure the drinks are ice cold.

▲ Providing appropriate music such as Jimmy Buffett, Caribbean steel band music, slow country tunes, or cool jazz.

▲ Allowing enough room for guests to kick off their shoes and dance if the mood hits them.

▲ Watching the sunset.

PIERSIDE MARYLAND STEAMED BLUE CRABS

3 dozen

Easy

1   cup beer or water

1   cup vinegar

3   dozen Maryland blue crabs

1   cup Chesapeake-style seafood seasoning

     cider vinegar, melted butter and crab seasoning for serving

254

◢ Plunge crabs into hot water for one minute.

◢ In a large crab pot with a rack, place the liquid in the bottom of the pan, just level with the bottom of the rack. If more liquid is needed, add more until the level is reached.

◢ Layer 6 crabs and 6 tablespoons of crab seasoning. Repeat until all of the crabs are in the pot. Bring to a boil uncovered. Reduce heat and simmer for 20 minutes, covered.

◢ Serve hot onto a table covered with a layer of newspaper. Eat the crab pieces plain or dip them in vinegar or melted butter.

◢ Extra crab seasoning may be sprinkled on the crabs if desired.

Chesapeake seafood seasoning is a regional specialty used in everything from seafood dishes to poultry and vegetables. The two most famous brands are Old Bay Seasoning and Wye River Seasoning.

Seafood

ANNAPOLIS HARBOR BOIL

Serves 8 - 10

Easy

¾ cup Chesapeake-style seafood seasoning

8 lemons, 4 - thinly sliced, 4 - wedged for condiments

1 large yellow onion, sliced in rings and separated

1 large bell pepper (any color) sliced lengthwise in ½" strips

5 pounds red potatoes, scrubbed and halved if necessary to make no larger than 4" circumference

1½ pounds smoked sausage, cut into 3" lengths and browned

8 small ears of corn, halved

2 pounds medium unshelled shrimp, deheaded and rinsed

1 pound drawn butter or margarine

1½ cups cocktail sauce

◢ Fill a 5 gallon crab pot ¾ full with hot water, add 6 ounces Chesapeake-style seafood seasoning and the 4 sliced lemons, bring to a rolling boil.

◢ Add onion, pepper and potatoes and boil for 20 minutes. Add sausage and boil an additional 20 minutes. Add shrimp and corn and allow to boil for 4 minutes, then turn off heat and leave for an additional 5 minutes in the water.

◢ Drain the entire mixture and ladle all items into 1 or 2 very large serving bowls. Serve immediately with butter and cocktail sauce.

EASTERN SHORE CIOPPINO

Serves 8

Average

A Chesapeake version of the San Francisco classic. Serve with thick crusty bread to mop up the sauce.

1½ pounds halibut

2 cups sliced onion

2 cloves garlic, finely chopped

¼ cup vegetable oil

1 (1 pound, 12 ounce) can Italian plum tomatoes, undrained

1 (8 ounce) can tomato sauce

1 cup water

¼ cup chopped fresh parsley

1 teaspoon salt

1 teaspoon dried basil

½ teaspoon oregano

¼ teaspoon fresh ground pepper

12 clams in shells, washed

½ pound medium shrimp, peeled and uncooked

1 pound lump crabmeat, shell and cartilage removed

parsley for garnish

◢ Cut halibut into 1½" chunks.

◢ In a large heavy dutch oven cook onion and garlic in oil until onion is tender. Add tomatoes, tomato sauce, water, parsley, salt, basil, oregano and pepper mixing well. Cover and simmer over medium low heat for 20 minutes.

◢ Add halibut chunks; cover and simmer gently for an additional 10 minutes.

◢ Add clams in shells and shrimp; cover and simmer over low heat for about 5 more minutes or until fish flakes easily when tested with a fork and clams are steamed open.

◢ Add lump crabmeat and serve.

PERFECT CRAB IMPERIAL

Serves 8

Easy

You'll never need another crab imperial recipe!

2   pounds cooked backfin crabmeat, shell and cartilage removed

½   cup diced red pepper

½   cup diced green pepper

½   cup minced onion

½   cup minced fresh parsley

2   eggs, lightly beaten

4   tablespoons melted sweet butter

4   tablespoons mayonnaise

4   teaspoons Worcestershire sauce

4   teaspoons dry mustard

4   teaspoons celery seed

2   tablespoons fresh lemon juice

3   teaspoons Chesapeake-style seafood seasoning or pulverized crab boil

1   cup white bread crumbs

4   tablespoons melted butter

▲ Combine all ingredients except bread crumbs and remaining 4 tablespoons melted butter.

▲ Divide crab meat mixture into buttered large scallop baking shells, sprinkle with bread crumbs and melted butter.

▲ Bake at 350° for 25 minutes.

An irascible crab is a torment to the unwary cook. My husband once attempted to put live crabs in the pot without gloves. One angry fellow promptly bit him on almost every finger! After a raucous battle, my husband shook him loose, whereupon the crab raced around the deck scattering our shrieking guests.

FIRST MATE'S FAVORITE VEGETABLE CRABCAKES

10 crabcakes

Average

Fresh tasting and colorful. A great way to use leftover corn on the cob.

1   egg, beaten

½   cup mayonnaise

¼   teaspoon dried parsley or 1 teaspoon fresh chopped parsley

1   teaspoon prepared mustard

¾   teaspoon Chesapeake-style seafood seasoning

2   teaspoons minced onion

½   cup fine bread crumbs

¼   cup diced red pepper

¼   cup diced celery

½   cup fresh cooked corn

1   pound backfin crabmeat, shell and cartilage removed

½   cup vegetable shortening

2   lemons, sliced

▲ Mix together egg, mayonnaise and seasonings. Add bread crumbs and vegetables. Stir well.

▲ Add crabmeat, stirring gently as to not to break up lumps. Shape into individual cakes.

▲ In a heavy skillet, melt shortening over medium heat. Brown crabcakes on each side until golden, approximately 4 minutes per side. Drain on paper towels. Serve with lemon slices.

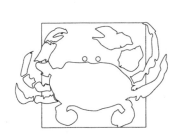

BEST MARYLAND CRABCAKES

Serves 4 - 6

Easy

*Best tasting crabcakes ever!
Serve with Old Bay seasoned
fries.*

4   slices white bread with
     crusts trimmed, or ½
     cup dry bread crumbs,
     or 6 saltines, crumbled

½   teaspoon dry mustard

½   teaspoon Chesapeake-
     style seafood seasoning

¼   teaspoon Accent

1   egg

½   cup mayonnaise

½   teaspoon lemon juice

½   teaspoon
     Worcestershire sauce

1   pound crabmeat, shell
     and cartilage removed

◢ Mix bread crumbs, mustard, seafood seasoning and Accent together and set aside.

◢ In another bowl, gently fold together egg, mayonnaise, lemon
juice, Worcestershire sauce and
bread crumb mixture. Add
crabmeat, and shape into individual cakes.

◢ Refrigerate for at least 2 hours to
avoid breaking apart when cooked.

◢ Place under broiler and broil until
brown, or fry in oil until brown and
drain on paper towels before serving.

259

SAUTÉED SOFTSHELL CRABS

Serves 3 - 6

Gourmet

The famous Chesapeake Bay delicacy. Serve alone or as a sandwich on sourdough bread.

½ cup flour

⅛ teaspoon Chesapeake-style seafood seasoning

¼ cup milk

6 soft-shelled crabs, cleaned

2-4 tablespoons vegetable shortening

⅓ cup butter

2 tablespoons fresh chopped parsley

1 lemon, quartered

◢ In a small bowl or brown bag, mix flour and Chesapeake-style seafood seasoning.

◢ Dip crabs in milk and dredge in flour. Shake to remove excess flour.

◢ Heat shortening over medium heat. Sauté crabs 3 minutes on each side until golden brown. Set aside.

◢ Drain off shortening from the pan and wipe clean. Melt butter in the same pan. Pour butter over the crabs and sprinkle with chopped parsley and lemon juice.

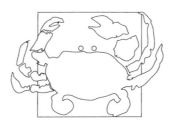

SEVERN RIVER CRAB SOUFFLÉ

Serves 2 - 4

Gourmet

*Perfect for a romantic dinner
or brunch with best friends!*

½ pound backfin
crabmeat, shell and
cartilage removed

¼ cup butter

¼ cup flour

1 tablespoon finely
chopped onion

⅛ teaspoon salt

¼ teaspoon crushed
tarragon leaves

⅛ teaspoon Chesapeake-
style seafood seasoning

1½ teaspoons parsley
flakes

⅓ cup grated medium
cheddar cheese

1 cup skim milk

3 eggs, separated

¼ teaspoon cream of
tartar

paprika for garnish

◢ Preheat oven to 325°. Butter soufflé
dish and set aside.

◢ Melt butter in a large saucepan over
low heat. Gradually stir in flour
until well blended. Cook over medium heat until mixture is bubbly.

◢ Add onion and spices. Stir in
cheese and milk and stir until
cheese has melted. Remove from
heat. Add crabmeat to mixture and
set aside.

◢ Beat egg yolks until thick and pour
into the crab mixture, stirring gently and set aside.

◢ Beat egg whites with cream of tartar until stiff. Gently fold egg
whites into crab mixture. Spoon
mixture into a greased soufflé dish.
Bake for 35 - 40 minutes or until a
knife inserted in the center comes
out clean.

SOUTH RIVER CRAB CASSEROLE

Serves 6

Average, can be made ahead
Serve with herb bread and
fresh green beans.

1 pound crabmeat, shell and cartilage removed

6 slices white bread, with crust removed

4 hard boiled eggs, grated

1¼ cups milk

1½ cups mayonnaise

¼ cup chopped onion

3 tablespoons chopped fresh parsley

1 (2 ounce) jar chopped pimentos

½ teaspoon Chesapeake-style seafood seasoning

½ teaspoon salt

¼ teaspoon white pepper

2 cloves pressed garlic

2 tablespoons sherry (optional)

½ pound grated cheddar cheese

◢ Break bread into small pieces and put into a bowl. Add eggs, milk, mayonnaise, onion, parsley, pimento, seasoning and sherry, mix well.

◢ Fold crabmeat into mixture and pour into a 9"x12"x2" casserole dish. Sprinkle cheese on top. Bake at 350° for 40 minutes.

◢ Can be made ahead and refrigerated overnight prior to cooking.

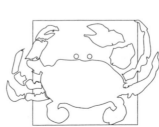

ANCHORS AWEIGH DEVILED CRAB

Serves 4 - 6

Average

Makes a good first course.

2   tablespoons butter, divided

2   tablespoons chopped onion

2   tablespoons mayonnaise

2   eggs, beaten

½   cup bread crumbs, divided

½   teaspoon dry mustard

1   teaspoon lemon juice

1   teaspoon Worcestershire sauce

⅛   teaspoon red pepper

1   pound crabmeat, shell and cartilage removed

    paprika

◢ Preheat oven to 450°. Sauté onion in 1 tablespoon butter. Remove from heat.

◢ Combine onion, mayonnaise, eggs, and ⅓ cup of the bread crumbs, mustard, lemon juice, Worcestershire sauce and red pepper. Add crabmeat and stir until just blended.

◢ Place crab mixture in cleaned crab shells or dishes. Sprinkle with bread crumbs and paprika. Dot with butter.

◢ Bake for 10 to 12 minutes until lightly browned. Serve immediately.

263

Marylanders pick crabs at record speed. It is a friendly tradition at area crabhouses for the locals to show struggling newcomers the precise way to wield knife and mallet to retrieve every piece of sweet crabmeat.

HOT BUTTERED CRAB

Serves 4

Easy

From colonial times to today, the classic recipe for the finest lump crabmeat.

1   pound lump backfin crabmeat, shell and cartilage removed

1   cup butter, do not substitute

1½   teaspoons dry white wine

⅛   teaspoon nutmeg or cayenne pepper

    salt and pepper to taste

▲ In a skillet, melt butter over low heat, add seasonings and wine. Stir well.

▲ Add crabmeat and sauté, turning carefully as not to break the lumps of crab. Sauté just until crab is warm. Serve immediately.

Seafood

BAKED ROCKFISH STUFFED WITH CRABMEAT

Serves 6

Gourmet, cannot be made ahead

An elegant dish for guests and the stuffing can be used to make crab cakes.

1   (5-8 pound) whole rockfish, scaled and gutted

Stuffing

1   medium onion, finely chopped

1   large stalk celery, finely chopped

2   tablespoons butter

1   pound crabmeat, shell and cartilage removed

2   cups soft bread crumbs

¾   cup mayonnaise

1   teaspoon dry mustard

1   teaspoon Chesapeake-style seafood seasoning

1   dozen finely chopped green olives

Topping

½   cup mayonnaise

½   cup sun-dried tomatoes

1   teaspoon basil

▲ For the stuffing, sauté onion and celery in butter until the onion turns clear. Place crabmeat, mayonnaise, mustard, seafood seasoning, olives and bread crumbs in a large bowl. Add onion and celery, mix well and set aside.

▲ To clean and stuff the rockfish; from the bottom, split the fish on both sides of backbone the full length of the fish from bottom up. Remove backbone. This may be done at the fish market. (If head is on, remove gill rakers).

▲ Rinse the fish and pat dry. Lay the fish open and coat the outside with mayonnaise, sun-dried tomatoes, basil, salt and pepper to taste. Spoon stuffing mixture over fish, close the fish and bind with twine. Lay fish on an aluminum foil covered broiling pan.

▲ Bake in a very hot oven (425 - 450°) uncovered for 10 minutes per inch of thickness of the fish, measured at the thickest point. (A 6 pound stuffed fish will take 30 - 40 minutes) The fish is done when a butter knife passes easily through the flesh.

MAHI MAHI WITH WHITE WINE AND FRESH MANGOES

Serves 4

Easy, cannot be made ahead
Great for a summer meal.

1	large mango, soft and fresh, peeled and sliced in long pieces
4	(¾" thick, 6 ounce) slices fresh mahi mahi
	salt and pepper to taste
¼	cup flour
1	lemon
4	tablespoons butter, divided
1	teaspoon vegetable oil
½	cup white wine
½	cup fish stock (may substitute chicken stock)
	coriander leaves for garnish

266

◢ Sprinkle the fish lightly with salt, pepper and a little lemon juice. Dust with flour.

◢ Heat 2 tablespoons butter and oil in a skillet, sauté fish for three minutes on each side. Remove from skillet and cover to keep warm.

◢ Add the remaining 2 tablespoons butter, wine, fish stock and lemon juice to the skillet and cook over high heat until all ingredients are reduced (about 20 minutes).

◢ Add mango slices and heat through. Toss fish gently in skillet until warm. Place fish on serving platter and garnish with coriander leaves.

◢ If mangoes are not available, use canned apricots without the juice.

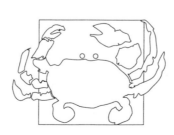

Seafood

GRILLED MARINATED SWORDFISH

Serves 6

Easy, must make marinade ahead

Mouthwatering flavor!

6 (1" thick) swordfish steaks

1 cup vegetable oil

1 lemon, juice only

4 cloves garlic, minced

2 tablespoons dried basil

1 tablespoons dried oregano

1 teaspoon celery salt

½ cup butter, melted

½ teaspoon ground black pepper

fresh parsley for garnish

◢ Combine oil, the juice of one lemon, garlic, basil, oregano, celery salt and pepper. Mix well. Brush both sides of the steaks generously with the mixture.

◢ Place the steaks in a shallow dish and pour remaining marinade over steaks. Refrigerate for 2 hours, turning steaks every half hour.

◢ Grill about 6 inches from the coals for 5 minutes. Turn and baste with marinade. Grill 6 to 7 more minutes.

◢ Serve brushed with melted butter and topped with fresh parsley.

Fish dinners are the men's task in my family. They catch 'em, clean 'em and cook 'em. And they start young. My eight-year old son startled my mother when he found her preparing a fish: "Grandma, I didn't know women cooked FISH."

CLASSIC SNAPPER VERONIQUE

Serves 2

Gourmet, cannot be made ahead

Impress your guests!

2   (7-8 ounce) snapper filets

¾   cup clam juice

¾   cup dry white wine

1   chopped shallot

¼   cup heavy cream

    salt and pepper to taste

    cayenne pepper

2   egg yolks

1   tablespoon heavy cream

½   cup sliced white grapes

½   cup sliced mushrooms

◢ Mix clam juice, white wine, shallot, cream, salt and pepper and cayenne pepper. Pour into fish poacher. Place fish on rack. Poach fish 3-4 minutes until fish is flaky. Remove fish from poacher and keep warm.

◢ Reduce poaching sauce by half.

◢ Whip egg yolks over a double boiler. Cook until ribbons form.

◢ Add cream to egg yolks and mix well. Pour egg yolk and cream mixture into reserved poaching sauce. Add mushrooms. Heat thoroughly, but do not boil.

◢ Pour over snapper, garnish with grapes. Place fish under broiler and brown slightly. Serve immediately.

268

SALMON WITH FRESH TOMATO BASIL SAUCE

Serves 4

Easy

Delicious with angel hair pasta.

4	(4 ounce) salmon fish filets
4	tablespoons olive oil, divided
1	medium finely chopped onion
4	medium tomatoes, peeled, seeded and chopped
½	cup heavy cream
1	bunch basil leaves, finely chopped
	salt and pepper

◢ Preheat oven to 350°. Lightly grease a baking pan big enough to hold the salmon.

◢ Heat 2 tablespoons olive oil in a medium skillet. Sauté onion until transparent. Add tomatoes and simmer, stirring often for 15 minutes.

◢ Add basil leaves and cream. Heat but do not boil. Season to taste with salt and pepper. Set aside and keep warm.

◢ In another skillet, heat remaining 2 tablespoons olive oil. Place salmon skin side down in the pan. Turn fish over in pan. While second side cooks, remove skin from salmon. Place in baking pan and bake 5 minutes or until done.

◢ Place tomato sauce on plate and place salmon on top of sauce.

269

Fresh fish will have little fishy odor and the color and eyes will still be bright and clear. Fish should be cooked within 48 hours.

SALMON AND SPINACH IN PUFF PASTRY WITH LEMON-HERB SAUCE

Serves 4 as a main dish, 8 as an appetizer

Gourmet, can be made ahead

An elegant presentation for salmon which even non-salmon lovers will like.

2	(10 ounce) salmon filets
2	sheets of puff pastry
1½	cups cooked white rice
1	package of frozen spinach, thawed and drained
1	clove crushed garlic
¼	cup white wine
⅓	cup sour cream
⅔	cup mayonnaise
3	tablespoons lemon juice
2	teaspoons dried parsley
1	teaspoon dried dill
½	teaspoon white pepper
1	egg, beaten
	fresh parsley or dill for garnish

▲ Preheat oven to 400°.

▲ Sauté spinach in a frying pan over medium heat with the white wine and garlic until the wine is almost evaporated. Remove from heat and mix with rice, set aside.

▲ Mix together the sour cream, mayonnaise, lemon juice, pepper and herbs, and set aside.

▲ Unfold the puff pastry. Place on a lightly floured board and gently roll out until approximately 2 inches larger on all edges. Lift off of board and place on a baking sheet. Fill one sheet at a time.

▲ Pat salmon filets dry with a paper towel. Spread one side of the salmon generously with the lemon-herb mixture. Reserve at least half of the mixture for garniture after baking. Place the filet face down in the center of the pastry sheet. Place ¾ of a cup of the spinach/rice mixture on top of the filet. Pinch edges shut and gently reverse pastry package so smooth edge faces up. Repeat with the second filet.

▲ Brush both pastries with the beaten egg. Bake for 45 minutes or until the pastry is golden brown. To serve, cut in 4 or 8 slices and garnish with 1 tablespoon of sauce and a sprig of fresh herb. Can be served hot or cold.

Seafood

GRILLED SALMON WITH PARSLEY LEMON DILL SAUCE

Serves 4

Easy

A fresh light taste, good enough for your in-laws.

4   salmon steaks

½   cup mayonnaise

½   cup sour cream

2   tablespoons lemon juice

1   tablespoon dried parsley or 4 tablespoons fresh chopped parsley

1   teaspoon dried dill

◢ Mix mayonnaise, sour cream, lemon juice and herbs together. Baste salmon steaks with half of the sauce.

◢ Grill for 3-4 minutes on each side. Serve with 1 tablespoon of remaining sauce on the side or on top of the steak.

Feathery-leafed dill is delicious with seafood and goes well in vegetable dishes. It imparts a distinctive, refreshing flavor to sauces. A fresh sprig leaves a delicate tracery of green for garnishes.

GRECIAN STYLE GROUPER

Serves 6

Easy, must make ahead

An inviting topping with a hint of lemon.

6   (6 ounce) grouper filets

⅓   cup lemon juice

1   medium chopped onion

1   medium chopped green pepper

3   tablespoons melted butter

2   medium diced tomatoes

    salt and pepper to taste

2½   cups shredded mozzarella cheese

½   cup sliced black olives

272

Place the filets in a shallow container. Pour lemon juice over fish and refrigerate for 2 hours.

Sauté onion and green pepper in butter for 5 minutes. Add tomatoes and cook an additional 2 minutes. Remove from heat and set aside.

Remove fish from lemon juice, place skin side down in a greased 13"x9"x2" baking dish. Sprinkle with salt and pepper. Bake uncovered at 350° for 30 minutes.

Spoon vegetable mixture over fish and sprinkle with cheese. Bake for an additional 15 minutes or until fish flakes easily with a fork. Sprinkle with olives and serve.

Seafood

ZESTY ORANGE ROUGHY ALMANDINE

Serves 4

Easy, cannot make ahead

Serve with brown rice and fresh vegetables for a delectable meal.

1   tablespoon plus 1 teaspoon sliced almonds

2   tablespoons margarine

2   tablespoons minced fresh parsley

1   tablespoon grated lemon rind

3   tablespoons lemon juice

¼   teaspoon salt

4   (6 ounce) orange roughy filets

▲ Brown almonds in a small non-stick skillet over low heat until lightly toasted, and set aside.

▲ Melt margarine in a skillet over low heat. Add parsley, lemon juice, rind and salt, stirring well. Remove from heat and set aside.

▲ Cover broiler pan with aluminum foil. Place in oven 6" from the heating element; preheat pan for 3 minutes. Arrange filets in preheated pan, and baste evenly with margarine mixture. Broil 6" from heat for 8 minutes or until fish flakes when fork tested.

▲ Sprinkle almonds over fish before serving.

Test sautéed or poached seafood for doneness when fish flakes easily when tested with a fork at the thickest part.

BROILED SOLE WITH SUN-DRIED TOMATO SAUCE

Serves 4

Average

Serve this scrumptious fish with rice or pasta.

½   cup sun-dried tomato paste

1   tablespoon butter ✓

1   medium clove garlic, minced

1   cup chicken stock, divided ✓

1   cup heavy cream

2   tablespoons vegetable oil

2   tablespoons chopped fresh basil

4   (½ pound) sole filets

274

▲ Melt butter over low heat and add paste. Stir until smooth, add garlic and cook for 30 seconds.

▲ Add ¾ cup stock, stir until smooth and bring to a boil, simmer uncovered over medium heat, about 10 minutes or until heated through.

▲ Add cream, bring to a boil, stirring, simmer until thick enough to coat spoon. Add filets just until heated, transfer filets to a warm plate.

▲ Add remaining stock to the skillet. Bring to a boil, stirring up pan juices, stir in basil, taste and adjust the seasonings.

▲ Place the filets on broiler tray, drizzle with sauce and broil for about 6 minutes, and serve.

▲ You may substitute orange roughy for the sole.

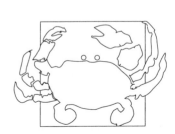

CRABMEAT STUFFED RED SNAPPER WITH ORIENTAL SAUCE

Serves 4

Average

A tangy and light alternative for stuffed fish.

1	(2 pound) dressed red snapper
¾	cup crabmeat, shell and cartilage removed
½	cup shredded carrots
1	thinly sliced green onion
1	teaspoon brown sugar
1	teaspoon corn starch
1	teaspoon soy sauce
1	teaspoon dry sherry

Poaching Sauce

¼	cup dry sherry
¼	cup soy sauce
1	teaspoon grated fresh ginger root
2	cups water

◢ Score fish with 6 diagonal cuts on each side, slicing almost to the bone.

◢ Combine crabmeat, carrot, onion, sugar, cornstarch, soy sauce and sherry. Spoon mixture into the fish cavity, patting mixture evenly. Place fish on greased rack of poaching pan. Lower rack into the pan.

◢ For poaching sauce, combine sherry, soy sauce, ginger root and water. Pour over fish. Simmer, covered, 20 minutes or until fish flakes. Transfer to platter; spoon some liquid on top.

◢ Can remove head and tail if necessary to fit fish into the poaching pan.

275

CHESAPEAKE PAELLA

Serves 10

Gourmet, may be started up to two days in advance.

This is the result of my husband's quest for the perfect paella when we toured Spain. It's a substantial one-dish meal for a crowd and always a hit! Serve with gazpacho and sangria.

276

8	boneless, skinless chicken breasts
1½	cups white wine
⅓	cup lime juice
⅓	cup Worcestershire sauce
⅓	cup soy sauce
7	cloves of garlic
¼	cup plus 6 tablespoons olive oil
3	chopped green peppers
3	sliced medium onions
1	pound fresh tomatoes, skinned and puréed or 2 (8 ounce) cans peeled tomatoes
6	sliced mild Italian sausages
½	pound crumbled hot sausage
1½	pounds sea scallops
1½	pounds large shrimp, peeled

▲ Up to 2 days ahead of time, cut the chicken into bite size pieces and marinate them in 1 cup of the wine, lime juice, Worcestershire sauce and soy sauce for 6 hours or overnight.

▲ Up to 1 day ahead of time, brown 2 cloves of crushed garlic in the olive oil over medium heat for one minute. Add green peppers and sauté them for 2 minutes. Add the onions to the mixture and sauté until clear. Add puréed tomatoes to the mixture and heat for 5 minutes.

▲ In a separate pan, sauté Italian sausages until well browned. Drain fat, add to the green pepper, onion and tomato mixture, cover and refrigerate.

▲ Sauté crumbled sausage until browned. Refrigerate sausage including the fat. The fat is important to the final dish. It will keep the rice and other ingredients moist. Many paellas get dry without the sausage fat added.

▲ Take the husks off the sea scallops (a small hard piece found on the outside of some scallops). Place scallops and shrimp on skewers.

▲ Mix mayonnaise, ¼ cup of olive oil, and 5 crushed cloves of garlic together. Brush the shrimp and scallops generously on both sides with the garlic sauce. Let sit for ½ hour then grill seafood until done. Remove from skewers, cover and refrigerate. The garlic sauce gives the seafood a light garlic flavor and keeps the seafood moist while grilling. Most of it will cook off.

▲ Place chicken pieces on skewers and grill until done. Reserve

CHESAPEAKE PAELLA (Continued)

1   pound mussels

15   medium clams

¾   cup mayonnaise

1   pound squid (optional)

1   cup peas

2½   cups rice

6   chicken bouillon cubes

7   cups water combined
    with chicken marinade

½   teaspoon ground
    saffron

1   tablespoon parsley

1   can artichoke hearts,
    quartered

1   tablespoon garlic
    powder

6   steamed crabs
    (optional)

Saffron has a pungent taste and is only used in small quantities. It gives a golden tint to the dish. Saffron goes particularly well with shellfish and is essential to paella.

remaining marinade and refrigerate. Remove chicken from skewers, cover and refrigerate. Clean and skin squid. Cut into strips.

◢ One hour before the meal: preheat oven to 350°. Put sausage, tomato, pepper and onion mixture in the bottom of a paella pan. Add peas. Heat on top of the stove over medium heat. Add chicken marinade, 5 cups of water/marinade mix, rice, 4 bouillon cubes and saffron. Cook, stirring frequently, for approximately 15 minutes or until rice is ¾ of the way done. Add squid if desired and place in oven for 45 minutes. After 30 minutes stir in chicken, shrimp, scallops, and quartered artichoke hearts.

◢ In two cups of water, bring clams to a boil and cook until shells open. Take off heat and set aside.

◢ As the paella cooks, clean mussels. In a stock pot combine 2 cups water, 2 chicken bouillon cubes, ½ cup white wine, parsley and garlic powder. Bring to a boil, add mussels, cover and cook for 10 to 12 minutes or just until the mussel shells open. Remove from heat and drain.

◢ Remove paella from oven and arrange mussels and clams around the edge of the pan. Serve straight from the oven.

◢ For a truly spectacular presentation, arrange the steamed crabs on top of the paella. Each guest should get a piece of crab along with a serving of paella.

CREOLE JUMBLE

Serves 12

Average, can make ahead

Gets better with each reheating!

3   medium diced onions

5   stalks chopped celery

2   green diced peppers

2   cloves garlic, pressed

2   cups cubed ham (honey baked makes the best flavor)

¼   cup butter

3   tablespoons flour

2   (12 ounce) cans tomatoes, chopped

1   (6 ounce) can tomato paste

2   cups uncooked rice

4   cups water

1½ pounds shrimp, cooked and peeled

1   pound kielbasa, cut into slices, sautéed until browned

2   tablespoons creole seasoning

    salt and pepper to taste

▲ In a dutch oven or paella pan, sauté onion, celery, green pepper, garlic and ham in butter until tender, 5 - 10 minutes. Sprinkle in flour to make a paste (or roux). If paste is too dry, add a little of the liquid from the canned tomatoes. Cook on medium heat, stirring constantly until roux is dark brown.

▲ Slowly add tomatoes with liquid, tomato paste, rice and water to roux. Cook on medium low heat until the rice is tender. Check frequently and stir so rice won't settle to the bottom and burn. Add more water during cooking if mixture gets too dry and starts to burn.

▲ Once rice is tender add shrimp, sausage and spices to taste. Cook just long enough to heat the shrimp and sausage through.

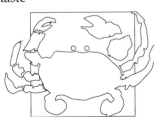

S P I C Y   S H R I M P   S C A M P I

Serves 4

Average, can be made ahead

Makes a beautiful presentation!

20	large shrimp, peeled and deveined
3	tablespoons margarine or butter
½	teaspoon curry
¼	teaspoon paprika
¼	teaspoon cayenne pepper
4	finely chopped green onions
1	red pepper, cut into strips
1	green pepper, cut into strips
1	stalk thinly sliced celery
1	cup sliced mushrooms
1	teaspoon flour
1	small can tomato sauce
¼	cup dry white wine
½	teaspoon tarragon
1	cup whipping cream
¼	cup dry vermouth

◢ Brown shrimp in 2 tablespoons butter with curry, paprika and pepper. Set shrimp aside, leaving butter in the pan.

◢ Add remaining tablespoon of butter to the skillet. Sauté onions, peppers, celery and mushrooms. Cook for 3 minutes over medium heat, then sprinkle flour over mixture. Stir, then gradually add wine and cream to the mixture, stirring constantly.

◢ Mix in tomato sauce, tarragon and vermouth. Cook for 5 minutes. Add shrimp and simmer for 3 minutes. Serve with rice.

SHRIMP AND ARTICHOKE TURNOVERS WITH ROASTED RED PEPPER SAUCE

Serves 4 as a main dish, 8 as an appetizer

Gourmet, can be made ahead partially

Tantalizing flavor and a spectacular presentation.

Velouté

½   tablespoon flour

½   tablespoon butter

1   cup chicken broth

Red Pepper Sauce

5   red peppers, roasted, seeded and peeled

½   tablespoon shallots

2   tablespoons white wine

2   tablespoons olive oil

4   tablespoons red wine vinegar

2   tablespoons chicken broth

1   tablespoon sugar

1   cup chicken velouté

▲ To make the red pepper sauce, combine butter and flour to make roux. Slowly add warm broth until blended. Simmer over low heat for 10 minutes.

▲ Add remaining ingredients along with the véloute and place in a food processor and purée. Reserve sauce. May be made up to 2 days in advance.

Continued on next page

280

Seafood

Turnovers

½	pound shrimp, 40 - 50 size, cooked and peeled
1	small can chopped artichoke hearts
1	tablespoon chopped garlic
3	sliced scallions
1	teaspoon minced fresh ginger
4	ounces Parmesan cheese
2	tablespoons chopped parsley
¼	teaspoon sesame oil
¼	cup mayonnaise
	salt to taste
4	puff pastry sheets
	toasted pumpkin seeds (optional)

◢ Cut puff pastry sheets into 3 inch squares. Combine remaining ingredients in a food processor. Fill each square with 1 tablespoon of turnover mix. Fold opposite corners, seal ends with a fork.

◢ Can be made ahead up to this point and frozen.

◢ Bake in a 375° oven until brown. If frozen, allow to reach room temperature prior to baking.

◢ Serve with red pepper sauce and garnish with toasted pumpkin seeds and fresh parsley.

281

SHRIMP IN CHAMPAGNE SAUCE

Serves 4

*Average, can partially be
made ahead*

Subtle and delightful flavor.

1   cup sliced mushrooms

1   tablespoon olive oil

1   pound medium
     shrimp, shelled

1½   cups champagne

¼   teaspoon salt

2   tablespoons minced
     shallots or scallions

2   diced plum tomatoes

1   cup heavy cream

1   pound dried angel hair
     pasta

3   tablespoons chopped
     parsley

282

◢ Sauté mushrooms in a medium saucepan in hot olive oil over medium high heat. Remove mushrooms and set aside.

◢ In same saucepan combine shrimp, champagne and salt. Over high heat, heat to simmer. When liquid just boils, shrimp are done. Remove shrimp from cooking liquid with a slotted spoon, and set aside.

◢ Add chopped shallots and tomatoes to cooking liquid. Boil over high heat until liquid is reduced to ½ cup, (approximately 8 minutes). When liquid is reduced, add ¾ cup heavy cream and boil one to two minutes until slightly thickened and reduced.

◢ Add shrimp and mushrooms to sauce, heat through. Add pepper to taste. Cook pasta according to label directions, return to pot and toss with remaining ¼ cup cream and parsley.

◢ To serve, divide pasta among plates. Spoon shrimp and sauce over pasta.

Put a slice of lemon in the water to give boiled or steamed seafood a fresh taste.

COCONUT SHRIMP WITH SPICY CITRUS SAUCE

Serves 4 as a main dish, 8 as an appetizer

Average, cannot be made ahead

Tasty for a casual dinner with friends.

1   pound medium shrimp, peeled and deveined

¼   cup Creole or Chesapeake-style seafood seasoning

¾   cup plus 2 tablespoons all-purpose flour

¼   cup plus 2 tablespoons beer

1   egg, beaten

½   teaspoon baking powder

1   (7 ounce) package flaked coconut

2   cups vegetable oil

Spicy Citrus Sauce

1   (12 ounce) jar orange marmalade

2   tablespoons horseradish

3   tablespoons lemon juice

2   tablespoons rough grain Dijon mustard

½   teaspoon grated lemon rind

▲ Combine flour, egg, beer and baking powder in a medium bowl, mix well and set aside for half an hour.

▲ Heat oil in deep fryer or skillet to 350°. Dip shrimp in seasoning, shake off excess seasoning. Dip seasoned shrimp into batter then dredge in coconut.

▲ Fry shrimp 6 at a time until golden brown, about 3 minutes. Drain on paper towels.

▲ Can keep warm in a 200° oven on a cookie sheet for up to one hour.

▲ For citrus sauce, combine all ingredients in a blender. Serve shrimp with sauce.

▲ Sauce will keep up to one month in the refrigerator.

283

TANGY SHRIMP TEMPURA

Serves 4 - 6

Average

*Great as an appetizer too!
You can also use uncooked
vegetables or boneless
chicken breast pieces.*

3   eggs, separated

1   (12 ounce) bottle beer

1   tablespoon vegetable
     oil

1   tablespoon soy sauce

1   teaspoon prepared
     mustard

1   cup flour

2   pounds peeled shrimp

Sauce

6   ounces currant jelly

3   ounces orange
     marmalade

1½   teaspoons white
     vinegar

2   teaspoons soy sauce

1   tablespoon lemon juice

▲ Mix egg yolks, oil, soy sauce, and mustard thoroughly. Blend in beer, then flour; mix should be medium thick.

▲ Beat egg whites to soft peaks, and fold into batter.

▲ Dip shrimp into batter, completely coat and drop into deep fat at 365° until nicely browned. Drain on absorbent paper. Serve with sauce.

▲ To make sauce, mix all ingredients in a blender a few seconds until smooth.

Seafood

BACON AND SHRIMP CREOLE

Serves 4 - 6

Average, sauce may be frozen and shrimp added at the last minute.

Perfect for a crowd, easily doubled.

2   pounds shrimp, peeled and deveined

4-8   slices bacon

4   cups canned tomatoes

1   chopped green pepper

1   cup chopped onion

1   cup chopped celery

1   (12 ounce) bottle chili sauce

2   tablespoons Worcestershire sauce

½   teaspoon black pepper

1   tablespoon bacon fat

2   teaspoons salt

3   tablespoons sugar

8   drops Tabasco sauce

Fry bacon and remove from pan to drain. Brown onion, celery, pepper in 1 tablespoon of bacon fat, and set aside.

In a large pot, place tomato, chili sauce, Tabasco, black pepper, salt, sugar and Worcestershire sauce. Mix well. Add browned ingredients to this and mix well. Cook very slowly for 2 hours, stirring occasionally.

Add shrimp to cooked sauce 30 minutes before serving. Break bacon into small bits and add to sauce in the last 10 minutes. Serve over rice.

CRAB STUFFED SHRIMP

Serves 4

Average

Elegant and deceptively easy.

1 dozen large shrimp, peeled, deveined and butterflied

½ medium finely chopped onion

½ medium chopped green pepper

½ cup finely chopped celery

1 pound fresh crabmeat, shell and cartilage removed

¾ cup finely crushed saltine crackers

½ cup mayonnaise

1 tablespoon Dijon mustard

2 teaspoons Worcestershire sauce

1 teaspoon lemon juice

⅛ teaspoon red pepper

1 egg, beaten

¼ cup melted butter

1 tablespoon butter

Chesapeake-style seafood seasoning to taste

◢ Sauté onion, pepper and celery in 1 tablespoon of butter, and set aside.

◢ Combine crabmeat, crackers, mayonnaise, mustard, Worcestershire sauce, lemon juice, red pepper and egg, stir in sautéed vegetables.

◢ Top each shrimp with crab mixture, stuffing lightly, sprinkle with Chesapeake-style seafood seasoning and drizzle with melted butter. Bake at 350° for 20 minutes or broil for 5 to 8 minutes.

To clean clams and mussels of sand, cover the shells with 1/3 cup of salt and 1 gallon of lukewarm water for 15 minutes. Repeat 2 or 3 times. The sand will filter to the bottom.

GRECIAN SHRIMP WITH FETA CHEESE

Serves 4 as a main dish, 8 as an appetizer

Easy

Fast and scrumptious.

½ cup olive oil

1 lemon, juice only

1 teaspoon oregano

¼ cup butter

1 sliced onion

4 ounces feta cheese

1 pound raw, peeled large shrimp, butterflied

▲ Sauté onion, lemon juice, oregano and butter in oil. Add shrimp and cook until pink. Before serving add feta cheese in large chunks into hot mixture.

▲ Can serve cold on a bed of romaine lettuce or hot over pasta.

287

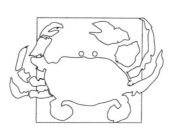

CURRIED SHRIMP AND SCALLOPS

Serves 8 to 10 as a main dish, up to 20 as appetizer

Gourmet, can be made ahead

A versatile dish for entertaining.

1	clove garlic, crushed
30	ounces frozen scallops or 3½ cups fresh
4	cups shrimp, cooked, cleaned, (6 pounds uncooked)
½	cup butter, divided
4	tablespoons curry powder
¾	cup flour
4	tablespoons white vinegar
1	quart whole milk
½	teaspoon ginger
¼	teaspoon nutmeg
¼	teaspoon cayenne pepper
2	teaspoons salt
3	chicken bouillon cubes
5	tablespoons parsley

Simmer ¼ cup of butter and garlic for 1 - 2 minutes. Add scallops, simmer an additional 5 minutes until scallops are opaque. Set aside.

Melt remaining ¼ cup of butter in a large saucepan over medium heat. Add curry, cook for 1 - 2 minutes to soften curry. Add flour and stirring constantly make a roux. Add vinegar, stir, add milk and stir. Add ginger, nutmeg, cayenne pepper, salt, and bouillon cubes. Heat mixture slowly, stirring constantly until boiling. Add parsley.

Reduce heat and add shrimp and scallops, plus all liquid cooked out of the scallops. Let cook at a high simmer for 5 - 8 minutes, stirring carefully several times.

Remove from heat and cover until cooked to room temperature. Refrigerate overnight, or for better flavor blending, refrigerate for 2 - 3 days.

Reheat slowly with frequent stirring. Serve in toast baskets, or over rice, as a main course; or as appetizer on toast rounds, crackers, or with heavy corn chips for dipping. If scallops are large, cut into halves or quarters.

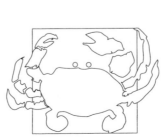

CREAMY SHRIMP AND SCALLOPS STROGANOFF

Serves 4 - 6

Average

Serve with our Cottage Dill Rolls.

1	pound jumbo shrimp, shelled and deveined
1	pound scallops, washed and drained
3	tablespoons butter, divided
½	pound mushrooms, sliced
2	tablespoons dry sherry
1	tablespoon flour
⅛	teaspoon pepper
1	envelope chicken flavored bouillon
1	(8 ounce) container sour cream
2	teaspoons minced fresh parsley
3-4	cups hot cooked noodles

◢ Rinse off shrimp and scallops with cold water and pat dry. In a 12" skillet, melts 2 tablespoons of butter. Sauté shrimp until pink, about 5 minutes. Remove from pan and set aside.

◢ Sauté scallops, about 5 minutes and remove from pan and set aside.

◢ Sauté mushrooms in remaining tablespoon of butter.

◢ Stir sherry, flour, pepper, and bouillon into 1 cup of cold water. Stir into mushrooms in skillet. Cook until sauce boils and thickens. Reduce heat to low. Stir in sour cream, and continue stirring until smooth.

◢ Return shrimp and scallops to the skillet, and continue cooking until heated through. Serve over hot noodles and garnish with parsley.

289

COQUILLE ST. JACQUES

Serves 4

Gourmet, can partially be made ahead

A proven classic, bake in individual scallop dishes for an impressive presentation.

1	cup water
½	cup dry white wine
2	chicken bouillon cubes
2	large shallots, peeled and minced
1	clove garlic, peeled and minced
1	bay leaf
½	teaspoon fresh fennel seeds, peeled and minced
¼	teaspoon dried crushed thyme
3	teaspoons fresh lemon juice, divided
½	pound mushrooms, trimmed, cleaned and thinly sliced
1	pound scallops, cut in half
½	cup milk
1	tablespoon plus 2 teaspoons all-purpose flour

◢ In a large saucepan, combine water, white wine, bouillon cubes, shallots, garlic, bay leaf, fennel seeds, thyme and 1 teaspoon lemon juice. Bring to a boil. Reduce heat to medium and cook for minutes. Add mushrooms and simmer 2 minutes. Add scallops and simmer for 2 more minutes. With slotted spoon, transfer mushrooms and scallops to a large plate and refrigerate.

◢ Bring cooking liquid to boil, then continue to cook at a low boil for 5 minutes to concentrate flavor. Strain and measure ½ cup of broth.

◢ In a medium saucepan, combine measured broth and milk. Bring to a boil. Sift flour over liquid and whisk to avoid lumps. Reduce heat, add salt, pepper and nutmeg and simmer for 5 minutes, stirring often to prevent scorching. Remove from heat and stir in parsley, mustard and remaining lemon juice.

Continued on next page

COQUILLE ST. JACQUES (Continued)

pinch of salt

¼ teaspoon freshly ground white pepper

¼ teaspoon freshly grated nutmeg

1 tablespoon minced fresh parsley

1 teaspoon Dijon mustard

½ cup grated white cheese

¼ cup fresh bread crumbs

1 teaspoon margarine

◢ In a medium bowl, combine mushrooms, scallops and sauce. Transfer to a shallow 1 quart baking dish and sprinkle with cheese then bread crumbs. Dot with margarine. Broil 6 inches from heat source for 5 minutes or until bread crumbs are lightly browned. Serve immediately.

291

SKEWERED SCALLOPS, ZUCCHINI AND ARTICHOKE HEARTS WITH SALSA

Serves 6

Average, can prepare ahead

A colorful and light patio dinner.

3   ounces fresh sea scallops

4   medium size zucchini, sliced into ½" rounds

6   large artichoke hearts, quartered, or 3 small jars

¼   cup olive oil

½   fresh lime

Salsa

2   minced large red-ripe or 4 small tomatoes

1   minced medium onion

2   cloves garlic, minced

1   lime, juice only

1   fresh jalapeño, seeded and minced

6   cilantro sprigs

     pinch of sugar

     salt and pepper to taste

▲ To prepare skewers: soak 8 wood skewers in water for 15 minutes. If using canned artichoke hearts, drain them and reserve the oil. Alternate the zucchini, scallops and artichokes on the skewers. Brush with oil or use reserve artichoke oil and squeeze a little lime juice over the skewers.

▲ Grill on an open grill over medium hot to red hot coals for a total of 6 - 8 minutes, turning carefully, until scallops are opaque. Drizzle with salsa to serve.

▲ To make the salsa, combine all ingredients in a bowl and mix well. Allow the salsa to stand at room temperature for 1 hour before serving.

▲ Salsa can be made up to 10 days in advance. Store in the refrigerator in a glass jar, with a tight fitting lid. To make the salsa milder, reduce the jalapeño to half.

Seafood

WATERCRESS SAUCE

Makes 2 cups

Easy

Particularly good with scallops or salmon.

1½ cups mayonnaise

¾ cup watercress leaves

1 tablespoon chopped dill

1 teaspoon fresh lemon juice

1 teaspoon grated onion

salt and pepper to taste

◢ Combine all ingredients in a blender or food processor and chill. Serve with poached cold fish or chicken.

CUCUMBER SAUCE

Makes 3 cups

Gourmet

Excellent with cold poached fish or scallops.

5 large thin cucumbers

1½ teaspoons salt

1 cup mayonnaise

1 cup sour cream

1 tablespoon Dijon mustard

2 tablespoons chopped fresh dill

salt and pepper to taste

◢ Peel cucumbers, cut them in half and scoop out the seeds. Chop the cucumbers in a food processor, fitted with steel blade on coarse. Remove mixture to a glass bowl and sprinkle with salt.

◢ Cover bowl with plastic wrap and chill for two hours. Drain cucumbers in a strainer squeezing out excess moisture. Pat with a paper towel.

◢ Combine remaining ingredients and add to cucumber mixture.

LEMON - GARLIC SEAFOOD MARINADE

Will marinate 2 pounds of seafood

Easy

Versatile for all types of seafood.

3   tablespoons extra virgin olive oil

3   lemons, juice only

2   tablespoons Dijon mustard

2   teaspoons freshly ground black pepper

¼   cup white wine vinegar

1½   teaspoons garlic, minced

½   teaspoon capers

1   teaspoon salt

▲ Blend ingredients. Select 2 pounds of your favorite seafood; cleaned squid, rockfish, shrimp, salmon.

▲ Marinade for 1 - 2 hours. Use extra marinade for basting.

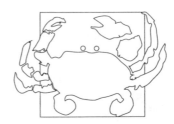

TARTAR SAUCE

Makes 1 1/2 cups

Easy, can be made ahead
A universal favorite.

1½ cups mayonnaise

1 tablespoon minced sweet gherkins

1 teaspoon Dijon mustard

1 teaspoon minced drained capers

1 teaspoon minced parsley

1 teaspoon minced chervil

1 teaspoon minced fresh tarragon

½ teaspoon anchovy paste

◤ Combine all ingredients well and chill. Serve with fish.

The Banneker-Douglas Museum celebrates African-American culture in Maryland. It is located in the elegant former sanctuary of the Mount Moriah A.M.E. Church. Mount Moriah was chartered in 1803, and the present building was constructed in 1874.

FRENCH DRESSING GRIBICHE

Makes 1 1/4 cups

Gourmet

Serve as an accompaniment to shellfish, fish, cold meats or poultry.

4	eggs, hard boiled
2	teaspoons Dijon mustard
½	teaspoon dry mustard
¼	teaspoon salt
⅛	teaspoon cayenne pepper
2	tablespoons tarragon vinegar
½	cup olive oil
3	tablespoons minced sour gherkins
1	teaspoon minced fresh parsley
1	teaspoon minced fresh tarragon
1	teaspoon minced fresh chives

◢ Separate egg yolks from the egg whites. Place the yolks in the food processor with the steel blade, and finely chop. Add mustards, salt and cayenne pepper.

◢ Turn the food processor on and gradually add the vinegar. Through the feed tube, add drop by drop the olive oil until well blended, scraping the bowl as needed.

◢ Remove contents of the work bowl to another bowl and add gherkins, herbs and 2 of the egg whites, chopped.

In a Minute

PASTA

A Summer Resort

For generations of Marylanders, Annapolis and Anne Arundel County were synonymous with summers spent in gentle leisure along the Chesapeake Bay. Cottages sprang up along the waterways as city dwellers sought to escape the heat and humidity of nearby Washington, D.C. and Baltimore. Vacationers would dine al fresco on the beaches and in the parks while those with boats would sail or fish in the rivers. The children learned to swim during afternoons spent exuberantly catapulting from docks or any conveniently floatable item.

Summer highlights during the early part of the 20th century included rides on the Chesapeake ferries — elaborate excursions for the extended family with heaping platters of food prepared by the ladies. These events were anticipated with much excitement. In the dusk after a busy day the exhausted guests would disembark, glowing from the summer sun, replete with good food and basking in the camaraderie of relatives and friends.

The ferries are long gone, and the summer resorts that were popular before the Chesapeake Bay Bridge gave vacationers easy access to the Atlantic Ocean beaches are now homes to year-round residents. Remnants of long-ago summer days still linger. Cottages have been converted to withstand the winter weather but continue to take advantage of the breezes that drift off of the water. Area residents fish and crab from the piers and bridges. Picnickers still use the parks and beaches. A new generation of children pokes around in the marshgrass and cannonballs joyfully into the cool river waters. Any weekend finds families gathered together to share good food and fellowship under the warm sun.

ANGEL HAIR FLANS

Serves 4

Gourmet

An elegant side dish for beef or lamb.

1   cup heavy cream

3   large eggs

1   teaspoon minced fresh thyme or ¼ teaspoon dried

½   teaspoon ground nutmeg

     salt and pepper to taste

1   cup freshly grated Parmesan cheese

6   ounces freshly cooked angel hair pasta

◢ Preheat oven to 350°

◢ Butter 4 half cup soufflé dishes or ramekins.

◢ Whisk cream, eggs, thyme and nutmeg in a medium bowl. Season generously with salt and pepper.

◢ Stir in ⅔ cup of Parmesan cheese.

◢ Divide pasta among the ramekins. Pour egg mixture over the pasta and sprinkle with remaining Parmesan cheese.

◢ Bake until flans are a golden brown, about 20 minutes.

◢ Run small sharp knife around sides of the soufflé dishes to loosen, unmold and serve.

PASTA WITH SHRIMP AND FETA CHEESE

Serves 6 - 10

Average

A quick delicious meal.

1   pound spaghetti, linguine, or fettuccine

1½ pounds shelled shrimp

1   stick butter

2   tablespoons olive oil

1   package sun-dried tomatoes

1   tablespoon each of chopped fresh dill and basil

1   (8 ounce) package crumbled feta cheese

½   cup white wine

3   cloves garlic

1   (14 ounce) jar artichoke hearts

◢ Cook pasta al dente according to directions, drain and return to pan. Quickly add olive oil to pasta.

◢ While pasta is cooking, sauté garlic and shrimp in butter, do not overcook. Add sun dried tomatoes and white wine. Bring to boil, remove from heat and set aside.

◢ Add cheese, artichoke hearts and shrimp mixture to pasta and toss. Add fresh herbs and toss.

◢ Serve immediately with salad and bread.

Pasta

EASY GOURMET SEAFOOD OR CHICKEN ALFREDO

Serves 12

Easy

Keep the ingredients on hand for emergency company. Tastes like three different recipes when made with clams, chicken or scallops.

1   pound fresh fettuccine

1   (6½ ounce) can minced clams, or 2-3 boneless, skinless chicken breasts, or 1 pound scallops

2   tablespoons oil for cooking

1   sliced red pepper

½   pound sliced fresh mushrooms

1   bunch sliced green onions

1   jar Alfredo sauce or Perfect Alfredo Sauce (Next page)

▲ Cook pasta according to package directions.

▲ Sauté clams, chicken or scallops in oil.

▲ Simmer alfredo sauce, add clams, chicken or scallops.

▲ Sauté onion, red pepper and mushrooms until onion is translucent and add to sauce. Serve immediately.

301

Try thinly sliced smoked salmon.

PERFECT ALFREDO SAUCE

Makes 1 1/2 cups

Average

Versatile and popular.

½ cup butter or quality stick margarine

1-2 tablespoons flour

2 tablespoons white wine

1 cup heavy cream or milk

1 cup Parmesan cheese

¼ teaspoon nutmeg

¼ teaspoon salt

¼ teaspoon coarsely ground pepper

Melt butter or margarine in 10 inch skillet over low to medium heat.

Whisk flour into butter until smooth. Use 1 tablespoon flour if using cream, 2 tablespoons for milk. Whisk white wine into mixture.

The sauce will seize briefly; when it does, start adding the cream or milk gradually, whisking constantly to make a smooth sauce.

Add the cheese, nutmeg, salt and pepper. Add some cream or milk if the sauce is too thick.

Pasta

GRILLED SHRIMP AND BASIL-LEMON PASTA

Serves 4

Average

A heavenly salad bursting with flavor.

¼ cup olive oil

½ cup dry white wine

½ teaspoon chopped garlic

½ teaspoon pepper

1½ pounds peeled and deveined medium shrimp

1 teaspoon marjoram

2 small peeled, seeded, quartered, ¼" sliced cucumber

4 medium peeled, ¼" sliced carrots

2 cups mayonnaise or salad dressing

1 cup fresh loosely packed basil leaves

¼ cup lemon juice

3 cloves minced garlic

½ teaspoon coarsely ground pepper

1 (8 ounce) package of angel hair pasta

◢ Marinate shrimp in olive oil, white wine, chopped garlic, marjoram and pepper for one hour. Do not marinate for longer than 2 hours.

◢ Place shrimp on skewer and grill for 5 to 6 minutes or just till the shrimp are pink. Remove from the heat.

◢ Cook carrots in boiling water just until tender. Remove from heat and drain.

◢ Chop basil leaves in food processor. Blend in mayonnaise, garlic and lemon juice, set aside.

◢ Cook pasta according to package directions. Immediately remove from heat, drain, and pour ½ of the sauce over hot pasta so the pasta will absorb the flavor of the sauce. Toss pasta. Chill pasta, shrimp and vegetables separately until ready to serve. Will keep for up to 24 hours.

◢ Put servings of pasta onto each plate. Arrange shrimp on the pasta in a line. Place one line of the cucumbers and one line of the carrots on either side of the shrimp. Drizzle with remaining sauce.

◢ Use fresh basil for a garnish if desired.

Basil is delicious in pasta and vegetable dishes. Its warm aromatic flavor is a natural complement to garlic.

FUSILLI WITH SAUTÉED SHRIMP AND MUSSELS

Serves 6

Gourmet

The ginger adds a nice accent.

8   tablespoons olive oil, divided

½   pound peeled medium shrimp (reserve shells)

1   small crumbled dry red chili pepper or ½ teaspoon chili powder

2   large finely minced garlic cloves

1½ teaspoons finely minced fresh ginger

6   small thinly sliced shallots

4   large peeled, seeded and chopped ripe tomatoes

2   teaspoons fresh oregano leaves

2   teaspoons fresh thyme leaves

    salt and freshly ground black pepper

2   small trimmed, quartered lengthwise and thinly sliced zucchini

½   pound corkscrew fusilli pasta

4   tablespoons finely minced fresh basil

◢ In a large, heavy skillet heat 2 tablespoons of olive oil over medium heat. When oil is hot, add the chili pepper and shrimp shells and sauté quickly until the shells turn bright pink. Remove the shells and chili pepper with a slotted spoon and discard.

◢ Add 1 tablespoon of oil to the skillet and when oil is very hot, add shrimp without crowding the pan. Sauté the shrimp until bright pink and lightly browned. Immediately remove shrimp from the skillet with a slotted spoon and reserve oil.

◢ Reduce the heat, add 2 tablespoons of oil to the skillet and add garlic, ginger and shallots. Cook until the shallots are soft but not browned. Add the tomatoes, oregano, thyme, salt and pepper, reduce the heat and simmer, covered until the ginger is very soft.

◢ In another heavy skillet, heat the remaining oil over medium-high heat. Add the zucchini and sauté quickly until lightly browned. Season with salt and pepper, add to the tomato sauce and simmer for 5 minutes. Keep the sauce warm.

◢ After shrimp have cooled dice and add to tomato-zucchini sauce and remove from heat.

◢ Bring plenty of salted water to a boil in a large pot. Add the fusilli and cook until al dente. Remove from heat. Immediately add 2 cups of cold water to stop further cooking.

Continued on next page

Pasta

2   tablespoons finely
    minced fresh Italian
    parsley

¾   cup crumbled mild
    goat cheese

3   pounds fresh washed,
    beards removed
    mussels

▲ Steam mussels in 2 cups water in a large covered pot. Discard any unopened mussels. Keep warm.

▲ Drain the fusilli well, return to the pot and toss with the shrimp, zucchini and ginger sauce. Add basil, minced parsley and goat cheese. Taste and correct the seasoning, if necessary.

▲ Transfer to a large pasta dish and arrange mussels, in their shells, around the edge of the dish. Serve immediately.

305

First dinners for new spouses can be more exciting than romantic. Our first meal ended in smoke and rubble when the neighbor's cat slipped in the window, and Otis, our dog, seized the opportunity for a vigorous chase through the house.

SPAGHETTI CARBONARA

Serves 4 - 6

Average

Serve with a crusty bread and spinach salad.

2   large chopped spanish onions

1   tablespoon olive oil

1   chopped clove garlic

1   pound spaghetti, linguine, or fettuccine

2   beaten eggs

½   pound fried crumbled bacon

1   bunch chopped parsley

1   cup Parmesan cheese

    cracked black pepper

 Cook onions slowly in olive oil until transparent.

 Add garlic and continue cooking until onions are brown.

 Cook pasta according to package directions, drain, do not rinse.

 Toss pasta with egg, coat well.

 Add bacon and parsley, stir in Parmesan cheese and sprinkle with cracked black pepper. Serve immediately.

SPICY SPAGHETTI SAUCE

Serves 8 to 10

Average

Ground turkey and turkey sausage may be substituted to make this dish lowfat. Can be made in a crockpot. Don't omit chili powder!

1½ pounds ground beef

½ pound Italian sausage

1 medium chopped onion

1 medium chopped green pepper

½ pound sliced mushrooms

3 (6 ounce) cans tomato paste

1 (32 ounce) can whole tomatoes, undrained and coarsely chopped

3 (8 ounce) cans tomato sauce

2 tablespoons Worcestershire sauce

2 teaspoons chili powder

2 teaspoons oregano

1 teaspoon Italian seasoning

¼ teaspoon garlic powder

⅓ cup red wine

1 cup water, optional

▲ Brown meat, onion, mushrooms, and green pepper in Dutch oven until vegetables are tender and meat is browned.

▲ Stir to crumble meat.

▲ Drain and add remaining ingredients.

▲ Cover, reduce heat, and simmer one hour, stirring occasionally.

▲ May need to add up to one cup water if sauce becomes too thick.

Warm precooked pasta noodles by plunging them into boiling water for a minute and draining.

ZITI SAUSAGE CASSEROLE

Serves 6 to 8

Easy, can be made ahead and frozen

Excellent for casual winter gatherings.

1	pound ziti noodles
3	pounds mild Italian sausages
1	medium chopped yellow onion
3	minced garlic cloves
2	large chopped green peppers
1	(2½ pound) can Italian style tomatoes, quartered, not drained
1	cup beef broth
1	tablespoon Italian seasoning
1	pound shredded mozzarella cheese

▲ Prepare pasta according to package directions, then set aside.

▲ Brown sausage in large skillet.

▲ Add onion, garlic and green pepper and sauté 5 minutes.

▲ Add tomatoes, broth and Italian seasoning and simmer covered for 30 minutes.

▲ Remove sausage and sauce from heat, remove sausages and cut them into 1½ inch lengths.

▲ Combine pasta, sausage and sauce in a large casserole dish and bake uncovered in 350° oven for 30 minutes.

▲ Stir in cheese and bake 15 minutes, serve warm.

THREE PEPPER PASTA WITH ITALIAN SAUSAGE

Serves 4 to 6

Average

A pasta lover's delight.

1 pound ½" sliced pieces of mild to medium Italian sausage

1 thinly sliced red pepper

1 thinly sliced yellow pepper

1 thinly sliced green pepper

1 pound fresh uncooked fettuccine

1½ cups grated Parmesan cheese

¼ fresh basil leaves

3 cups heavy cream

2 tablespoons sherry to taste

salt and pepper

◢ Brown sausage and sauté peppers in skillet, drain and set aside.

◢ Cook pasta as directed, drain and rinse.

◢ Place pasta in a large saucepan, stir in Parmesan cheese, basil, cream, sherry, salt and pepper. Cook over low heat, stirring constantly until thoroughly heated.

◢ Top with sausage and pepper mixture and serve immediately.

309

Ham, chicken or seafood may be substituted for the sausage. Fresh asparagus and mushrooms may be added or substituted for the peppers.

W I N T E R P A S T A

Serves 8

Average

A hearty pasta dish with robust taste.

6   boneless chicken breasts, cut into 1" cubes (may substitute 1½ pounds of Italian sausage)

¼   cup olive oil, divided

2   teaspoons oregano

8   ounces sliced mushrooms

¼   cup butter or margarine

¼   cup white wine

½   teaspoon garlic powder

1   pound fresh linguine noodles

8   ounces crumbled feta cheese

6   slices cooked, drained, and sliced bacon

1   (14 ounce) can drained and sliced artichoke hearts

1   large can drained and sliced pitted black olives

¼   cup pine nuts

     fresh ground black pepper

◢ Place chicken in a frying pan with a tablespoon of olive oil and the oregano. Brown until cooked, drain and set aside.

◢ In the same skillet, sauté mushrooms with butter, white wine and garlic powder. Remove from heat.

◢ Cook pasta according to package directions, adding a teaspoon of olive oil in the water to keep the noodles from sticking together. Drain pasta and place in serving bowl.

◢ Pour the remaining olive oil and feta cheese over pasta and toss until well coated.

◢ To pasta mixture, add chicken, bacon, artichoke hearts, mushroom mixture, olives and pine nuts. Toss well.

◢ Sprinkle with fresh pepper and serve immediately. May be refrigerated and served cold.

CHICKEN PECAN FETTUCCINE

Serves 6

Average

A delicious pasta which will become a family favorite.

10   ounces fresh fettuccine

1   pound boneless, skinless chicken breasts, cut into ¾ inch pieces

¾   cup butter, divided

3   cups sliced fresh mushrooms

1   cup sliced green onions

¾   teaspoon salt, divided

½   teaspoon white pepper, divided

½   teaspoon garlic powder

1   egg yolk

⅔   cup half and half or milk

2   tablespoons chopped fresh parsley

½   cup grated fresh Parmesan cheese

1   cup toasted chopped pecans

◢ Cook fettuccine in boiling salted water until al dente. Drain well.

◢ Melt ¼ cup butter in a large skillet, sauté chicken until lightly browned. Remove chicken and set aside.

◢ To drippings in skillet, add mushrooms, green onions, ½ teaspoon salt, ¼ teaspoon pepper, ¼ teaspoon garlic powder. Return chicken to skillet and simmer for 20 minutes or until chicken is done.

◢ Melt ½ cup butter and combine with egg yolk, half and half, parsley, and remaining salt, pepper and garlic powder. Stir butter sauce into fettuccine. Sprinkle with cheese, tossing until well mixed.

◢ Add chicken and mushroom mixture, toss until combined.

◢ Arrange fettuccine on a warm platter and sprinkle with toasted pecans and sprinkle with fresh ground black pepper and parsley. Serve immediately.

311

We enjoy making homemade pasta and often invite our guests to participate in making the noodles and sauces. Hanging fettuccine all over the kitchen makes for a festive atmosphere!

GRILLED CHICKEN FETTUCCINE IN MUSHROOM AND PEPPER SAUCE

Serves 4

Gourmet, may be partially made ahead

A great pasta for entertaining.

½ cup olive oil

½ cup minced fresh basil, divided

3 tablespoons lemon juice

2 teaspoons minced fresh garlic

1½ pounds boneless, skinless chicken breasts

1 medium red bell pepper

1 medium yellow bell pepper

3 tablespoons unsalted butter, divided

½ cup dry white wine

½ cup chicken broth

2 cups heavy cream

4 ounces sliced fresh mushrooms (approximately 1 cup)

½ teaspoon salt

12 ounces freshly cooked and drained fettuccine

½ cup freshly grated Parmesan cheese

◢ Mix oil, ¼ cup basil, lemon juice, and garlic in a shallow dish. Add chicken, turn to coat. Cover and marinate in refrigerator at least 3 hours or overnight.

◢ To make sauce, peel bell peppers with vegetable peeler, reserve skins. Cut peppers into very thin strips.

◢ Melt 1½ tablespoon butter in a small saucepan over low heat. Add pepper peels and cook 2 minutes or until tender. Stir in wine and chicken broth. Increase heat to high and boil until only 1 tablespoon of liquid remains.

◢ Add cream, stir constantly, and cook for 4 minutes or until mixture is reduced by half and thick enough to coat the back of a spoon.

◢ In a large skillet, melt the remaining 1½ tablespoon of butter over medium-high heat. Add mushrooms and cook about 2 minutes until browned.

◢ Pour in cream sauce through a sieve. Remove from heat, stir in salt, then pepper strips. (Can be refrigerated at this point, warm over low heat when ready.)

◢ Drain chicken, broil or grill, turning once until opaque. Cut in chunks or slices.

◢ Add to hot pasta in large bowl. Stir remaining basil and cheese into warm sauce. Pour sauce over chicken and pasta. Toss and serve.

Pasta

CHICKEN TARRAGON PASTA WITH GORGONZOLA AND ASPARAGUS

Serves 4 - 6

Easy

Absolutely delicious!

1 pound fresh asparagus

¾ pound linguine or fettuccine

2 tablespoons butter

1½ cups thin strips of chicken

1 cup heavy cream

⅛ teaspoon red pepper flakes

3 tablespoons finely chopped shallots

⅛ teaspoon nutmeg

¼ pound cubed Gorgonzola cheese

2 tablespoons fresh tarragon or ½ teaspoon dried

½ cup freshly grated Parmesan cheese

Trim and clean asparagus and cut along diagonal into 1½ inch lengths. Drop into boiling water to blanch, drain and set aside.

Cook pasta until al dente and drain.

Heat butter in large pan, add chicken and stir fry until cooked, whisk in cream, red pepper, shallots, nutmeg and blend.

Add Gorgonzola cheese and cook just to melt. Add tarragon and asparagus, add pasta to sauce and toss well.

Turn into warmed casserole dish. Serve immediately with freshly grated Parmesan cheese.

313

ANGEL HAIR PASTA WITH WALNUT SAUCE

Serves 6

Average

A terrific nut sauce with a little zip.

¾	pound angel hair pasta
1	can drained and rinsed flat anchovy filets
6	minced garlic cloves
6	tablespoons olive oil
½	cup pine nuts
¾	cup chopped walnuts
4	tablespoons raisins
3	tablespoons minced parsley
¾	teaspoon dried basil
¼	teaspoon oregano
¼	teaspoon crushed red pepper
½	cup freshly grated Parmesan cheese
2	tablespoons minced fresh parsley

▲ In a skillet sauté anchovy filets with minced garlic in olive oil until anchovies are melted, do not brown.

▲ Add the nuts, raisins, parsley, basil, oregano and red pepper.

▲ Cook pasta according to package directions.

▲ Drain and toss pasta immediately with 1 tablespoon olive oil.

▲ Pour in sauce mixture and toss.

▲ Serve immediately, topped with Parmesan cheese and chopped parsley.

PASTA WITH AURORA SAUCE

Serves 4

Average

This creamy sauce with a hint of tomato is wonderful over stuffed ravioli or tortellini.

1	chopped tomato
¼	tablespoon butter
2	tablespoons flour
¼	cup white wine
1½	cups milk or cream
½	cup Parmesan cheese
1	minced garlic clove
1	teaspoon parsley
½	teaspoon basil
½	teaspoon white pepper
1	tablespoon tomato paste
1	package stuffed ravioli or tortellini

◢ Melt butter in a shallow pan, whisk in flour. Gradually add white wine, then milk or cream, whisking constantly.

◢ Add chopped tomato, Parmesan, garlic, herbs and tomato paste.

◢ Cook over low to medium heat, stirring frequently, until thickened.

◢ Toss with freshly cooked tortellini or spoon over ravioli. Serve immediately.

315

When preparing a pasta dish which is not a casserole, reheat the pasta and the sauce separately and combine at the last minute so all the sauce will not absorb.

PENNE WITH FRESH TOMATO SAUCE

Serves 6

Easy

Good hot or cold. Dynamite with garden tomatoes.

4   ripe peeled, cored and chopped tomatoes

12   fresh chopped basil leaves

2   garlic cloves

⅓   cup olive oil

½   cup white wine

ground black pepper to taste

½   teaspoon crushed red pepper

1   pound penne noodles

◢ Toss tomatoes, basil, white wine and olive oil together in a bowl.

◢ Place garlic cloves in garlic press and press over tomatoes. Sprinkle with crushed red pepper and black pepper. Let sit for at least one hour.

◢ Cook pasta according to package directions, drain.

◢ Toss tomato mixture with hot pasta, serve immediately. May garnish with fresh basil leaves.

PASTA WITH BRIE

Serves 8

Easy

A colorful and simple pasta. The sauce is also tasty as an appetizer on baguette slices.

4   large peeled, cored and cubed tomatoes

1   pound brie cheese

1   cup washed and dried fresh basil

3   large minced garlic cloves

1   cup olive oil

2½   teaspoons salt

½   teaspoon pepper

1½   pounds linguine noodles

     Parmesan cheese

◢ Remove rind from brie cheese and cut into small pieces.

◢ Cut basil in strips.

◢ Combine tomatoes, basil, brie, garlic with olive oil and salt and pepper. Cover and let sit at room temperature for 2 hours.

◢ Cook pasta according to package directions. Drain and put on platter.

◢ Cover with sauce and sprinkle with cheese.

317

R O A S T E D   V E G E T A B L E   P A S T A

Serves 6

Easy, can be made ahead

A good pasta for buffets.

2   pounds quartered leeks with greens

¼   cup olive oil

3   cloves minced garlic

¼   cup chicken broth

2   tablespoons fresh thyme leaves or 1 teaspoon dried

1   tablespoon coarse sea salt

coarsely ground black pepper to taste

6   ripe quartered tomatoes

½   pound sliced ¼" round yellow squash slices

½   cup pitted black olives

⅓   cup chopped flat leaf parsley

1   pound cooked fettuccine

▲ Preheat oven to 400°.

▲ Place leeks and minced garlic in a shallow pan and drizzle with olive oil and chicken broth. Sprinkle with thyme, salt and pepper. Cover with aluminum foil and bake for 30 minutes.

▲ Remove foil, add tomatoes, squash and olives. Bake uncovered for 45 minutes more until vegetables are tender, tossing vegetables once or twice.

▲ Remove vegetables from oven and adjust seasonings.

▲ Toss with parsley and cooked pasta in a large bowl. Serve hot or at room temperature.

ZITI WITH VODKA SAUCE

Serves 4

Easy

A delicate pink sauce delicious on all pastas.

2   tablespoons margarine

½   cup cream or low-fat sour cream with a little milk

½   cup Parmesan cheese

2   cloves garlic

1   teaspoon basil

2-3 tablespoons tomato sauce

     dash white pepper

8   ounces ziti pasta

1½   shots vodka

◢ Brown garlic in melted margarine.

◢ Add rest of ingredients, except vodka and pasta.

◢ Cook pasta according to package directions, drain.

◢ Add vodka to the sauce, pour over pasta and serve.

319

HERBED LASAGNA

Serves 12

Gourmet, can be made ahead
Fennel and rosemary give
this dish a wonderful flavor.

1   tablespoon olive oil

1½   finely chopped onions

1   chopped green pepper

1   clove minced garlic

1   (28 ounce) can crushed
     tomatoes

1   (6 ounce) can tomato
     paste

1   cup water

1   bay leaf in 2 pieces

1½   tablespoons fresh basil
     or 1½ teaspoons dried

1½   tablespoons fresh
     fennel or 1½ teaspoons
     dried

½   teaspoon ground black
     pepper

     salt to taste

1½   pounds hamburger or
     ground turkey

½   pound ground pork or
     ground turkey

1   tablespoon fresh
     rosemary or 1 teaspoon
     dried

1   tablespoon fresh
     oregano or 1 teaspoon
     dried

2   tablespoons olive oil

320

◢ For sauce, heat oil and add onion, green pepper and garlic. Sauté for 5 minutes.

◢ Add tomatoes, tomato paste, water, bay leaf, basil, fennel, pepper and salt. Bring to boil and simmer for 45 minutes.

◢ For meat, brown both meats in oil, add rosemary and oregano. When meat is fully cooked, drain and set aside.

◢ For filling, mix ricotta, mozzarella cheese, eggs, pepper and parsley in medium bowl.

◢ Preheat oven to 375°.

◢ To assemble lasagna, use either very large lasagna pan or two medium ones.

Continued on next page

HERBED LASAGNA (Continued)

1 pound ricotta cheese

1 pound grated mozzarella cheese

2 eggs

¼ teaspoon pepper

¼ cup finely chopped fresh parsley

1 pound cooked lasagna

½ cup grated Parmesan cheese or ¼ cup each of Parmesan and Romano cheese

▲ Begin by layering sauce, noodles, meat and cheese, ending with sauce. Sprinkle with ½ cup grated Parmesan cheese and bake for 45 minutes.

I prepared lasagna for my husband on our first date. It was so good he ate three helpings and suffered an attack of I-ate-too-much. He left early, and I was sure he was bored and wouldn't ask me out again. He still loves lasagna, and me.

MEXICAN LASAGNA

Serves 8 to 10

Average, can be made ahead

Stupendous lasagna that improves with age.

1   tablespoon olive oil

⅓   cup finely diced yellow onion

2   cloves minced garlic

1   pound ground beef or ground turkey

1   package taco seasoning

    water

1   (28 ounce) can Italian style tomatoes

1   cup salsa

1   teaspoon dried crumbled basil

½   teaspoon red pepper flakes

½   teaspoon salt

¼   teaspoon pepper

1   package wide lasagna noodles

1   (15 ounce) container ricotta cheese

1   egg

1   teaspoon cilantro

½   teaspoon red pepper

1   chopped jalapeño pepper

1   cup grated Monterey jack cheese with jalapeños

◢ Cook onion, garlic and meat in a large saucepan, until meat is completely browned.

◢ Add taco seasoning package and water according to directions.

◢ Mix well, add tomatoes, basil, red pepper, salt and pepper and simmer over low heat for 40 minutes, covered.

◢ Cook pasta according to package directions, rinse with cool water and set aside.

◢ Mix ricotta cheese, egg, cilantro, red pepper and jalapeño pepper together in a bowl and set aside.

◢ To assemble, place 2 to 3 tablespoons of salsa on bottom of 10 x 12 x 2 inch pan and smooth over bottom. Next layer lasagna noodles, spread cheese mixture over noodles to completely cover. Spread meat mixture on top of cheese mixture.

◢ Repeat this sequence two more times, then top with grated Monterey jack cheese. Bake at 350° for 50 minutes, serve warm.

Pasta

JULIE'S VEGETABLE LASAGNA

Serves 8 to 12

Easy, can be made ahead

A tasty alternative to a meat dish.

1   (16 ounce) package of large lasagna noodles

2   thawed packages chopped spinach

2   cups grated Parmesan or Romano cheese

2⅔ cups ricotta cheese

1   teaspoon salt

1   teaspoon pepper

½   teaspoon ground nutmeg

2   cloves minced garlic

1   large chopped onion

3   tablespoons olive or salad oil

1   (30 ounce) can tomato sauce

¼   cup dry red wine

½   teaspoon basil

½   teaspoon oregano

▲ Cook noodles according to package directions, drain and rinse twice in cold water, set aside.

▲ Squeeze excess moisture from spinach. In bowl, mix spinach and 1½ cups Romano/Parmesan cheeses.

▲ Add ricotta cheese, salt, ½ teaspoon pepper and nutmeg, mix well. Spread mixture along each noodle and roll in jelly roll.

▲ Stand rolled and filled noodles up on end, making sure they are not packed in, in 9 x 13 inch buttered baking dish.

▲ Sauté garlic and onion in oil on medium heat.

▲ Add tomato sauce, wine, basil, oregano and remaining ½ teaspoon pepper.

▲ Simmer uncovered for 10 minutes, spoon sauce on top of each noodle and pour remaining sauce on top.

▲ Bake uncovered at 350° for 30 minutes. After cooking, sprinkle leftover grated cheese on top.

THYME PESTO

Makes 1 cup

Average

Use over pasta or drizzle over grilled flank steak. Basil can be substituted for thyme.

1½   cups loosely packed fresh parsley

½   cup loosely packed fresh thyme leaves or 1 tablespoon crumbled dried leaves and ½ cup additional fresh parsley

½   cup grated Parmesan cheese

½   cup toasted pine nuts or walnuts

2   cloves garlic

½   cup olive oil

▲ Finely chop first 5 ingredients in food processor.

▲ With machine running, gradually add ½ cup olive oil. Continue processing until pesto is almost smooth.

▲ Season to taste with salt and pepper. Cover tightly and refrigerate.

▲ Pesto can be prepared up to 1 week ahead.

324

SUN-DRIED TOMATO PESTO

Serves 4

Easy

Serve over pasta or meat.

2   packages sun-dried tomatoes (3 to 4 ounce each) or 2 jars sun-dried tomato bits

1   (8 ounce) package toasted almonds

½   cup fresh Parmesan cheese

1½   cups extra virgin olive oil

▲ Boil whole tomatoes until just softened or use tomato bits straight from the jar. (Soften whole tomatoes or you'll burn up your food processor).

▲ Mix all ingredients in the food processor, add olive oil until well lubricated and process until nuts disappear.

APRICOT PASTA SALAD

Serves 6 to 8

Easy

Perfect for a summer luncheon.

4	ounces corkscrew pasta
¾	pound fresh quartered apricots
1	piece cooked, skinned, shredded chicken breast
½	pound julienned zucchini
1	julienned red pepper
2	tablespoons white wine vinegar
1	tablespoon sugar
¼	vegetable oil
3	tablespoons fresh basil or 1 tablespoon dried

◢ Cook pasta according to package directions, drain and cool.

◢ Combine pasta, chicken, zucchini, and red pepper in large bowl.

◢ To make dressing, combine apricots, white wine vinegar and sugar in blender, whirl until blended. Continue whirling slowly adding vegetable oil. Whirl until thick and smooth, stir in basil.

◢ Pour dressing over pasta mixture and toss.

325

Add a small amount of the dressing to pastas immediately after cooking to allow the flavors to absorb.

ORIENTAL PASTA SALAD

Serves 4 to 6

Easy, must be made ahead
Delicious and different.

⅓ cup rice wine vinegar

¼ cup soy sauce

1 tablespoon minced fresh ginger root

1 teaspoon minced garlic

⅓ cup sesame oil

⅓ cup vegetable oil

hot chili oil to taste

1 teaspoon sugar

½ teaspoon salt

½ teaspoon black pepper

1 pound spaghetti

8 ounces snow peas

1 cup finely chopped green onions with some green tops

½ cup coarsely chopped dry-roasted peanuts

½ cup chopped fresh parsley

1 thinly sliced sweet red pepper

1 head of lettuce

▲ To make vinaigrette, mix rice wine, soy sauce, ginger root, garlic, sesame oil, vegetable oil, hot chili oil, sugar, salt and pepper in jar and let stand at room temperature overnight.

▲ Cook pasta according to package directions, drain and rinse in cold water.

▲ Put pasta in bowl with ½ of vinaigrette and toss well, cool to room temperature and stir occasionally.

▲ Add snow peas, green onions, peanuts, sweet pepper, parsley and remaining vinaigrette, toss gently.

▲ Serve at room temperature on bed of leaf lettuce.

GRECIAN PASTA SALAD

Serves 8 to 12

Average

The dressing is also good for green salads with crumbled feta cheese.

¼ cup salad oil

2 tablespoons lemon juice

½ teaspoon salt

¼ cup wine vinegar

⅛ teaspoon pepper

1 teaspoon dried oregano leaves

1 (8 ounce) package corkscrew pasta

1 cup sliced green peppers

1 large sliced tomato

½ cup finely chopped green onion

½ pound crumbled feta cheese

½ cup sliced black olives

1 teaspoon dried dill weed

2 peeled, halved, seeded, and sliced cucumbers

◢ Mix together salad oil, lemon juice, salt, wine vinegar, pepper, and oregano in a jar and shake.

◢ Cook pasta according to package directions, drain, and put into bowl.

◢ Add dressing and mix, let cool.

◢ Add rest of ingredients to the pasta when cooled, cover and refrigerate 1 hour before serving.

327

Oregano and its sweeter cousin marjoram are almost indispensable to pasta dishes. These herbs go particularly well with tomatoes and vinaigrette.

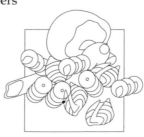

SESAME NOODLES WITH CHICKEN AND PEANUTS

Serves 6 - 8

Easy, can be made ahead

Can serve for a luncheon or buffet style, letting guests serve their own noodles, chicken and dressing separately.

¼ cup water

3 tablespoons sesame seed paste or peanut butter (½ of each)

3 tablespoons peanut oil

3 tablespoons red wine vinegar

1 teaspoon sugar

3 tablespoons light soy sauce

1 tablespoon sesame oil

1 pound fresh egg noodles, cooked and chilled 2 hours

1-2 cups shredded cooked chicken meat

½ cup chopped roasted peanuts

2 tablespoons toasted sesame seeds

¼ cup minced green onion or chives

▲ Combine water, sesame paste, peanut oil, red wine vinegar, sugar, light soy sauce, sesame oil, blend well and set aside. If substituting peanut butter for sesame seed paste, heat before blending.

▲ Place chilled noodles on serving dish and top with chicken, peanuts, sesame seeds and green onions.

▲ Drizzle dressing over and serve.

Pasta

MEXICAN CHICKEN FUSILLI SALAD

Serves 6 to 8

Average

You will love the taste of lime and spices.

3   tablespoons fresh lime juice

1½ tablespoons white wine vinegar

2   large minced garlic cloves

1-2 seeded and chopped jalapeño chilies (wear rubber gloves) or Tabasco juice to taste

1½ teaspoons ground cumin

⅔   cup olive oil

½   pound corkscrew fusilli pasta

2   grilled, skinned and chopped chicken breasts

1   finely chopped red bell pepper

1   finely chopped yellow bell pepper

1   quartered and thinly sliced red onion

1   can sliced black olives

⅓   finely chopped fresh coriander

    shredded romaine lettuce for garnish

2   peeled and diced avocados for garnish

▲ In a blender or food processor, blend together the lime juice, vinegar, garlic, jalapeños, cumin, salt and pepper until the mixture is smooth. With the motor running add the oil in a stream and blend the dressing until it is emulsified.

▲ In a large saucepan, bring plenty of salted water to a boil and cook pasta until al dente, drain and let cool.

▲ In a large bowl toss pasta with chicken, peppers, onion, black olives, coriander and dressing.

▲ Arrange romaine lettuce on a large platter, spoon the salad over it and scatter the avocados on top.

▲ Serve immediately.

SUN-DRIED TOMATOES AND SPINACH FETTUCCINE SALAD

Serves 4

Average

Also works well as a hot entree.

11   fresh basil leaves

2   large garlic cloves

5   oil-packed sun-dried tomato halves, drained

6   tablespoons olive oil

¼   cup balsamic vinegar

1   teaspoon salt

½   teaspoon sugar

¼   teaspoon dried red pepper flakes

2   pounds seeded and chopped ripe plum tomatoes

8   ounces cooked, drained spinach fettuccine

5   drained and chopped oil packed sun-dried tomatoes

5   basil leaves cut in thin strips

◢ To make dressing, place basil and garlic in food processor, using the steel blade. Scrape down sides of bowl.

◢ Add sun-dried tomato halves and finely chop. Add olive oil, vinegar, salt, sugar, and red-pepper flakes.

◢ Process for 2 minutes or until ingredients are puréed. Can be prepared 8 hours ahead, whisk before using.

◢ To make salad, place fettuccine, plum tomatoes, and sun-dried tomatoes in large bowl.

◢ Pour dressing over and toss, garnish with basil strips.

◢ Salad can be tossed 2 hours before serving. Bring to room temperature before serving.

Final Bows

DESSERTS

The Performing Arts

Colonial Annapolis was the center for the arts in the mid-Atlantic area. During the busy social season, visitors from Maryland and neighboring colonies gathered in Annapolis to see the latest plays from England and to hear the finest colonial musicians perform on the harpsichord. Over succeeding years, Annapolis has continued the reputation as a strong cultural arts center. A home to symphony, opera, and ballet companies at Maryland Hall for the Arts, Annapolis has a lengthy tradition of relishing the arts.

In addition to the classic performing arts, Annapolis is home to musical ensembles ranging from Renaissance music to cool jazz. The King of France Tavern offers performances by celebrities such as Ethel Ennis, Charlie Byrd, and the Ink Spots in an intimate setting. The superb acoustics of the Naval Academy Chapel and the Great Hall of St. John's College echo with exquisite choral and chamber music. Modern performers recreate the lively songs of the colonial period in historic settings.

Local theatre companies abound. Comedy clubs, dinner theatres, theatre-in-the-round, and theatre troupes at the Naval Academy, St. John's College, and Anne Arundel Community College provide many opportunities for area residents to enjoy topnotch productions ranging from Shakespeare to Gilbert and Sullivan to Broadway plays and musicals. Each fall, the Maryland Renaissance Festival recreates merry Tudor England with a cast of characters extending from Queen Elizabeth and her court to bawdy peasants peddling their wares.

The scenic vistas in and around Annapolis provide inspiration for every type of visual artist. Local guilds include watercolor artists, quilters, potters, sculptors, and jewelers. There is also a large contingent of oil painters and portrait artists who have lived in the area beginning with the famous colonial portrait artist, Charles Willson Peale. Boat designers and naval architects who are world renowned also claim Annapolis as their residence.

Interest in the arts extends to the youngest Annapolitans. Ballet, theatre, youth symphony orchestra, and an education program that offers summer camps for students of string, band, and chorus are only some of the cultural programs that are readily provided for talented area children.

Desserts

APPLE-FRANGIPANE TART

Serves 8

Gourmet

An elegant dessert for family and friends.

Crust

1¼ cups flour

⅔   cup sugar

¾   cup whole butter

1   egg

▲ Blend flour, sugar, whole butter, and egg. Blend quickly.

▲ Press into 9 inch springform pan bottom and half way up sides.

Frangipane

¾   cup almonds

2   tablespoons sugar

1   egg

6   tablespoons butter

½   cup flour

1   tablespoon amaretto

1   teaspoon almond extract

▲ Grind almonds and sugar until fine.

▲ Cream butter and sugar. Add egg and mix. Add ground almonds, flour, amaretto and almond extract.

▲ Spread onto crust. Marzipan paste may be substuted for frangipane.

Filling

3   yellow delicious apples

1   egg

½   cup sugar

½   cup heavy cream

1   teaspoon cinnamon

2   tablespoons kirsch

▲ Core and peel apples. Slice and arrange on top of frangipane.

▲ Cover with a mixture of egg, sugar, cream, cinnamon, and kirsch. Bake at 375° for 45 minutes.

BAKED ORANGE-CARDAMOM APPLES

Serves 4

Easy, can be made ahead

Delicious served over vanilla ice cream.

3   medium Granny Smith apples, peeled, quartered, cored and cut into ½ inch slices

2   tablespoons honey

2   tablespoons frozen orange juice concentrate

½   teaspoon fresh ground cardamom

1   tablespoon butter or margarine

▲ Arrange apples in an overlapping circle in a greased 9 inch pie pan.

▲ Stir together honey, orange concentrate and cardamom. Pour over apples and dot with butter.

▲ Bake in 375° oven, basting once with pan juices for 25 to 30 minutes or until tender.

The scarred wooden table in my parents' kitchen was the heart of our family's life. It served as a center for meals and homework, the daily discussion of activities, and late night conversations when we came home from dates. We celebrated in the dining room, but we grew up in the kitchen.

Desserts

GEORGE WASHINGTON APPLE PIE

Serves 8

Easy, can be made ahead

A classic dessert honoring Annapolis's most famous visitor.

5   cups pared, thinly sliced apples (5-6 apples)

1   cup sugar

1   tablespoon flour

1   teaspoon cinnamon

½   teaspoon nutmeg

1   teaspoon lemon juice

1   prepared double crust pastry

Preheat oven to 425°. Line 9 inch pie pan with pastry. Mix 1 tablespoon of sugar with flour and sprinkle over pastry.

Mix remaining sugar with spices and lemon juice. Fill shell with alternative layers of apples and sugar mixture. Dot with butter.

Cover with top of pastry. Cut several steam vents. Cover edges of pastry with narrow strips of foil (to prevent over browning of pie crust).

Bake at 425° for 30 to 40 minutes or until crust is nicely browned.

FRESH STRAWBERRY PIE

Serves 8

Easy, must be made ahead

A colorful pie that also makes elegant tarts.

¾ cup sugar

2 tablespoons cornstarch

1½ cups water

¼ cup regular strawberry jello (½ of 3 ounce box)

1 quart fresh strawberries, washed and hulled

1 baked 9 inch pastry

336

Mix sugar and cornstarch in small saucepan. Stir in water. Heat over medium heat until mixture is clear.

Add jello and stir well. Let cool. Fill pastry shell with fresh strawberries.

Pour sauce over all and let sit until sauce has thickened. Refrigerate.

Desserts

FOURTH OF JULY BLUEBERRY CREAM PIE

Serves 6

Average, must be made ahead

Take your family blueberry picking & make this treat to reward their work.

1	cup sour cream
2	tablespoons all-purpose flour
¾	cup sugar
1	teaspoon vanilla
¼	teaspoon salt
1	egg
2½	cups fresh blueberries
1	unbaked 9 inch pie shell
3	tablespoons flour
1½	tablespoons butter
3	tablespoons chopped pecans (optional)

◢ Combine sour cream, all-purpose flour, sugar, vanilla, salt, and egg in large bowl. Beat with electric mixer about 5 minutes or until smooth.

◢ Fold in blueberries. Pour into shell and bake at 400° for 25 minutes. Remove from oven.

◢ Combine flour, butter, chopped pecans, stir well with fork. Sprinkle over pie, bake for an additional 10 minutes. Chill before serving.

337

CREAMY PEACH-BLACKBERRY COBBLER

Serves 8

Average

A distinctive custardy fruit dish.

Topping:

1	cup all-purpose flour
½	cup sugar
6	tablespoons softened butter
1	teaspoon vanilla extract

Filling:

⅔	cup all-purpose flour
1¾	cups sugar
¼	teaspoon cinnamon
5	eggs
1	teaspoon vanilla extract
2	cups milk
½	cup whipping cream
4	cups peaches, peeled and cut in ¼ wedges
2	cups blackberries, rinsed
	butter for greasing dish
2	cups whipping cream, optional
2	tablespoons powdered sugar, optional

◢ To make the topping, combine flour and sugar, cut in butter until mixture resembles coarse cornmeal. Add vanilla extract, mix thoroughly and set aside.

◢ Preheat oven to 400°, lightly butter a 13 x 9 x 2 inch baking pan.

◢ To make filling, combine the flour, sugar, cinnamon, eggs, vanilla extract, milk and ½ cup of cream in a blender or food processor.

◢ Line the dish with the peaches and berries.

◢ Carefully pour the custard filling over the fruit and bake for 30 minutes.

◢ Sprinkle the topping over the cobbler and bake 15 to 20 minutes, until the topping is brown and a knife inserted comes out clean.

◢ Serve warm. If desired, sweeten 2 cups cream with powdered sugar and serve on the side.

338

Desserts

BANANAS FOSTER

Serves 4

Average, cannot be made ahead

A show stopper for an intimate dinner.

4	tablespoons butter
½	teaspoon cinnamon
4	bananas, cut in half lengthwise, then halved
1	cup brown sugar
4	tablespoons banana liqueur
4	scoops vanilla ice cream
¾	cup of rum

◢ Melt butter over an alcohol burner in a flambé pan or attractive saucepan. Add the sugar, cinnamon, and banana liqueur and stir to mix.

◢ Heat for a few minutes, then place the halved bananas in the sauce.

◢ Add the rum and allow it to heat well, then ignite the sauce with a match. Allow the sauce to flame until it dies out, tipping the pan with a circular motion to prolong the flame.

◢ Carefully lift the bananas from the pan onto the ice cream, then spoon the hot sauce from the pan over the bananas.

CRÊPES WITH LEMON LISBON SAUCE

Serves 12 to 14

Gourmet, can be made ahead, partially

An elegant dessert that will have your guests begging for more.

Crêpes

3½ cups flour

¾ cup sugar plus 2 tablespoons

12 eggs

4 tablespoons oil

1½ quarts milk

1 pinch of salt

¼ cup orange flavored liqueur

Lisbon Sauce

¾ cup sugar (or more)

2 tablespoons grated lemon peel

1 stick butter

¼ cup brandy

¼ orange flavored liqueur

2 tablespoons lemon juice

thin lemon slices & mint leaves to garnish

◢ Mix crêpe ingredients in blender until smooth; let stand for 1 hour.

◢ Use crêpe pan or small frying pan over medium heat, butter pan with paper towel (keep butter to a minimum) and wipe off excess.

◢ Pour 1 tablespoon of batter into pan and swirl pan making batter cover entire pan with very thin mix.

◢ Turn when light brown.

◢ Stack crêpes, cover with plastic wrap. Crêpes can be frozen, do not refrigerate.

◢ Mix butter, brandy, orange flavored liqueur and lemon juice and heat.

◢ Place crêpes in oven proof dish, folding them in half and then half again.

◢ Arrange in dish placing one on top of another around the dish, making a circular or oval pattern. Sprinkle liberally with sugar and lemon peel.

◢ Can be made ahead to this point on the same day as serving, cover tightly with plastic wrap, can be kept at room temperature.

◢ Pour a little of the sauce over the crêpes.

◢ Place in broiler 5 inches from heat until sugar is melted and bubbling.

◢ Serve remaining sauce with crêpes, garnish with lemon slices & mint leaves.

◢ Allow 4 to 5 crêpes per serving.

◢ For a variation, fill crêpes with orange marmalade and dust with powdered sugar.

Desserts

RASPBERRY FLAMBÉ

Serves 6

Easy, can be made ahead
Sophisticated & colorful.

1 package (10 ounces) frozen raspberries

½ cup orange juice

1 tablespoon cornstarch

⅓ cup brandy

◢ Thaw raspberries, drain and reserve liquid. Combine liquid and cornstarch in saucepan. Add orange juice. Bring to a boil, stirring 2 to 3 minutes.

◢ Add raspberries, stirring gently.

◢ In a small pan heat brandy until bubbles form around edge of pan. Ignite with a match and pour over raspberry sauce. Serve the flaming sauce over ice cream in individual heat resistant dishes.

LEMON CHIFFON CAKE

Serves 8-10

Average, can be made ahead
A refreshing dessert that tastes as good as it looks.

48 ladyfingers

4 eggs, separated

2 grated lemon rinds

½ cup lemon juice

1 can condensed milk

¼ cup sugar

1 cup whipping cream to garnish

◢ Preheat oven to 500°, spray 9 inch springform pan with a nonstick vegetable spray. Line sides of pan with ladyfingers, tear remaining ladyfingers into pieces and sprinkle on the bottom of pan.

◢ Beat egg yolks. Add lemon rind, lemon juice and milk to egg yolks and beat well.

◢ Beat 2 whites until stiff and fold into yolk mixture, pour into pan.

◢ Make meringue by beating remaining 2 egg whites with sugar until stiff.

◢ Cover pan with meringue.

◢ Turn off oven, place in oven for 40 minutes, cool completely before removing sides of pan, chill.

◢ Serve with whipped cream, best served the day prepared.

KEY LIME MOUSSE

Serves 6

Gourmet

A light as air dessert perfect for a luncheon or shower.

1	package unflavored gelatin
2	tablespoons white wine
⅓	cup key lime juice
2	tablespoons grated lime rind
3	eggs
3	tablespoons sugar
5	tablespoons sugar
1	cup of whipping cream
8	thin ¼ slices of lime

◢ Bring the eggs to room temperature by placing in a bowl filled with warm water for five minutes. Separate, beat egg yolks with 3 tablespoons of sugar.

◢ Warm white wine in a double boiler, stir in gelatin until it starts softening, then add the white wine and lime juice, cook until the gelatin is dissolved.

◢ Gradually stir in egg yolks, remove from heat and stir in lime rind. Let cool, but not beyond pourability stage.

◢ Whip cream in a chilled bowl, set aside.

◢ Beat egg whites until they form soft peaks, gradually add 5 tablespoons of sugar until the whites form stiff peaks.

◢ Fold whipped cream into the egg whites, gradually fold in the cooled lime gelatin mixture, thoroughly blend.

◢ Spoon the mousse into individual sherbet glasses and garnish with a lime slice, chill for 3 hours before serving. Serve with powdered tea cookies.

TANGERINE MOUSSE WITH CHOCOLATE SAUCE

Serves 6

Gourmet, must be made ahead

A tempting blend of citrus and chocolate.

1   package unflavored gelatin

2   tablespoons triple sec

⅓   cup tangerine juice (2 to 3 tangerines)

3   eggs at room temperature

3   tablespoons sugar

5   tablespoons sugar

1   cup of whipping cream

6   ounces chocolate chips

1½   tablespoons butter

1   tablespoon triple sec

12   fresh mint leaves

◢ Separate eggs. Beat egg yolks with 3 tablespoons of sugar.

◢ Warm triple sec in a double boiler, stir in gelatin until it starts softening, then add the tangerine juice, cook until the gelatin is dissolved. Gradually stir in egg yolks, remove from heat, let cool. Whip cream in a chilled bowl, set aside.

◢ Beat egg whites until they form soft peaks, gradually add 5 tablespoons of sugar until the whites form stiff peaks. Fold whipped cream into the egg whites, gradually fold in the cooled tangerine gelatin mixture, thoroughly blend.

◢ Spoon the mousse into individual molds, chill for 3 hours before serving.

◢ To serve, melt the chocolate chips and butter in a double boiler over low heat.

◢ Remove from heat and stir in the triple sec.

◢ Gently unmold each mousse by placing the mold briefly on a towel moistened with warm water and loosening edges with a knife.

◢ Reverse onto the dessert plate and drizzle chocolate sauce around the mousse. Garnish the top of the mousse with two mint leaves.

Final Bows

STRAWBERRY WALNUT SQUARES

Serves 12 to 15

Easy, must be made ahead and frozen

Refreshing summer dessert trimmed with fresh strawberries.

1   cup flour

¼   cup packed brown sugar

½   chopped walnuts

½   cup melted butter or margarine

2   egg whites

¾   cup sugar

2   tablespoons lemon juice

1   (10 ounce) package frozen strawberries, thawed & drained

1   cup whipped cream or 4½ ounces frozen whipped dessert topping, thawed

▲ Preheat oven to 350°

▲ Mix flour, brown sugar, walnuts, and butter together. Spread evenly in a 9 x 13 x 2 inch pan. Bake 20 minutes, stirring occasionally.

▲ When lightly browned, remove from oven, let cool. Put aside ⅓ of this mixture for garnish.

▲ Leave remaining ⅔ of baked mixture sprinkled in same baking pan.

▲ Combine egg whites, sugar, strawberries and lemon juice. Beat at low speed until mixture thickens (approximately 2 minutes.) Beat at high speed until stiff peaks form (approximately 10 to 12 minutes.)

▲ Fold in whipped cream or dessert topping. Spoon evenly into pan onto crumbled mixture. Top with remaining crumb garnish.

▲ Freeze 6 hours or overnight. Serve with fresh strawberries if desired.

Desserts

MOCHA RASPBERRY TRIFLE

Serves 12

Average, can be made ahead

A rich variation of classic English trifle.

1   box brownie mix

4   egg yolks

¼   cup cornstarch

¾   cup sugar

1½   cups milk

1   tablespoon instant coffee dissolved in 1 tablespoon water

1   tablespoon vanilla extract

1½   pints whipping cream

⅓   cup kahlua

12   ounces fresh or frozen raspberries

1   ounce grated dark chocolate

▲ Make brownies per instructions, bake in two 9 inch cake pans, cool.

▲ Custard: Whisk egg yolks, cornstarch and sugar together in saucepan until smooth.

▲ Heat milk separately and gradually stir into yolk mixture, cook, stirring constantly until mixture boils and thickens.

▲ Add combined coffee, water, and vanilla extract. Cover surface with plastic wrap to prevent skin forming and cool to room temperature.

▲ Beat cream until soft peaks form and fold ½ into custard.

▲ Place one pan of brownies in bottom of large glass bowl. Pour evenly ½ kahlua over top.

▲ Add layer of ½ raspberries and sprinkle with ⅓ of grated chocolate.

▲ Spread on half the custard, repeat layers.

▲ Decorate with rest of whipped cream, remaining chocolate and rest of raspberries.

CHOCOLATE MOUSSE TORTE

Serves 8

Average, must make ahead

This chocolate lover's delight will become a family favorite.

1 package chocolate wafers (3 cups)

½ cup melted butter

2 cups whipping cream

¼ cup sugar

4 eggs, separated

12 ounces semisweet chocolate

2 whole eggs

2 tablespoons almond liqueur or extract

1 teaspoon vanilla extract

whipped cream & chocolate shavings for garnish

◢ Spray a ten inch spring form pan with cooking spray.

◢ Crumble chocolate wafers in food processor, add butter and mix thoroughly. Press on sides and bottom of pan, put in freezer while making rest of recipe.

◢ Whip cream until soft peaks form, add sugar and beat until combined. In separate bowls, beat 4 egg whites until stiff.

◢ Melt chocolate in double boiler over medium heat, cool to lukewarm.

◢ To make egg mixture, beat 2 whole eggs, then one at a time, add the 4 remaining egg yolks. Add chocolate.

◢ Add flavorings or extracts and 1 cup of beaten egg white to egg mixture. Fold remaining egg whites into whipped cream, add chocolate mixture until completely incorporated.

◢ Turn into prepared crust, chill overnight (at least 6 hours), or freeze and thaw ½ hour at room temperature before serving.

◢ Serve with whipped cream and chocolate shavings.

Desserts

CINNAMON CHOCOLATE TORTE

Serves 6

Gourmet, can be made ahead
All your favorite tastes!

2 eggs, separated

¼ teaspoon salt

½ cup sugar

½ teaspoon white vinegar

2 teaspoons cinnamon

6 ounces semi-sweet chocolate bits

¼ cup water

¾ teaspoon cinnamon

1 cup whipping cream

¼ cup sugar

walnuts for garnish

▲ Combine egg whites, salt, ½ cup sugar, ½ teaspoon white vinegar and 2 teaspoons cinnamon, beat until stiff.

▲ Spread meringue on brown paper making sides 1 inch high, bake at 275° for one hour. Turn off heat and let meringue dry for two hours.

▲ Melt chocolate bits and spread 2 teaspoons over cool meringue shell.

▲ To rest of chocolate add 2 egg yolks and ¼ cup of water, beat together, chill until thick.

▲ In a separate bowl whip 1 cup whipping cream with ¼ cup sugar and ¾ teaspoon cinnamon. Put half of this whipped cream on top of chocolate in meringue shell.

▲ Fold other half of whipped cream into chocolate/egg yolk mixture and spread on top of second layer (whipped cream).

▲ Garnish with walnuts.

COFFEE ALMOND MACAROON DELIGHT

Serves 6

Average, must make ahead

Almond macaroon cookies are sometimes difficult to find but are worth the trouble. Check with your bakery or in the freezer dessert section.

1 (4 ounce) package sliced almonds

butter

½ gallon coffee ice cream

2 dozen almond macaroon cookies

¼ cup rum

12 ounces whipping cream

◢ Soften coffee ice cream.

◢ Brown almonds in butter, save for topping.

◢ Crumble enough macaroon to line bottom of serving dish into a bowl, mix with rum, line bottom of serving dish with macaroons.

◢ Put coffee ice cream in a layer over macaroons. Put whipping cream in a layer over ice cream, sprinkle with almonds.

◢ Put in freezer for 1 to 2 hours before serving.

348

FUDGIE ICE CREAM SQUARES

Serves 9

Easy

Great for a children's party!

24 chocolate sandwich cookies

4 tablespoons melted butter

1 quart softened ice cream

1 cup commercial chocolate fudge topping

1 cup whipping cream

¼ cup powdered sugar

½ cup chopped nuts, optional

◢ Crush cookies (filling included) in blender or by hand to make 2¼ cups crumbs. Combine with butter, pat in 9 inch square pan.

◢ Cover with layer of ice cream, freeze.

◢ Remove from freezer, cover with fudge topping.

◢ Whip cream with powdered sugar, spread on top of dessert. Sprinkle with chopped nuts.

◢ Cover, freeze until ready to serve.

349

CHEESECAKE ALMANDINE

Serves 16

Average, must make ahead

This sour cream cheesecake has a delicate flavor.

1½ cups finely crushed vanilla wafer crumbs

1¼ cups sugar

½ cup finely chopped pecans

½ teaspoon grated lemon rind

¼ cup melted margarine

3 (8 ounce) packages softened cream cheese

3 eggs

¾ teaspoon almond extract

⅔ cup chopped almonds, blanched

1 cup dairy sour cream

⅓ cup sliced toasted almonds

◢ Combine wafer crumbs, 2 tablespoons sugar, pecans, lemon rind and melted margarine. Press into the bottom of greased 8 inch springform pan and refrigerate.

◢ Mix cream cheese and 1 cup sugar until light and fluffy. Add eggs, one at a time, beating well after each addition.

◢ Blend in ½ teaspoon almond extract and chopped almonds, pour into chilled crust. Bake at 375° for 45 minutes and cool 30 minutes.

◢ Blend sour cream, remaining 2 tablespoons sugar and ¼ teaspoon almond extract.

◢ Spread over cooled filling. Bake for another 10 minutes and then sprinkle with almonds and cool. Refrigerate overnight before serving.

1 ounce of low-fat cottage cheese (blenderized) or 1 ounce low-fat cream cheese can be used as a partial or total substitute for 1 ounce cream cheese.

Desserts

WHITE CHOCOLATE BLACKBERRY CHEESECAKE

Serves 8-10

Gourmet, must make ahead

Your guests will rave about this cheesecake. Other berries work well, too!

1½ cups chocolate cookie crumbs

3 tablespoons sugar

6 tablespoons melted butter

1 teaspoon raspberry liqueur

3 (8 ounce) packages softened cream cheese

3 eggs

2 tablespoons flour

1 cup sugar

4 ounces white chocolate

2 tablespoons butter

1 tablespoon raspberry liqueur or extract

1 pint blackberries, washed and drained

½ cup blackberry or raspberry preserves

◢ Preheat oven to 375°. Spray 10 inch springform pan with cooking spray.

◢ Combine cookie crumbs, 3 tablespoons sugar, 6 tablespoons melted butter and liqueur in a small bowl with a fork.

◢ Turn into pan and gently press from center around sides to make crust.

◢ Melt white chocolate and 2 tablespoons butter in a double boiler over medium low heat, set aside to cool.

◢ Beat cream cheese until fluffy, gradually add eggs, 1 cup sugar and flour at low speed. Add white chocolate mixture and raspberry liqueur.

◢ Gently spread into pan and bake for 45 minutes or until lightly browned.

◢ When cake is done, turn off heat. After 10 minutes, open oven slightly, but keep in oven until completely cool.

◢ Arrange berries on top and glaze with preserves, keep in refrigerator for at least 8 hours. Can be made up to two days ahead.

◢ Unmold from springform pan just before serving.

BLACK RUSSIAN CAKE

Serves 8 to 12

Easy, can be made ahead
Packed with flavor!

1   package dark chocolate cake mix

½   cup salad oil

1   (4½ ounce) package instant chocolate pudding

¾   cup strong coffee

3   ounces kahlua

3   ounces creme de cacao

4   eggs, room temperature

Glaze:

1   cup sifted powdered sugar

2   tablespoons strong coffee

2   tablespoons kahlua

2   tablespoons creme de cacao

◢ Combine cake mix, salad oil, pudding mix, coffee, kahlua, creme de cacao and eggs in a large mixing bowl. Beat 4 minutes at medium speed or until smooth.

◢ Spoon into well greased bundt pan and bake at 350° for 45 to 50 minutes.

◢ Remove cake from pan when cool.

◢ Punch holes in cake with cake tester or meat fork.

◢ Combine powdered sugar, coffee, kahlua, cream de cacao and mix well. Spoon topping over cake and let set before serving.

Substitute 1/2 cup nonfat plain yogurt for 1 egg and 3 tablespoons oil or 2 tablespoons oil and 2 tablespoons nonfat yogurt for 1/4 cup oil in cake or brownie mixes.

BLACK WALNUT CAKE

Serves 8-12

Average, can be made ahead

A rich, moist cake with great taste.

¼ cup softened butter

¼ cup softened margarine

¼ cup shortening

2½ cups sugar

5 eggs

2 teaspoons vanilla extract

3 cups flour

½ teaspoon salt

½ teaspoon baking powder

1 cup milk

1 cup chopped black walnuts

◢ Grease 10 x 4 inch tube pan.

◢ Cream together butter, margarine, and shortening until light and fluffy.

◢ Add sugar and cream until light. Add eggs, one at a time, beat well. Add vanilla extract.

◢ Sift flour, salt and baking powder. Add this to the creamed mixture, alternating with milk.

◢ Beat well, until batter looks like cream.

◢ Fold in black walnuts, pour into pan. Bake at 350° for 1 hour and 30 minutes, starting with a cold oven.

353

I've always enjoyed wandering down to the kitchen after goodnights have been said and the house becomes quiet and dark. Some of the best conversations I have had with family members have been over some cake and milk in the midnight stillness.

FABULOUS CHOCOLATE SHEET CAKE

Serves 20

Average, can be made ahead and frozen

Make this ahead for your next birthday party.

2 cups sugar

2 cups unsifted all purpose flour

1 stick margarine

3½ tablespoons cocoa

½ cup shortening

1 cup water

2 eggs

1 teaspoon vanilla extract

½ cup buttermilk

1 teaspoon baking soda

1 stick margarine

3½ tablespoons cocoa

⅓ cup milk

1 box powdered sugar, sifted

1 cup chopped pecans

1 teaspoon vanilla extract

◢ Mix sugar and flour.

◢ Place 1 stick of margarine, cocoa, shortening and water in saucepan and bring to boil. Pour over sugar and flour mixture and stir.

◢ Add eggs, vanilla extract, buttermilk and soda.

◢ Mix well and pour into ungreased sheet pan 11 x 18 inch or two smaller pans. Bake about 20 minutes at 400°.

◢ Start cooking frosting 5 minutes before cake is done.

◢ Bring 1 stick of margarine, cocoa and milk to a boil.

◢ Remove from heat and add powdered sugar, nuts and vanilla extract.

◢ Pour over hot cake you have removed from oven. When cool, cut in squares.

Desserts

GRAND MARNIER POUND CAKE

Serves 12

Average, can be made ahead

Excellent for brunch or a shower.

1½ cups softened butter or margarine

3 cups sugar

5 eggs

3½ cups flour

1 teaspoon cream of tartar

1½ teaspoons baking powder

¾ cup milk

¼ cup orange juice

¼ cup Grand Marnier

1 teaspoon vanilla extract

1 teaspoon almond extract

2 tablespoons grated orange rind

▲ Cream butter, add sugar and mix in blender until light and fluffy. Add eggs one at a time, beating after each addition.

▲ Sift flour, cream of tartar, and baking powder.

▲ Add flour mixture to creamed mixture alternating with milk, orange juice and Grand Marnier.

▲ Stir in flavorings and orange rind.

▲ Pour into greased and floured bundt pan. Bake at 325° for one hour and 20 minutes until cake springs back to the touch.

▲ Cool on wire rack, remove from pan onto serving plate.

To reduce fat content use 3/4 cup vegetable oil for 1 cup shortening or butter in baking.

ITALIAN CREAM CAKE

Serves 10-12

Gourmet, can be made ahead
Good enough to serve to
your most particular guests.

¾   cup softened butter or margarine

¼   cup shortening

2   cups sugar

5   eggs, separated

2   cups self rising flour

1   teaspoon baking soda

1   cup buttermilk

1   teaspoon vanilla extract

1   small can flaked coconut

1   cup chopped pecans

1   (8 ounce) package softened cream cheese

½   cup softened butter or margarine

1   (16 ounce) box powdered sugar

1   teaspoon vanilla extract

1   cup finely chopped pecans

▲ Preheat oven to 350°, grease and flour three 8 inch cake pans.

▲ Cream ¾ cup butter and ¼ cup shortening. Add sugar and beat until mixture is smooth.

▲ Add egg yolks and beat well.

▲ Combine flour and baking soda and add to creamed mixture, alternating with buttermilk.

▲ Stir in 1 teaspoon vanilla extract, add coconut and pecans.

▲ Fold in egg whites. Pour batter into cake pans and bake for 25 minutes or until cake tests done. Cool completely.

▲ Beat cream cheese and ½ cup butter until smooth.

▲ Add powdered sugar and mix well.

▲ Stir in 1 teaspoon vanilla extract.

▲ Spread on cake between layers and on top, sprinkle with finely chopped pecans.

DREAMY CHOCOLATE LOAF CAKE

Serves 8

Easy

A delectable cutting cake.

1 cup flour

1 cup sugar

½ cup cocoa

4 tablespoons butter

1 cup boiling water

1 teaspoon baking soda

1 egg

½ teaspoon vanilla extract

¼ teaspoon salt

◢ Mix together and hollow out flour, sugar and cocoa.

◢ Add remaining ingredients into hollow, making sure not to "cook" the egg with the boiling water.

◢ Stir by hand or mix with beaters until smooth and thoroughly mixed.

◢ Pour into greased and floured loaf pan.

◢ Bake at 350° for 45 minutes. Remove from oven and cool.

357

3 tablespoons dry cocoa powder and 1/2 tablespoon liquid oil is a low-fat substitute for 1 square of chocolate.

PINEAPPLE CARROT CAKE

Serves 8-10

Average

The best carrot cake you have ever tasted.

2   cups sugar

1¼ cups vegetable oil

4   eggs

2¼ cups flour

2   teaspoons baking soda

2   teaspoons cinnamon

2   cups finely grated carrots

1   (8 ounce) can crushed pineapple, well drained

½   cup butter

1   (8 ounce) package softened cream cheese

1   (16 ounce) package powdered sugar

1   teaspoon vanilla extract

1   cup chopped pecans

◢ Preheat oven to 350°, grease and flour three 8 inch cake pans.

◢ Cream sugar and oil, add eggs one at a time, beat after each addition.

◢ Sift together flour, baking soda and cinnamon, add to cream mixture, blend until mixed.

◢ Fold in carrots and pineapple.

◢ Pour into cake pans and bake for 30 minutes. Remove from oven and cool.

◢ Mix butter, cream cheese and sugar until creamy.

◢ Stir in vanilla extract and pecans.

◢ Frost between layers, tops and sides of cake.

PUMPKIN ROLL

Serves 10

Average, can be made ahead

Try this instead of pumpkin pie at Thanksgiving.

3   eggs

1   cup sugar

⅔   cup pumpkin

1   teaspoon lemon juice

¾   cup flour

1   teaspoon baking powder

1   teaspoon ginger

2   teaspoons cinnamon

½   teaspoon nutmeg

½   teaspoon salt

1   cup finely chopped pecans or walnuts

2   cups powdered sugar

1   (8 ounce) package softened cream cheese

½   cup softened butter or margarine

½   teaspoon vanilla extract

◢ Preheat oven to 375°, grease and flour a 15 x 10 x 1 inch jelly roll pan.

◢ Beat eggs on high speed for 5 minutes. Gradually beat sugar into egg mixture. Stir pumpkin and lemon juice into egg mixture.

◢ Sift together flour, baking powder, ginger, cinnamon, nutmeg and salt. Fold dry ingredients into pumpkin mixture. Spread into pan and top with chopped nuts.

◢ Bake for 15 minutes, remove from oven and turn out on towel sprinkled with powdered sugar.

◢ Starting at narrow end, roll towel and cake together. Let cool, and unroll.

◢ Combine sugar, cream cheese, butter and vanilla extract, beat until smooth. Spread over cake and roll back up.

◢ Store in the refrigerator until ready to slice and serve.

Nutmeg is a pungent spice most often used in baking and in cheese dishes. Used sparingly, it also adds depth to vegetable dishes and stews.

SOUR CREAM BANANA CAKE

Serves 16

Gourmet

A good cake for after school snacks.

¼   cup shortening

1⅓ cups sugar

2   eggs

1   teaspoon vanilla extract

2   cups flour

1   teaspoon baking powder

1   teaspoon baking soda

¾   teaspoon salt

1   cup sour cream

1   cup mashed bananas

½   cup chopped pecans

1   (8 ounce) package softened cream cheese

¼   cup melted butter

1   teaspoon vanilla extract

1   (16 ounce) box powdered sugar

◢ Preheat oven to 350°.

◢ Cream shortening and sugar until fluffy. Add eggs and vanilla, blend thoroughly.

◢ Combine flour, baking powder, baking soda, and salt, add to creamed mixture, alternating with sour cream. Add bananas and pecans, stir to blend.

◢ Pour into greased and floured 13 x 9 inch pan, bake for 45 minutes.

◢ Mix 8 ounces of softened cream cheese, ¼ cup melted butter, 1 teaspoon vanilla, and 1 (16 ounce) box of powdered sugar, blend until creamy.

◢ Spread frosting on cake when cool.

After Hours

COOKIES & OTHER TREATS

St. John's College

St. John's College, situated on the banks of College Creek in Annapolis, is the third oldest institution of higher learning in the United States. It was established by royal charter in 1696 as King William's School. After the American Revolution the royal assets were seized and St. John's College was chartered in 1784. Four of the trustees were signers of the Declaration of Independence. Early alumni include Francis Scott Key, President Washington's adopted grandson, two nephews of Washington, and four governors of Maryland.

Today the historic college is best known for its renowned liberal arts curriculum based on the great books of western civilization. Its serene campus in the heart of the Historic District contains many points of historic interest. The only surviving Liberty Tree in this country stands on front campus. More than 400 years old, this stately tulip poplar was the meeting site for the Sons of Liberty before the American Revolution. Ironically, it was the celebration of American independence which saved this green monument. Around 1840, the tree was dying of a parasite. One Fourth of July, some enterprising youngsters placed gunpowder in a hollow in the venerable tree and set the tree on fire. Annapolis' citizens rushed to quench the fire and punish the miscreants. The fire killed the pests, however, and the Liberty Tree, newly invigorated, sent forth new shoots the next spring. It still continues to grow.

The central building on campus, McDowell Hall, constructed from 1742 to 1784, was originally designed to be the colonial governor's mansion. It was abandoned after Governor Bladen's budget ran out for his grand mansion and the colonial legislature refused to allocate more funds. Known as "Bladen's Folly", it was given to the College after the Revolution.

St. John's is still a center for community activities in Annapolis. In addition to lectures, art exhibitions, and concerts, St. John's hosts a spirited annual croquet match with its military neighbor, the midshipmen of the U.S. Naval Academy. Held the last Saturday in April, the mids in their yachting dress and the St. Johnnies in attire that ranges from Gatsbyesque to bohemian meet under the Liberty Tree for a best three out of five matches. Spectators dressed in boaters or blazers, lovely spring dresses, or shorts and cotton tops sip champagne and dine on strawberries and pate while jazz music plays in the background. The civilized air shouldn't fool the spectator. Johnnies have been known to steal the Navy goat before the match and distract the midshipmen's attention with a "Designated Temptress." Mids have attempted a number of pranks in return. It all ends in a friendly waltz party in McDowell Hall that evening.

Cookies & Other Treats

ALMOND BUTTER COOKIES

Makes 24 cookies

Easy, can be made ahead

My Swedish Grandmother's secret recipe!

1	stick softened salt-free butter
1	cup sugar
¼	cup flour
1	egg, separated
1	cup chopped unblanched almonds
	salt

◢ Preheat oven 350° and lightly grease a 10" x 15" jelly roll pan with cooking spray.

◢ Mix together butter, sugar, and flour; mix in egg yolk.

◢ Spread mixture onto jelly roll pan; roll lightly with rolling pin; flour hands and pat evenly to edges.

◢ Pour the unbeaten egg white on top; tilt pan to spread egg white thoroughly over dough; pour off excess.

◢ Sprinkle salt lightly on top; sprinkle crushed almonds on the top; take another cookie sheet of the same size on top and press down almonds lightly into dough.

◢ Bake 10 to 12 minutes until medium brown; remove from oven; immediately cut into ½ inch squares; cool on rack. Will keep in closed container for 2 to 3 weeks.

For my daughter's wedding both mothers and all the grandmothers made cookies from family recipes. Each table of guests had a plate of the "Family Cookies." These almond cookies were among them.

CHEESECAKE DIAMONDS

Makes 16 cookies

Average, can be made ahead

Delightful for special occasions.

5 tablespoons butter or margarine

⅓ cup brown sugar

1 cup sifted all purpose flour

¼ cup chopped walnuts

½ cup granulated sugar

1 (8 ounce) package softened cream cheese

1 egg

2 tablespoons milk

1 tablespoon lemon juice

½ teaspoon vanilla extract

◢ Preheat oven 350°.

◢ Cream butter and brown sugar; add flour and nuts; mix well.

◢ Set aside 1 cup of this mixture for topping; press remainder in bottom of an 8"x8"x2" baking pan. Bake 12 to 15 minutes.

◢ Blend sugar and cream cheese until smooth; add egg, milk, lemon juice and vanilla; beat well; spread over bottom crust.

◢ Sprinkle with reserved cup of topping; return to oven.

◢ Bake for 25 more minutes; cool, then chill; cut into diamonds.

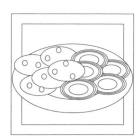

Cookies & Other Treats

CREAMY CHOCOLATE MACADAMIA COOKIES

Makes 3 dozen

Average

Meltingly good!

2 cups flour

½ teaspoon baking soda

¼ teaspoon salt

1 cup light brown sugar

3 tablespoons granulated sugar

½ cup softened salted butter

4 ounces cream cheese

1 large egg

2 teaspoons vanilla

½ cup whole macadamia nuts

½ cup semi-sweet chocolate chips (or white chocolate).

▲ Preheat oven 300°.

▲ In a medium bowl combine flour, soda and salt; mix well with wire whisk.

▲ In a large bowl blend sugars well using electric mixer at high speed; add butter and cream cheese; mix to form a smooth paste.

▲ Add egg and vanilla; beat at medium setting until light and soft.

▲ Add flour mixture; combine in nuts and chocolate chips; drop onto ungreased cookie sheet.

▲ Bake 20 to 23 minutes.

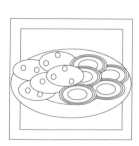

GRANDMOTHER'S CINNAMON SQUARES

Makes 4 dozen

Average, can be made ahead

A terrific addition to a holiday cookie assortment or a "care package".

1	cup sugar
2	cups sifted flour
1	tablespoon cinnamon
	dash salt
1	cup shortening (½ or all butter)
1	unbeaten egg yolk
1	slightly beaten egg white
	sliced almonds for garnish

◢ Preheat oven 325°. Blend sugar, flour, cinnamon and salt and cream into shortening; add egg yolk.

◢ Divide the dough into thirds and refrigerate the thirds you are not working with until needed.

◢ Spread ⅓ of the dough on a cookie sheet; spread until it is uniform and as thin as possible.

◢ Brush egg white over dough; sprinkle sliced almonds on top.

◢ Bake 15 to 20 minutes or until evenly browned; remove from oven; slice into squares quickly and remove from cookie sheet immediately. Repeat with other two-thirds of dough.

These squares keep a long time or may be kept frozen.

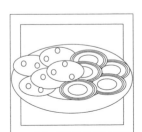

HOLIDAY FRUIT DROPS

Makes 160 cookies

Gourmet

Even children will love this colorful tasty cookie.

1	pound cut-up candied cherries
1	pound cut-up pineapple
1	pound chopped dates
½	pound raisins
6	cups chopped pecans
4	eggs, separated
3	cups sifted flour
1	tablespoon cinnamon
1	tablespoon nutmeg
1	teaspoon cloves
1	cup brown sugar
½	cup butter
1	tablespoon baking soda
½	cup red or white wine (orange or lemon juice may be substituted or a little added if mixture is too thick).
3	tablespoons sour milk

◢ Preheat oven to 325°. Dredge chopped fruit with 1 cup flour; cream butter and sugar; add beaten egg yolks and mix well.

◢ Add sifted flour, spices and baking soda alternately with milk and wine.

◢ Beat egg whites and fold into mixture; mix this with the chopped fruit; drop in tablespoons on cookie sheet.

◢ Bake for 20 to 25 minutes.

367

I always thought the holiday cookies I decorated were the most beautiful ones. I never wanted anyone to eat them, but I would usually let my grandma have one.

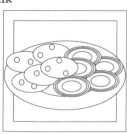

GLAZED CARROT COOKIES

Makes 60 cookies

Average, can be made ahead

A delectable treat for a Halloween party.

1   cup shortening

1   cup sugar

2   eggs

1   teaspoon vanilla extract

1   teaspoon orange extract

2   cups flour

2   teaspoons baking powder

½   teaspoon nutmeg

¼   teaspoon salt

2   cups finely shredded carrots

1   teaspoon orange juice

½   cup lightly toasted chopped nuts

Icing

2   cups sifted powdered sugar

1   orange (juice and grated rind)

½   teaspoon orange extract

◢ Preheat oven to 350°.

◢ Cream shortening and sugar; add eggs and extracts; beat well.

◢ Combine flour, baking powder, nutmeg and salt; add alternately carrots and flour mixture to the shortening and sugar mixture; mix well.

◢ Add nuts and orange juice. Drop in tablespoonfuls on ungreased cookie sheet.

◢ Bake for 10 to 12 minutes; cool on wire rack.

◢ Mix icing ingredients; ice when cool.

PRALINE PUMPKIN COOKIES

Makes 4 - 5 dozen

Average, can be prepared ahead

Delicious and different!

1   cup shortening

1   cup sugar

1½ cups pumpkin purée

1   egg

2   cups flour

1   teaspoon soda

1   teaspoon cinnamon

½   teaspoon salt

1   cup butterscotch bits

1   cup pecan pieces

1   cup raisins

Frosting

3   tablespoons butter

4   teaspoons milk

½   cup brown sugar

1   cup powdered sugar

¾   teaspoon vanilla extract

◢ Preheat oven to 375°.

◢ Cream shortening and sugar; add pumpkin and egg.

◢ Combine flour, soda, cinnamon and salt; add and mix into creamed mixture.

◢ Stir in butterscotch bits, nuts and raisins; spoon the dough onto ungreased cookie sheet.

◢ Bake 10 to 12 minutes; remove and cool on wire rack.

◢ Combine butter, milk and brown sugar in saucepan; cook until sugar is dissolved; cool then stir in powdered sugar and vanilla.

◢ Frost cookies while they are warm.

369

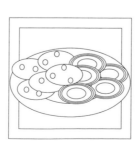

MINT CHOCOLATE CHIP M&M COOKIES

Makes 3 dozen

Easy, can be made ahead

A special treat for after-school conversations with Mom.

1 cup softened butter

¾ cup sugar

¾ cup firmly packed brown sugar

2 eggs

1 teaspoon peppermint extract

1 teaspoon vanilla extract

½ teaspoon salt

1 teaspoon baking soda

1¾ cups all purpose flour

1 cup mint chocolate chips

1 cup M&M's candy coated chocolate candies or regular chocolate chips

 Preheat oven 350°.

 Cream butter and sugar; add eggs and extracts.

 Add salt, soda and flour; mix well.

 Add mint chocolate chips and M&M's; mix until evenly distributed; drop by spoonfuls onto ungreased baking sheet.

 Bake 10 to 12 minutes until golden brown; cool slightly; remove from baking sheet.

370

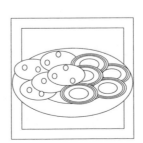

Cookies & Other Treats

ORANGE DROP COOKIES

Makes 28 - 30 cookies

Gourmet

Pretty and fresh tasting. Delightful after-dinner cookie.

1½ cups firmly packed brown sugar

1 cup butter or margarine

2 eggs

1 tablespoon grated orange peel

1 teaspoon vanilla extract

3 cups presifted flour

2 teaspoons baking powder

1 teaspoon baking soda

½ teaspoon salt

¾ cup buttermilk

Icing

1 tablespoon grated orange peel

3 tablespoons orange juice

3 tablespoons butter

3 cups sifted powdered sugar

▲ Preheat oven to 350°.

▲ Cream brown sugar and butter; add eggs, orange peel and vanilla; beat till fluffy.

▲ Sift together flour, baking powder, soda and salt; add to creamed mixture alternately with buttermilk; beat after each addition.

▲ Drop on ungreased cookie sheet.

▲ Bake for 10 to 12 minutes.

▲ For icing, combine peel, juice and butter; stir in powdered sugar; ice cookies as they cool.

OATMEAL AND TOFFEE COOKIES

Makes 12 cookies

Easy, can be made ahead

These cookies have a satisfying crunchiness; great with milk!

¾ cup brown sugar

¾ cup butter or margarine

½ cup sugar

1 egg

1 teaspoon vanilla extract

1½ cups Old Fashioned oatmeal

1 cup flour

½ teaspoon baking soda

dash salt

¾ cup chopped pecans

6-7 ounces chopped chocolate covered English toffee

◢ Preheat oven 350°.

◢ Mix brown sugar, butter, sugar, egg and vanilla until fluffy.

◢ Add oats, flour, baking soda and salt; stir in pecans and English toffee.

◢ Mound dough by ¼ cupfuls onto greased cookie sheets, 2" apart; flatten slightly with fingers.

◢ Bake for 20 minutes; remove from oven and let cool awhile on cookie sheet; when cooled transfer to rack.

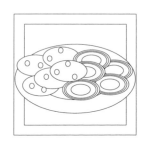

PEANUT BUTTER CUP COOKIES

Makes 2 dozen

Average, can make ahead

A favorite of the midnight snack crowd.

2¼ cups all purpose flour

⅓ cup unsweetened cocoa powder

1 teaspoon baking soda

½ teaspoon salt

1 cup softened margarine

¾ cup creamy peanut butter

¾ cup firmly packed light brown sugar

¾ cup granulated sugar

1 teaspoon vanilla extract

2 eggs

5 (1.6 ounce) packages peanut butter cups, cut into 8 pieces

1 (6 ounce) package semi-sweet chocolate chips

◢ Preheat oven 350°.

◢ Combine flour, cocoa powder, soda and salt; set aside.

◢ Using medium speed, beat margarine, peanut butter, brown sugar, granulated sugar and vanilla about 3 minutes or until light and fluffy; add eggs, one at a time; beat after each addition.

◢ Reduce speed to low; gradually beat in flour mixture until smooth; stir peanut butter cup pieces and chocolate chips into dough.

373

◢ Drop dough (approximately 3 tablespoons per cookie) onto ungreased cookie sheet; approximately 1" apart.

◢ Bake 13 to 15 minutes. Cool 1 minute and remove from cookie sheet.

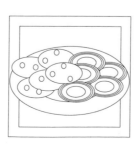

SOFT GINGER COOKIES

Makes 2 - 3 dozen

Easy, can be made ahead and frozen

Send these heartwarming cookies to your favorite college student to help them survive exams.

2¼ cups flour

1 teaspoon ground ginger

1 teaspoon baking soda

½ teaspoon cinnamon

¼ teaspoon ground cloves

¼ teaspoon salt

¾ cup margarine, butter or shortening

1 cup sugar

1 egg

¼ cup molasses

◢ Preheat oven 350°.

◢ Combine flour, ginger, soda, cinnamon, cloves and salt.

◢ Mix butter, sugar, eggs till fluffy; add molasses and dry ingredients.

◢ Shape into 1 to 1½ inch balls; roll in 2 tablespoons sugar; place on ungreased cookie sheet.

◢ Bake for approximately 10 minutes; DO NOT OVER BAKE; let stand before removing from cookie sheet.

My mother would send an assortment of goodies to my roommate and me before exams. Homemade chocolate chip and soft ginger cookies, cinnamon rolls, and other treats were carefully wrapped in wax paper and shipped in a shoe box. How we looked forward to our mail!

374

AMARETTO SUGAR COOKIES

Makes 4 dozen 2-inch cookies

Average

Cut into flower shapes for a spring tea!

1   cup softened butter or margarine

1½   cups powdered sugar

1   egg

1   teaspoon vanilla extract

½   teaspoon almond extract

2½   cups all purpose flour

1   teaspoon baking soda

1   teaspoon cream of tartar

Frosting

1   cup powdered sugar

1-2 tablespoons amaretto

▲ Cream together butter and sugar; add egg, vanilla, and almond extract; blend in flour, baking soda and cream of tartar; mix well.

▲ Cover and chill dough 2 to 3 hours; preheat oven 375°.

▲ Divide dough in half; keep one half chilled until ready to shape; roll each half ³⁄₁₆" thick on lightly floured cloth; cut dough into desired cookie shapes; place on lightly greased baking sheet.

▲ Bake at 375° 7 to 8 minutes or until light brown on edge; remove from oven; let cool.

▲ Mix frosting of powdered sugar and Amaretto until easily spreadable and frost cookies.

375

TRUFFLE BALLS

Makes 4 dozen

Easy, can be made ahead

Rich and crumbly, a special cookie!

1¼   cups butter

1   cup powdered sugar

½   cup cocoa

2   cups all purpose flour

1   teaspoon vanilla extract

1   cup chopped pecans

powdered sugar to dust cookie tops

 Preheat oven 350°.

 Cream butter and sugar; add cocoa, flour, and vanilla, mix in pecans. Chill dough in refrigerator 1 hour.

 Roll chilled dough into size of large marble and place 1" apart on an ungreased cookie sheet.

 Bake 16 minutes; remove from oven while warm and roll in confectioner's sugar; when cool, sift confectioner's sugar over cookies to dust.

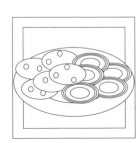

AUTUMN APPLE SQUARES

Makes 18 bars

Easy, can be made ahead

A tasty treat for school lunches.

1   cup melted butter

2   cups sugar

2   eggs

6   medium cooking apples (pared, cored and sliced thin)

1   cup chopped nuts

2   cups flour

1   teaspoon baking powder

2   teaspoons cinnamon

1   teaspoon baking soda

▲ Preheat oven 350°.

▲ Mix butter, sugar and eggs; beat well, stir in apples; add nuts.

▲ Sift flour, baking powder, cinnamon and baking soda; blend with apple mixture; turn into a greased 9" square pan.

▲ Bake for 40 to 45 minutes.

The Charles Carroll House, on the grounds of St. Mary's Catholic Church, was built between 1725 and 1735. It contains an unusual wine cellar under the porch.

377

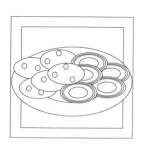

BUTTERSCOTCH BROWNIES

Makes 16 brownies

Easy, can be made ahead and frozen

Serve warm on a cold winter day.

½   cup melted butter

2   cups dark brown sugar

2   eggs

½   teaspoon salt

1½ cups flour

 2   tablespoons baking powder

1   teaspoon vanilla extract

1   cup chopped nuts

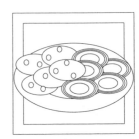

▲ Preheat oven 350°.

▲ Mix all the ingredients together, combining them well, spread in a buttered 9" square cake pan.

▲ Bake 35 to 40 minutes or until dry on top and almost firm to the touch; remove from oven; cool for 10 to 15 minutes; cut into squares.

CARAMEL PECAN BARS

Makes 20 bars

Easy

My husband's favorite!

⅔ cup vanilla caramels
(approximately 12)

⅓ cup margarine or
butter

2 tablespoons milk

¾ cup sugar

2 eggs

½ teaspoon vanilla
extract

¾ cup all purpose flour

½ teaspoon baking
powder

¼ teaspoon salt

½ cup chopped pecans

▲ Preheat over 350°.

▲ Combine in 2 quart saucepan caramels, margarine and milk; heat and stir over low heat until caramels have melted; remove from heat.

▲ Stir in sugar; add the eggs and vanilla; stir until well blended.

▲ In mixing bowl combine flour, baking powder and salt; add this to saucepan mixture; stir until well blended; stir in pecans; turn in a greased 9"x9"x2" baking pan.

▲ Bake 20 to 25 minutes or until a toothpick inserted in the center comes out clean; let cool, cut into bars.

379

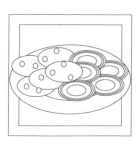

CHOCOLATE CARAMEL OAT MELTS

Makes 2 1/2 dozen

Average, must be made ahead

Your family will be fighting for seconds before you put them in the oven.

1½ cups flour

1½ cups oats (old-fashioned or quick)

1½ cups brown sugar

½ teaspoon baking soda

¼ teaspoon salt

1½ sticks chilled unsalted butter (cut into spoon sized pieces)

1 (12 ounce) bag semi-sweet chocolate morsels

½ cup heavy cream

1 (14 ounce) bag caramels

 Preheat oven 350°.

 Combine flour, oats, brown sugar, baking soda and salt in a mixing bowl; cut in butter pieces with pastry knife until mixture begins to stick; press all but 2 cups of mixture into a 9"x13" ungreased baking pan; sprinkle chocolate morsels over this crust mixture in pan; set aside.

 In saucepan over medium heat bring cream to a simmer; add caramels stirring until melted and smooth; pour this over crust mixture and chocolates in baking pan; sprinkle on top remaining 2 cups of crust mixture.

 Bake 15 to 20 minutes or until edges are golden brown; remove from oven; let cool and cut into squares; refrigerate until well chilled (approximately 3 hours); serve chilled. Not recommended for outdoor functions.

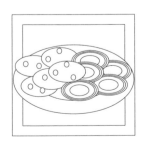

Cookies & Other Treats

ENGLISH MATRIMONIALS

Makes 1 1/2 dozen

Easy, can be made ahead

Try these with peach or blackberry jam. Serve a variety for a bridal shower.

1¼ cups flour

1 cup brown sugar

1¼ cups rolled oats

½ teaspoon salt

¾ cup butter

¾ cup red raspberry jam

◢ Preheat oven to 350°.

◢ Mix flour, brown sugar, oats, salt and butter until crumb-like consistency.

◢ Place half mixture into 6"x9"x2" greased pan; press into firm layer; cover with jam and top with remaining crumb mixture.

◢ Bake for 40 to 45 minutes; cool and cut into squares.

CHOCOLATE HAZELNUT TRUFFLES

Serves 16 Truffles

Easy

A decadent nibbler great for gifts.

8 ounces bittersweet chocolate, chopped

7 ounces almond paste

2 tablespoons fresh, strong, hot coffee

2 tablespoons hazelnut liqueur

sprinkles or cocoa powder

◢ Place chopped chocolate in bowl of food processor, process until finely ground.

◢ Add almond paste, cut in pieces, process until smooth. With motor running, add coffee and liqueur. Process until mixture forms soft ball.

◢ Pour into medium mixing bowl, chill for 30 minutes.

◢ Form into ¾ inch balls, roll in sprinkles or cocoa powder.

◢ Place in small paper cups. Chill until ready to serve.

FROSTED COCONUT NUT SQUARES

Makes 12 squares

Easy

Incredibly tasty!

½ cup softened butter

1 cup flour

2 eggs

1½ cups brown sugar

2 tablespoons flour

½ teaspoon salt

1 teaspoon baking powder

1 teaspoon vanilla extract

½ cup shredded coconut

1 cup chopped walnuts or pecans

Frosting

¼ cup softened butter

2 cups sifted powdered sugar

1 tablespoon lemon juice

¼ teaspoon salt

2 tablespoons cream or evaporated milk

▲ Preheat oven 350°.

▲ Cut butter into flour with a pastry knife; press mixture down in ungreased 9" square baking pan.

▲ Bake 15 minutes until light brown; remove from oven.

▲ Beat together eggs and brown sugar, set aside; mix together 2 tablespoons flour, salt, baking powder, vanilla, coconut and nuts; add mixture to eggs and brown sugar; spread on top on baked crust.

▲ Return to oven 20 to 25 minutes; remove from oven, let cool.

▲ Cream together butter and sugar until soft and smooth; (sugar must be added gradually); add lemon juice and salt; gradually work in cream or evaporated milk until smooth; spread on top of cooled baked mixture.

GRAND CHAMPION GINGERBREAD

Makes 12 squares

Average, can be made ahead

A grand champion ribbon winner at the county fair.

2½ cups all purpose flour

2 teaspoons baking soda

½ teaspoon salt

1 teaspoon cinnamon

1½ teaspoons powdered ginger

¼ teaspoon ground cloves

½ teaspoon dry mustard

½ teaspoon ground black pepper

8 tablespoons butter

½ cup dark brown sugar

2 eggs

1 cup molasses

1 cup boiling water

▲ Preheat oven to 350°.

▲ Combine flour, soda, salt and spices; sift together on piece of waxed paper; set aside.

▲ Beat butter and sugar until well blended; add eggs to butter and sugar mixture and beat well; beat in molasses; add boiling water and dry ingredients and beat until the batter is smooth; pour into greased and floured 8" square pan.

▲ Bake 35 to 45 minutes; remove from oven and let cool in pan for 5 minutes; turn onto wire rack; serve warm or at room temperature.

383

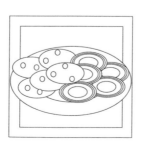

MARBLE BROWNIES

Makes 3 dozen

Average

Substitute raspberry, orange or almond liqueur or extract for the vanilla extract for different flavors.

1   (8 ounce) package softened cream cheese

2¼ cups sugar, divided

1   teaspoon cinnamon

5   eggs

2½ teaspoons vanilla extract, divided

1   cup butter or margarine

4   ounces unsweetened chocolate

1½ cups flour

½   teaspoon salt

1   cup coarsely chopped nuts (optional)

Preheat oven to 350°.

In small bowl, beat cream cheese, ¼ cup sugar, cinnamon, 1 egg, and 1½ teaspoons vanilla for 2 minutes; set aside.

Heat butter and chocolate over low heat until melted; cool.

In large mixing bowl, beat chocolate mixture, remaining sugar, eggs and vanilla on medium speed 1 minute, scraping bowl occasionally; beat in flour and salt on low speed, about 30 seconds; beat on medium speed about 1 minute; stir in nuts.

Spread half the batter into pan; spread the cream cheese filling over batter; lightly spread the remaining batter over the cream cheese filling; gently swirl through batter with a spoon in an over-and-under motion to create a marbled effect.

Bake for 55 to 65 minutes, or until pick inserted into center comes out clean; cool and cut into bars.

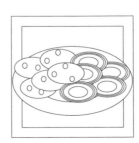

CHUNKY HONEY CHOCOLATE BARS

Makes 24 bars

Easy

A satisfying treat for your crew.

1 (21½ ounce) package of fudge brownie mix, plus the ingredients listed to make brownies.

½ cup honey

¼ cup creamy peanut butter

¾ cup chopped salted peanuts

1 (6 ounce) package semi-sweet chocolate chips

◢ Prepare brownies and bake according to package directions.

◢ Combine honey and peanut butter in a small saucepan over low heat, stirring often.

◢ Immediately after taking brownies from oven sprinkle with peanuts and chocolate chips; drizzle peanut/honey mixture over brownies; let cool and cut into squares.

385

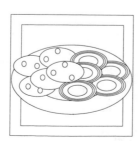

CHOCOLATE FROSTED PEANUT BUTTER BARS

Makes 3 dozen

Easy, can be made ahead
An easy weekday dessert.

½ cup butter

½ cup sugar

½ cup brown sugar

1 egg

⅓ cup peanut butter

½ teaspoon baking soda

½ teaspoon vanilla extract

1 cup flour

1 cup rolled oats

1 (12 ounce) package milk chocolate chips

◢ Preheat oven to 350°.

◢ Mix together all ingredients except chocolate chips; spread mixture into a greased 9"x13 pan.

◢ Bake for approximately 20 to 25 minutes until light brown around edges; remove from oven.

◢ Spread chocolate chips evenly on top; allow to melt; let cool, cut into bars.

My brothers were notorious traders of Mom's homemade desserts on the school playground. They accumulated a huge collection of marbles on the quality of her brownies and cookies.

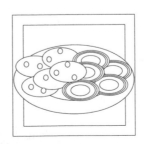

ROCKY CHOCOLATE BARS

Makes 30 bars

Average, can be made ahead

Buttery and delicious. Try ½ cup of toffee bits and ½ cup of pecans as a topping also.

2   sticks sweet butter

1   cup light brown sugar

1   egg yolk

2   cups flour

1   teaspoon vanilla extract

1   (12 ounce) package semi-sweet chocolate chips

1   cup coarsely chopped pecans

▲ Preheat oven 350°.

▲ Cream butter and sugar; add egg yolk; beat well.

▲ Sift in flour; stir in vanilla; mix well; spread batter in greased 13"x9"x2" rectangular baking pan.

▲ Bake 25 minutes; remove from oven; cover with chocolate chips; return to oven for 4 minutes; remove from oven; smooth chocolate evenly; sprinkle with nuts; cool completely before cutting into bars.

387

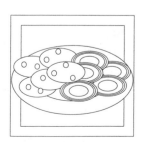

CHOCOLATE COVERED STRAWBERRIES

Makes 15 - 20

Easy, can be made ahead

Also wonderful with dried apricots, fresh cherries or kiwi slices.

2-2½ pints fresh
strawberries (rinsed
and dried)

16 ounces semi-sweet
chocolate

12 ounces German sweet
chocolate

1½ cups light table cream

2 tablespoons brandy or
favorite liqueur

toothpicks

◢ Melt chocolate in microwave; add chocolate to warm cream and brandy; stir until combined and smooth over low heat.

◢ Insert a toothpick into each strawberry and individually dip and swirl into chocolate mixture; refrigerate to harden chocolate.

◢ Eat within 2-3 days for best results.

Cookies & Other Treats

CREME DE MENTHE SQUARES

Makes 144 1-inch x 1/2-inch squares

Gourmet, must be made ahead

Makes nice gift candy!

1¼ cups softened butter, divided

½ cup cocoa powder

3½ cups sifted powdered sugar (divided)

1 beaten egg

1 teaspoon vanilla extract

2 cups graham cracker crumbs

1½ cups semi-sweet chocolate chips

⅓ cup green creme de menthe

Bottom layer - in saucepan combine ½ cup butter and cocoa powder; heat; stir until blended; remove from heat; add ½ cup powdered sugar, egg, and vanilla; stir in graham cracker crumbs; mix well; press mixture in bottom of ungreased 9"x13" baking pan.

Middle layer - melt ½ cup butter in small bowl; combine butter and creme de menthe; using low mixer speed, beat in remaining sugar until smooth; spread over crumb layer; chill 1 hour.

Top layer - combine in saucepan remaining butter and chocolate chips; cook and stir over low heat until melted; spread over middle layer; chill 1 to 2 hours; cut into small squares and serve.

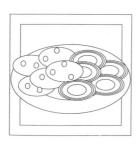

GRAND MARNIER SPICED PECANS

Makes 3 cups

Easy, can be made ahead

An elegant nibbler for holiday parties. Keep on hand for gifts.

1½ cups sugar

½ cup sour cream

1 tablespoon grated orange rind

½ teaspoon nutmeg

½ teaspoon clove

1 teaspoon cinnamon

1 tablespoon Grand Marnier

1 pound whole pecans

◢ Line 2 cookie sheets with waxed paper.

◢ Mix sugar, cinnamon, nutmeg, clove and sour cream in a small saucepan; bring to a boil; continue boiling for 5 minutes, stirring frequently.

◢ Remove from heat; stir in orange rind and Grand Marnier; add nuts and stir until the nuts are coated.

◢ Pour onto the waxed paper; using two forks, separate the pecans quickly; let cool thoroughly and store in an airtight container.

◢ Will keep for up to two months.

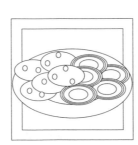

PECAN PRALINES

Makes 30 pralines

Gourmet, can be made ahead

This will only be successful and harden if done on a dry day. If it is humid and/or raining then pralines will not harden.

1¼ cups granulated sugar

¾ cup light brown sugar

2 tablespoons light corn syrup

½ cup evaporated milk

2 cups pecan halves

1 teaspoon vanilla extract or bourbon

2¾ tablespoons margarine

◢ Combine granulated sugar, brown sugar, corn syrup and evaporated milk in a saucepan; cook on low heat for 10 minutes, stirring constantly.

◢ Add pecans; continue cooking for approximately 20 more minutes, stirring constantly.

◢ Test for soft ball stage with candy thermometer, when it reaches soft ball temperature quickly remove from heat.

◢ Add vanilla or bourbon and margarine; stir quickly until color and texture begins to change.

391

◢ Put on wax paper by the tablespoonful; after putting on wax paper keep sliding the wax paper around to prevent sticking; it will harden in about 2 to 3 hours, sometimes overnight; dry completely before wrapping.

Cinnamon is a universal favorite among spices. It is used extensively in baking, is good in chili and stews, and is also delicious in fruit and chicken salads.

TANGY TOASTED NUTS

Serves 6 - 8

Easy, can be made ahead and stored in an airtight container.

Great for Super Bowl gatherings.

2 tablespoons Worcestershire sauce

2 tablespoons melted butter

2 tablespoons Parmesan cheese (fresh if available)

½ teaspoon red pepper

1½ cups walnuts, pecans, or clean and dry pumpkin seeds

▲ Preheat oven to 350°.

▲ Mix Worcestershire, butter, Parmesan cheese and pepper.

▲ Coat nuts with sauce mixture and spread on a cookie sheet or jelly roll pan.

▲ Toast for 15 minutes for nuts or 30 minutes for seeds.

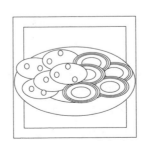

On the Go,

A PROVISIONING GUIDE FOR BOATING, CAMPING, & VACATIONS

The Sailing Capital

The protected natural harbor that first led the colonists to establish a settlement at the mouth of the Severn also turned Annapolis into a major center for maritime commerce, a heritage that has lasted through the centuries. The description that William Eddis wrote of Annapolis in the 18th century is still accurate today. "The courthouse, situated on an eminence at the back of town, commands a variety of views highly interesting; the entrance of the Severn, the majestic Chesapeake, and the eastern shore of Maryland, being all united in one resplendent assemblage. Vessels of various sizes and figures are continually floating before the eye; which, while they add to the beauty of the scene, excite ideas of the most pleasing nature."

Today, Annapolis' harbor draws hundreds of thousands of people content to watch the boats dancing in the water, to shop for nautical items, and to daydream. Once a major boatbuilding center for the colonies, Annapolis is still the heart of the modern maritime industry. World-class racing sailors have located their businesses here, and in October Annapolis hosts the premier industry shows: the U.S. Powerboat Show and the U.S. Sailboat Show. Floating docks are set up in the inner harbor and several thousand current and prospective boat owners flock to Annapolis to inspect the latest boat models, exchange sea-stories, and enjoy the sight of hundreds of pristine vessels bedecked in nautical flags under the crisp blue autumn sky.

For the local boater, Annapolis is the homeport from which to bask in the familiar local rivers and coves, to explore the Chesapeake, or venture into the Atlantic. Annapolis-to-Bermuda and Annapolis-to-Newport are biennial racing events drawing challengers from all over the East Coast. At any time in the year, sailing and yacht clubs are conducting races all over the Chesapeake. Sailing schools offer seamanship courses to beginning sailors or those who wish to improve their skills. Cruising boaters board their boats late on Fridays or early on Saturday mornings, eager to reach one of the charming Eastern shore towns or to disappear to their favorite hidden anchorage for a swim, a simple but elegant dinner, and a restful sleep interrupted only by the gentle lapping of a passing boat's wake. To wake up in the quiet stillness of a cove and enjoy the jewel-like brilliance of the morning sun on the water or to dip your hand in the water at night and trace patterns in the moonlit phosphorescence is to know why Annapolis continues to bring boaters and dreamers to its harbor.

A Provisioning Guide for Boating, Camping or Vacations

PLANNING STRATEGIES

Menu planning is essential for a successful carefree vacation whether you rent a house at the beach or in the mountains, go camping, or enjoy boating. Spend time in the kitchen before you leave. Plan menus for each meal of the day that you plan to be away, including snacks. Choose recipes that can be prepared ahead, easily cooked or completed. Look for recipes that share common ingredients to minimize storage and transportation concerns as well as your grocery bill. Use this chart to help you plan.

Day _____

Breakfast _____

_____

Lunch _____

_____

Dinner _____

_____

Snacks _____

_____

Drinks _____

_____

Day _____

Breakfast _____

_____

Lunch _____

_____

Dinner _____

_____

Snacks _____

_____

Drinks _____

_____

Day _____

Breakfast _____

_____

Lunch _____

_____

Dinner _____

_____

Snacks _____

_____

Drinks _____

_____

Day _____

Breakfast _____

_____

Lunch _____

_____

Dinner _____

_____

Snacks _____

_____

Drinks _____

_____

Make a copy of this chart for each trip

On the Go

Day _____
Breakfast _____
_____

Lunch _____
_____

Dinner _____
_____

Snacks _____
_____

Drinks _____
_____

Day _____
Breakfast _____
_____

Lunch _____
_____

Dinner _____
_____

Snacks _____
_____

Drinks _____
_____

Day _____
Breakfast _____
_____

Lunch _____
_____

Dinner _____
_____

Snacks _____
_____

Drinks _____
_____

Day _____
Breakfast _____
_____

Lunch _____
_____

Dinner _____
_____

Snacks _____
_____

Drinks _____
_____

Make a copy of this chart for each trip

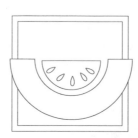

A Provisioning Guide

Planning Suggestions

◢ Sharing a vacation with several people? Have every person pick a night to cook or clean up. Make it fun by having a gourmet cookoff and start with a delicious dinner yourself. By the end of the week the meals will be spectacular!

◢ Measure and pack dry ingredients and store in plastic bags. Just pour into a bowl and add the liquid ingredients. Don't forget the recipe!

◢ Take almost empty condiment bottles and spice jars home at the end of a trip and refill. This will prevent garbage and duplicates.

◢ Make a list before you leave the boat or camper at the end of a trip of which supplies need replenishing.

◢ Pack matches, salt and dry goods in plastic bags to guard against moisture.

◢ Make sandwiches after breakfast before the boat starts moving or people head out to the beach. Everyone can eat on their own schedule and the kitchen only needs to be cleaned once.

◢ Buy chopped vegetables and fruits at the grocery store salad bar to save preparation time.

Cooler Storage

◢ Label everything clearly.

◢ Invest in water-tight stackable containers. Pack meats and other fresh foods in these containers before placing in cooler in reverse order of use. They will keep food fresh and will make the fullest use of your cooler. They are also good for leftovers and reduce garbage on board.

◢ Buy plastic baskets for breads, cheeses, and fruits. Sort by food category into these containers to minimize hunting for an item in the cooler. The less time the cooler is open, the colder it will stay.

◢ Bag packages in plastic zipper bags to seal against moisture.

◢ Prepare main dishes ahead and freeze them in sizes that will fit the boat/camper oven. They will help keep the cooler cold as they defrost and cut down on the need for ice.

▲ Put meats and foods close to the ice blocks and vegetables and fruits further away.

▲ Use boneless meats for cooking. They create less garbage and smell on board.

▲ Chop vegetables and tear salad greens at home. Rinse and dry thoroughly. Place in an airtight container or plastic bag. Greens will keep for up to three days.

▲ Dress salads at the last minute to prevent the vegetables from turning yellow or soggy and to prevent the dressing from leaking into the cooler.

▲ Keep clean gallon and half-gallon plastic jugs on hand. Before packing for a trip, fill to 1½ inches from the top with water and fruit juice and freeze until solid. Placed in a cooler, the jugs will act as ice-blocks to keep food cool and will not create a wet mess at the bottom of the cooler. As they melt, you will have cool fresh water or juice. Because they are solid masses, they will not melt as quickly as ice cubes.

▲ Keep drinks in a separate cooler so the food cooler does not have to be opened frequently.

▲ Use dry ice for long voyages.

▲ Scramble eggs and season, then place in zipper plastic bags for each meal.

▲ Place a single serving of soup in a zipper plastic bag. Boil in water as needed.

▲ Chill foods in refrigerator before packing the cooler.

▲ Preheat thermos containers with hot water or chill with cold water to keep beverages and soups at the proper temperature.

▲ Keep cooler in a cool, shady place. Cover with blankets.

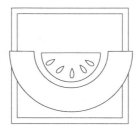

A Provisioning Guide

Supply checklists

Use these checklists for supplies and utensils to remember items you may have to bring for cooking. Some rental homes and charter boats are well equipped, others are not. Check with your rental agency before you leave. These lists are also useful for setting up a first kitchen.

Kitchen Utensils and Pans

☐ 1 small frying pan
☐ 1 large frying pan with a lid
☐ 1 5-quart Dutch oven
☐ 2 saucepans with lids
☐ 1 cookie sheet (fitting the boat or camper oven)
☐ 1 9x9 baking dish
☐ 1 9x12 baking dish
☐ 1 colander or drainer
☐ 2 large serving bowls
☐ 1 coffee pot
☐ 1 utility knife

☐ 1 paring knife
☐ 1 tongs
☐ 1 wire whisk
☐ 1 rubber spatula
☐ 1 metal spatula
☐ 1 can opener
☐ 1 corkscrew/bottle opener
☐ 3 large serving spoons
☐ 1 ice pick
☐ 1 set measuring cups
☐ 1 set measuring spoons
☐ 1 chopping board

Items not to forget

☐ sponge
☐ kitchen soap
☐ hand soap
☐ paper towels
☐ foil/plastic wrap

☐ plastic bags
☐ toilet paper
☐ garbage bags
☐ dishwasher detergent

Staples

☐ flour
☐ sugar
☐ baking powder
☐ baking soda
☐ butter/margarine
☐ shortening

☐ cornstarch
☐ vegetable oil
☐ other _____
☐ other _____
☐ other _____
☐ other _____

Make a copy of this chart for each trip

On the Go

Herbs, Spices, and Flavorings

- [ ] salt
- [ ] pepper
- [ ] allspice
- [ ] basil
- [ ] bay leaves
- [ ] bouillon cubes
- [ ] chili powder/cumin
- [ ] cinnamon
- [ ] ground cloves
- [ ] curry
- [ ] dill
- [ ] garlic powder
- [ ] ginger
- [ ] marjoram

- [ ] nutmeg
- [ ] onion powder
- [ ] oregano
- [ ] parsley
- [ ] rosemary
- [ ] seasoned salt
- [ ] tarragon
- [ ] thyme
- [ ] vanilla extract
- [ ] other_____
- [ ] other_____
- [ ] other_____
- [ ] other_____
- [ ] other_____

Condiments

- [ ] barbeque sauce
- [ ] jelly/jam
- [ ] ketchup
- [ ] lemon juice
- [ ] maple syrup
- [ ] mayonnaise
- [ ] mustard, Dijon
- [ ] mustard, regular
- [ ] peanut butter

- [ ] soy sauce
- [ ] steak sauce
- [ ] vinegar
- [ ] Worcestershire sauce
- [ ] other_____
- [ ] other_____
- [ ] other_____
- [ ] other_____
- [ ] other_____

Make a copy of this chart for each trip

Acknowledgements & Contributors

The Junior League of Annapolis would like to thank our provisional, active and sustaining members, families and friends for their recipes, assistance in testing, editing, and prepublication work. These people made OF TIDE & THYME a reality, and we are very grateful to them. Following are the contributors, cookbook committee members, and typists for the book.

Cathy Aadnesen
Beth Aiello
Lorraine Allerson
Jennifer Alphin
Jean Andrews
Caroline Cather Aras
John A. Aras
Pamela Henery Arey,
  Typing Coordinator
Kara Arnold
Alice Ashley-Hall
Sandra M. Askew, *Section*
  Editor
Nancy H. Voorhees Balenske
Lisa Barteldes
Carolyn Teague Bates
Nancy Dunlap Baudean
Heather Bauer
Susan Bissell Beach
Angie Beaver*
Lesly Ann Bell, *Section Editor*
Karen M. Bennett
Nancy N. Bennett
Heidi Berry
Ariel H. Biddle
Marilyn Miller Blandford
Linda Oehlschlager Blessed
Marty Bonds*
Jane Bowen
Kay Boylan
Valerie J. Brady
Melynda Branch
Noelle Buttarazzi*
Katherine H. Caldwell
Torii Campbell
Mary Canny
Kathryn Carroll
Jane H. Carter
Kacky Carter
Katherine Carter
Diane Goff Cather
Amy Chalstrom
Carol Chambers
Diane Cikanovich
Emily Clark
Stephanie Clark
Linda Constand

Anne DelTufo
Harriett Diakoulas
Joyce Dougherty
Dottie Douglas
Nancy Douglas
Lois F. Duffy, *Section Editor*
Kathy C. Ebner
Lorraine Ellerson
Sarah Evans
Pat Farrell
Karen Fine
Melissa Flaherty
Lisa Fletcher
Elizabeth Fralin*
Carole Frantz
Donna Frantz
Linda T. Fuller
Greshen Gwendolyn Gaines
Janet Gambarani
Elizabeth Gamble*
Cathy Gaudreau
Donna German*
Helen Gilbert
Edie Gillis
Sally Gingell
Donna Broyles Glazer
Mrs. Kent Chapman
  Guernsey, *Section Editor*
Joene Gwin
H.H. Leonards
D.J. Hall
Ann Hunter Pierce Haller*
Linda Hammer
Donna R. Harrington
Cathy Leahy Harrison
Celeste Ann Hartman,
  Cookbook Chair 1994-1995
Carolyn Heim
Patti Heisman
Lynn Helder
Anne Treadwell Henderson
Pam Henel, *Section Editor*
Catherine Hewes
Caroline Nunan Hill
Joann Hoffman
RoJean S. Holler
Reed Holmes*

Dotty Holoubek
Dianne Hood
Edie Hopkins
Anna von Oesen Hughes
Gretchen Hunter
Barbara A. Interlandi
Sue James
Lisa L. Jones
Marian Dohoney Kaufman*
Lisa Kennedy
Sue Kimmel
Theresa Klem
Margie Kling
Tina Kotseas
Patricia Anderson Lambrow
Kim Lank
Nancy Lank
Susan Joyce Latonick
Susan Leshner
Beverly Liddick
Sarah Macindoe
Julie Madden
Catherine Adams Masek
Ann Maxfield
Emory Furniss Maxwell
Jane O'Neal McAfee
Diane McClatchy
Heidi B. McCree
Maggie McDowell
Pat McHold
Wendy McIntyre
Paul Meredith
Pat Merkert
Zana Metelski*
Kim Neihold Michie
Dianne Minderline
Kathy Mogelinski
Beth Morgan
Ruth Lottman Morgan,
  Cookbook Chair 1992-1994
Tim Morgan
Bonnie V. Morris
Theresa Moyer*
Teresa Musgrave
Marcia Myers
Melissa Myers
Susan Myron

(continued)

Katherine Niepold
Linda Ransom O'Bannon
Ellen P. O'Boyle
Robin O'Connell
Mrs. William Sterling
    Ogden, Jr.*
Amy M. Olmert
Katherine Willson Ostberg
Sarah Ann Parsons
Pam Pavlik
Mary T. Preas
Angela Pumphrey
Claire Purnell
Jean H. Rademacher,
    Section Editor
Rogies Randall
Marilyn Muhleman Rausch
Eleanor Reed
Gale Genzen Reed,
    Section Editor
Sally Reed
Joyce Reinhart
Deborah D. Richardson
Victoria A. Ricketts,
    Section Editor
Catherine A. Roberts
Elizabeth Rogers
Valerie Rogers

Charles E. Ruch, Jr.
Grace Wolohon Ruch
Joan Dawson Ruch, *Editor*
Susan Gwin Ruch
Catherine Rutland
Beth Marshall Ryan,
    Cookbook Chair 1995-1996
Marie Scalisi
Trina Schafer
Nancy Clayton Schall
Lee Schwall
Vicki Scott
Gail Sewell
Sheila Spainhour Shaffer*
Elizabeth Shemer
Helen McKenna Sherman
Side Street Framers
Katye Skeath
Laura Smith*
Sherrie Burton Smith,
    Copy Editor
Mary Stansfield*
Kay Peacock Steinfeld
Kathy L. Sterritt
Mabel McK. Stinner
Cindy Strady
Jan Sutton
Cheryl Taylor

Susan Dierdorf Taylor
Leslie M. Thomas
Joann M. Thompson
Susie Bonner Tighe*
Kimberly Todd
LuAnne O. Tyler*
Patricia Ulep
Liz Ulvila
Carol Walker
Robin L. Wallace
Colleen Waters
Barbara Ann Watson*
Kathleen Watson
Betsy Weatherby
Donna Weaver
Trudy M. Weeks
Jennifer Heyd Wharton
Collette W. Wheatley
Donna Sposato Williams
Heather Williams
Lacy Williams,
    Typing Coordinator
Windows Resteraunt
Kristin Witzenburg
Ann Otto Warfield
Karen Nygren Wright
Harriet Yake

*Cookbook Committee Member

Index

Index

Index

406

D

E

Index

Index

Index

Index

Index

Index

Index

Index

Order Form

OF TIDE
THYME

Thank you for supporting the purpose and community projects of the Junior League of Annapolis, Inc.

Please send me_____copies @ $18.95   each_____

Maryland residents add 5% sales tax   @ $ .95   each_____

Postage & handling   @ $ 3.00   each_____

Each additional book to the same address @ $ 1.50   each_____

*Gift wrap & enclosure card   @ $ 2.00   each_____

If shipping to multiple addresses please attach list. Please send to:

Name_____

Address_____City_____State_____Zip_____

❏ Check or money order enclosed. Make check payable to Junior League of Annapolis

❏ Visa /Mastercard #_____Exp. Date_____Signature_____

Send to Jr. League of Annapolis, Inc. 19 Loretta Ave. Annapolis, Md 21401 Phone (410)224-8984 Fax (410)573-9236

Order Form

OF TIDE
THYME

Thank you for supporting the purpose and community projects of the Junior League of Annapolis, Inc.

Please send me_____copies @ $18.95   each_____

Maryland residents add 5% sales tax   @ $ .95   each_____

Postage & handling   @ $ 3.00   each_____

Each additional book to the same address @ $ 1.50   each_____

*Gift wrap & enclosure card   @ $ 2.00   each_____

If shipping to multiple addresses please attach list. Please send to:

Name_____

Address_____City_____State_____Zip_____

❏ Check or money order enclosed. Make check payable to Junior League of Annapolis

❏ Visa /Mastercard #_____Exp. Date_____Signature_____

Send to Jr. League of Annapolis, Inc. 19 Loretta Ave. Annapolis, Md 21401 Phone (410)224-8984 Fax (410)573-9236

Order Form

OF TIDE
THYME

Thank you for supporting the purpose and community projects of the Junior League of Annapolis, Inc.

Please send me_____copies @ $18.95   each_____

Maryland residents add 5% sales tax   @ $ .95   each_____

Postage & handling   @ $ 3.00   each_____

Each additional book to the same address @ $ 1.50   each_____

*Gift wrap & enclosure card   @ $ 2.00   each_____

If shipping to multiple addresses please attach list. Please send to:

Name_____

Address_____City_____State_____Zip_____

❏ Check or money order enclosed. Make check payable to Junior League of Annapolis

❏ Visa /Mastercard #_____Exp. Date_____Signature_____

Send to Jr. League of Annapolis, Inc. 19 Loretta Ave. Annapolis, Md 21401 Phone (410)224-8984 Fax (410)573-9236

I would like to see *Of Tide & Thyme* in the following stores in my area. (Please include phone number or address.)

_____

_____

_____

_____

_____

I would like to see *Of Tide & Thyme* in the following stores in my area. (Please include phone number or address.)

_____

_____

_____

_____

_____

I would like to see *Of Tide & Thyme* in the following stores in my area. (Please include phone number or address.)

_____

_____

_____

_____

_____